CW01460959

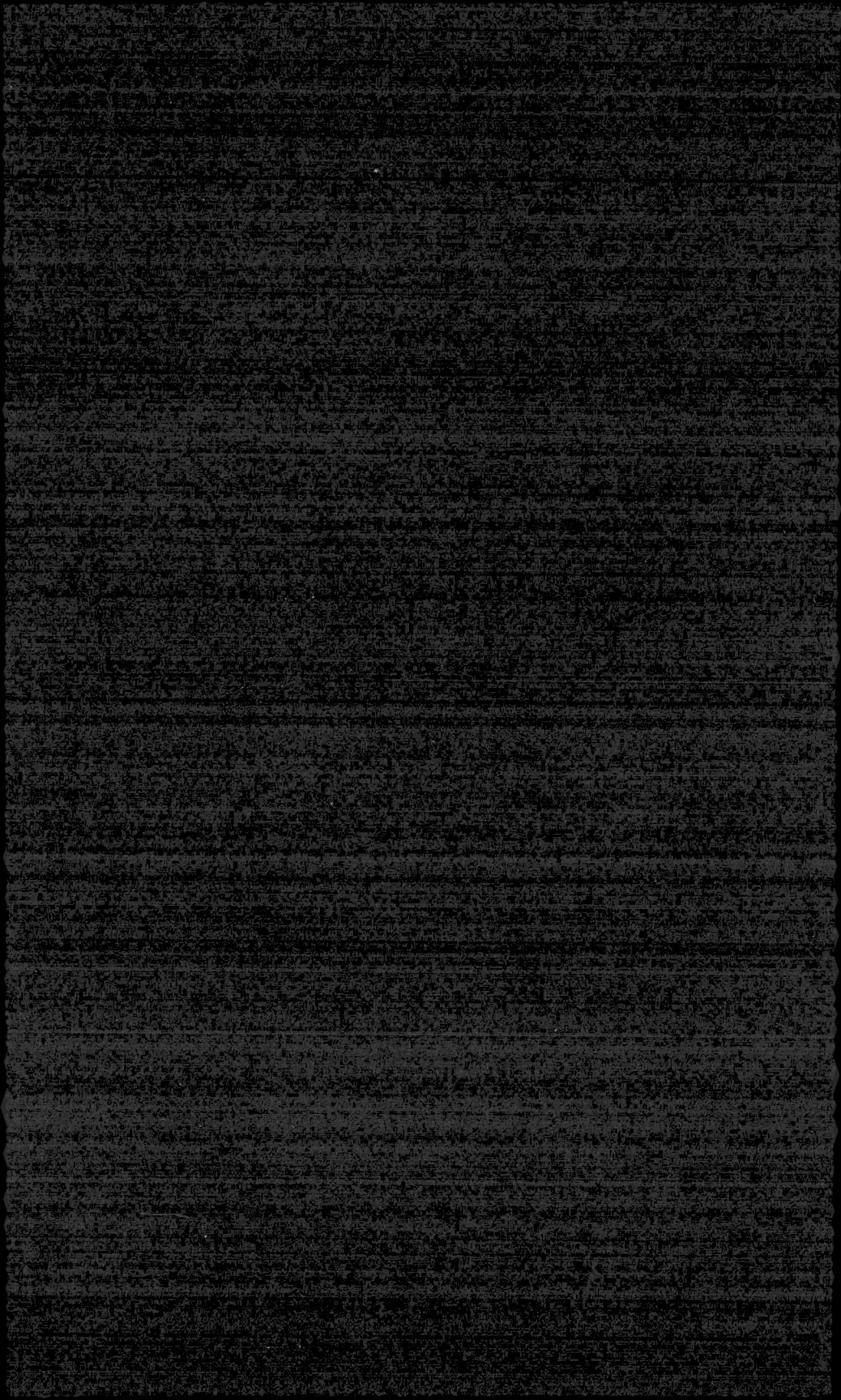

THE
ORPHIC
HYMNS

About the Author

Patrick Dunn (Chicago, IL) is a poet, linguist, Pagan, and university English professor with a PhD in modern literature and language. His understanding of semiotics and the study of symbols arises from his training in linguistics and literary theory. He has practiced magic since childhood. Visit him online at Pomomagic.nfshost.com.

To Write to the Author

If you wish to contact the author or would like more information about this book, please write to the author in care of Llewellyn Worldwide Ltd. and we will forward your request. Both the author and the publisher appreciate hearing from you and learning of your enjoyment of this book and how it has helped you. Llewellyn Worldwide Ltd. cannot guarantee that every letter written to the author can be answered, but all will be forwarded. Please write to:

Patrick Dunn
℅ Llewellyn Worldwide
2143 Wooddale Drive
Woodbury, MN 55125-2989

Please enclose a self-addressed stamped envelope for reply,
or $1.00 to cover costs. If outside the U.S.A., enclose
an international postal reply coupon.

Many of Llewellyn's authors have websites with additional
information and resources. For more information,
please visit our website at http://www.llewellyn.com

PATRICK DUNN

THE
ORPHIC
HYMNS

A NEW TRANSLATION
FOR THE OCCULT PRACTITIONER

Llewellyn Publications
Woodbury, Minnesota

FIRST EDITION
Third Printing, 2022

Cover design by Kevin R. Brown

Llewellyn Publications is a registered trademark of Llewellyn Worldwide Ltd.

Library of Congress Cataloging-in-Publication Data
Names: Dunn, Patrick, translator.
Title: The Orphic hymns : a new translation for the occult practitioner /
    Patrick Dunn.
Other titles: Orphic hymns. English.
Description: Woodbury, Minnesota : Llewellyn Publications, 2018. | Includes
    bibliographical references.
Identifiers: LCCN 2018036769 (print) | LCCN 2018040661 (ebook) | ISBN
    9780738755847 (ebook) | ISBN 9780738753447 (alk. paper)
Subjects: LCSH: Orphic hymns.
Classification: LCC PA4259 (ebook) | LCC PA4259 .E5 2018 (print) | DDC
    292.3/8dc23
LC record available at https://lccn.loc.gov/2018036769

Llewellyn Publications
A Division of Llewellyn Worldwide Ltd.
2143 Wooddale Drive
Woodbury, MN 55125-2989
www.llewellyn.com

Printed in the United States of America

Other Books by Patrick Dunn

The Practical Art of Divine Magic
(Llewellyn, 2015)

Cartomancy with the Lenormand and the Tarot
(Llewellyn, 2013)

δ δ᾽ ὄλβιος, ὅν τινα Μοῦσαι
φίλωνται: γλυκερή οἱ ἀπὸ στόματος ῥέει αὐδή.
—Homeric Hymns 25:4–5

This book is dedicated to Richard

Contents

FOREWORD

There's something to be said for scholarly objectivity. A scholar who cannot remain objective has a tendency to see what isn't there, to project and distort. But there's also something to be said for subjectivity, for examining something from within. Such subjectivity allows a deeper grasp than objective observation. To speak objectively of Bacchic euphoria misses the entire point of the experience, and is nothing like speaking of such frenzy after feeling the presence of Dionysos.

I am not an objective scholar in regard to these hymns. For one thing, I have a weird love for the ancient Greek language, and it's hard not to take a certain personal glee in feeling a sentence fall into place. But more importantly, I *believe* in the gods who are the subjects of these hymns.

The exact manner in which I believe in them changes from day to day and moment to moment. Sometimes they are abstract laws with a consciousness of their own existence, not much more personal than gravity. Sometimes they are psychological functions—metaphors and stories that give a life a mythographic shape. And other times they are individuals, as real and singular as anyone I pass in the street: Pan pressing his hooves in the loam; Artemis stalking with her silver bow between the trees; Poseidon in the deep, wreathed in kelp, sporting with dolphins; and always, of course, Zeus on high, stepping from the mountain tops to strike the earth with his bolts.

I suspect the gods are all those things and more, just as I myself am many different people and many different kinds of people. And my felt sense of these hymns, having lived with them for a while now, is that Orpheus had a similar multifarious view of the gods. Sometimes they're mythological figures, but at the same time, he's not above praising an abstract concept with no recourse to mythological allusion. Rather than a lack of imagination, I think this displays a keen theological mind, who can see the gods not *only* as blessed and distant immortals, and not *only* as statues in temples, and not *only* as the sky, moon, sun themselves, but as all of these things at once.

I would not have wanted to be an Orphic, or any kind of ascetic for that matter. But their hymns—if indeed these are the hymns of an "orthodox" ascetic sect of Orphism—speak to me regardless. I hope they speak to you as well and that you find them to be of use in your work, in your devotions, or even just as a satisfaction to your curiosity.

I am in debt to several people for this book's existence. First, I'm grateful to have the opportunity to thank my Richard, who was supportive of this occasionally obsessive project, and puts up with my ranting and mumbling about particular fine grammatical points in ancient Greek. Second, I thank Monica, who has not only been a gracious hostess while I was working on the revisions of this book, but also provided a place for me to work in peace and quiet away from my other responsibilities, to finalize the finished copy. I also thank Elysia, my long-suffering and understanding editor, who patiently awaited the final version and believed in the project from the beginning.

Finally, I owe a debt of gratitude to Keith Jones, who looked over my translations and compared them to the Greek. His understanding of Greek far exceeds mine, and his comments and suggestions were more helpful than he knows in correcting my errors both small and sometimes quite large. Any errors that remain are my fault. I also thank Kitos Digiovanni for his assistance and encouragement, and his kind gift of a Big Liddell.

I began this project because I wanted to have what you now hold in your hands: a new translation of the hymns I could use in my own devotions and work. I hope that you enjoy it, and an additional dose of gratitude goes to you, the reader.

Evoe!

Patrick Dunn
Santa Barbara, California
8 July 2017

INTRODUCTION
TO THE ORPHIC HYMNS

The Orphic Hymns are eighty-eight (or eight-seven, depending on how you count them) devotional hymns written in a dialect of Greek known as Homeric or Epic Greek, in dactylic hexameter. They were probably composed at some point in the first four centuries of the common era near the region of Anatolia, in what is now Turkey. It is widely accepted that they were used as the liturgy of a particular Orphic cult, a mystery religion dedicated to the god Dionysos. The earliest manuscript to return to Europe was probably brought, as many ancient Greek texts were, by Giovanni Aurispa from Constantinople to Venice in 1423. Unfortunately, this manuscript is now lost, but it is usually considered the archetypal manuscript from which all other copies in the West derive. Thirty-six manuscripts, probably copies of the Aurispa archetype, survive, some in fragmentary form.[1] These manuscripts are the sources for the Quandt edition, which is reproduced here with the kind permission of Olms Weidmann Verlag.

The Orphic Hymns are named for Orpheus, mentioned twice in the corpus of the hymns: once in the title of the first introductory hymn, and once in a coda to the hymn to Fate. Orpheus, the son of Apollon and the muse Kalliope (by some accounts, at least), was born in Thrace. He became renowned as a musician whose skill at the lyre could command inanimate objects and beasts. He fell in love with Eurydike, but shortly after the wedding, she died from a venomous snake bite. He

---

1. Apostolos N. Athanassakis and Benjamin M. Wolkow, *The Orphic Hymns* (Baltimore: Johns Hopkins UP, 2013), ix.

followed her into the underworld, the realm of Hades, where he played for Plouton, the god of the dead. He played so well that Plouton wept iron tears and granted Orpheus's request to have her back for the full span of her life, but on one condition: he must not look at her until they had departed the realm of Hades. She followed him up the steep ascent, but once he stepped out into the light, he could no longer resist and looked behind him. But she was still in the darkness of the underworld, and now he had broken the condition. She was taken from him one last time. In grief he wandered the world until he encountered a group of women maddened in the worship of Dionysos. These Mainades, as they were called, tore him limb from limb. The Mousai gathered up his limbs and buried them; where they laid them, oracles sprang up. His head, by some accounts, washed up on the isle of Lesbos, where it prophesied after death.

The Orphic cult found this myth inspirational for its concept of descent and return from death. Their mystery rites may have contained some element of reenactment of this myth. The central god of Orphism, perhaps surprisingly considering his role in the myth, is Dionysos, god of wine. Stories of women maddened by his worship were common. Called Mainades or Bakchai, these followers of Dionysos were sometimes regarded as a danger, capable of tearing a man apart and consuming his flesh. Euripides's play *The Bakchai,* recounts the death of the blaspheming King Pentheus, who is killed by his own mother in a Bacchic frenzy.

There were indeed celebrations of Bakchos that involved dancing, drinking, and frenzied states of enthusiasm, and perhaps even the consuming of raw meat in honor of the god. But much of what we know about these Bacchanalia comes from sources critical of the practice, so it is impossible to know what is and what is not propaganda or slander. It is interesting that many of the criticisms of Bacchic mystery religions involve the same allegations laid, even at the same time, against Christianity: cannibalism, frenzy, madness, drunkenness, sexual license, and so on.

Also feeding into the stream of Orphic religious practices was the probably older mystery religion of Demeter of Eleusis. In this myth, recounted in the Homeric Hymn to Demeter, the god of the underworld, Plouton or Hades, kidnaps Demeter's daughter, called Kore or Persephone. He takes her to the underworld, where he keeps her captive. Demeter is enraged and heartbroken, and she wanders the earth refusing to eat. Since she is the goddess of grain, the earth begins to die until she comes to Eleusis and is employed by Queen Metaneira as a nurse for her infant child. Demeter tries to give immortality to the baby by nursing him on ambrosia and setting him in the fire to burn off his mortality but is caught by Metaneira, who misunderstands this ritual. Demeter reveals her true form, rebukes Metaneira, but then relents and promises to teach the rites of immortality to the people of Eleusis. Eventually, Persephone is returned to the world of the living but only for half of the year, leaving the other half barren and dead while Demeter mourns.

The rites of Eleusis are mentioned in the Orphic hymns, but we do not know what they entailed exactly because, being mystery religions, they were secret. We know that they occurred every five years, involved a lengthy initiation, and at the end of it, purportedly banished all fear of death.

Death is a perpetual concern in all mystery religions; or more accurately, *immortality* is a primary concern. The goal of these mystery religions appears to be a shared one: ward off the sting of death by giving some certainty about what awaits in eternity. The Orphic hymns refer to sleep as a practice or training for death, and the sequence of hymns ends (quite appropriately) with a hymn to Thanatos, the personification or daimon of Death.

While death is a chief concern, the hymns also refer to other, more life-affirming goals. They ask repeatedly for blessings, prosperity, piety, and so on. They also ask for very ordinary things: clear weather, protection for travelers, and the like. In this, they are halfway between praise poems and incantations, and they bear a slight resemblance to the Artharvaveda, Indian hymns to particular deities for specific magical effects.

It is possible that the hymns represent a single all-night ritual, with a particular sequence of initiatory steps. Albrecht Dieterech identified the sequence as a kind of liturgy as early as 1891. Fritz Graf carries on that idea to what appears to me to be a logical conclusion: the hymns are arranged as a ritual in themselves, with distinct parts. He points out that the first two hymns (after the introductory prayer), are hymns to Hekate as guardian of gates, suitable for initiates or worshippers entering into a temple.[2] Similarly, the hymn to Night occurs fairly early in the sequence, while the hymn to Eos or Dawn occurs later. The hymn to Night explicitly mentions all-night vigils. I think it is quite likely that these hymns were used more or less as Graf represents, which means that we have in them the liturgy if not the ritual actions of an entire initiation into a mystery religion.

We do not know if the hymns were sung or chanted, but it seems likely that the rituals included some kind of musical accompaniment. I have experimented myself with setting some of them to music with moderate success, both in modern scales and reconstructed Greek modes. I encourage experimentation along those lines. Those seeking inspiration can look at the Seikilos Epitaph, an inscription containing the only surviving complete Greek song with lyrics, probably dating from the first century of the common era. I would be happy to hear from those who have experimented musically with the hymns, and they may contact me in care of my publisher.

Whatever the Orphics may have done with them, the hymns also have a tradition in contemporary occult and Neopagan practices. Thomas Taylor was the first person to translate the hymns into English in 1792. Taylor, a devoted Neoplatonist, wrote and translated extensively on ancient Greek sources and philosophy. His poetic translation is enlivened by footnotes and an extensive introduction laying out his own interpretation of the purpose of the hymns. While his understanding is now dated by more contemporary research, it is still interesting and informative. Many people like his translations for their poetry, although others are less pleased by the common practice of translating Greek names into their sometimes approximate Latin equivalents. His translations are included at the end of this book, although I have not reproduced his notes or extensive introduction.

---

2. Fritz Graf, "Serious Singing: The Orphic Hymns as Ritual Text" in *Kernos* 22, (2009). http://journals.openedition.org/kernos/1784.

ON TRANSLATION

In translating these hymns I have relied predominately on the standard Greek edition of Guilelmus Quandt, *Orphei Hymni*, 1955. For context and analysis, I have referred to Anne-France Morand's *Études sur les Hymnes Orphiques*. I have also relied on her analysis of the various incenses and fumigations, and occasionally preferred her readings of the manuscripts over Quandt's.

The hymns are written, as mentioned before, in the Epic dialect, the same dialect used by Homer and Hesiod. This fact should not be taken as evidence of their antiquity. Imitation of the Epic dialect is common right up through late antiquity. Moreover, the imitation is not perfect; in fact, it is somewhat inconsistent between poems. This inconsistency may be evidence of multiple authors, which to me seems likely. For example, most of the hymns prefer the modal particle ἄν, which is commonly used in several dialects of Greek including Attic and Koine. The synonymous modal particle κέ, used predominately in the Epic dialect, is relatively rare in the Orphic hymns. Other choices, such as whether or not to employ the augment prefix for past tense (optional in Epic; mandatory in other dialects), are also inconsistent. However, most of this inconsistency could be explained by the authors' metrical concerns, aiming for a short or long syllable in order to fill out a line.

The meter, in fact, is very regular, often assisted by the use of formulaic utterances, repeated phrases to help fill out a metrical line. It appears that the author(s) were making a concerted effort to imitate Homer and Hesiod's own formulaic composition. In short, the ancient Homeric epics were originally composed orally, more or less extemporaneously, by stitching together formulas (like "grey-eyed goddess

Athene") to fill out metrical lines. Albert Lord showed that this practice was still very much alive in the twentieth century, though not in Greece but in Yugoslavia, where oral poets known as *guslars* composed very long oral epics by stringing together such formulas.[3] If the Orphic poet(s) imitated Homer in this way, they may have imitated his orality in order to impart a sense of antiquity and gravitas to their work, even though the hymns were almost certainly composed by literate people in writing.

In translating these hymns, I aimed for accuracy overall but also wanted to capture the effect of the poems as much as possible. I have tried never to sacrifice accuracy for effect, but when given some freedom by the Greek idiom or the richness of English, I have made choices that imitate the effect. For example, the hymn to Zeus the Thunderer contains a long string of harsh initial consonant clusters, particularly doubled plosives, an effect impossible to replicate in English. But I could choose words beginning with plosives rather than sibilants or liquids, and in some places did so in order to hint at the effect of the original. I have done this sort of thing with an extremely light hand, however, despite occasional temptations to impose my own poetic sensibilities on the work.

The Ancient Greek language presents an interesting set of challenges to the translator. The Greek verb, like its Proto-Indo-European ancestor, displays a complex morphology. The Greek verb can encode much more than the English verb, including three voices, two different kinds of irrealis moods, and an array of aspects and tenses. Moreover, the participles and infinitives can also mark tense, voice, and aspect in a way that English participles and infinitives cannot. This complexity allows a Greek participle or infinitive to enfold almost all the functions of a conjugated verb, meaning that a single participle can do the work that in English must be done with a subordinate clause or completely new sentence. Similarly, nouns can mark gender, number, and case, which allows very complex sentences, appositives, or participial phrases without concern for strict word order.

---

3. Albert B. Lord, *The Singer of Tales* (New York: Atheneum, 1973).

Many of the hymns consist predominately of participles and nouns, strung together in a stack, without clear connective tissue other than their declensions. In many places, this leaves room for interpretation. My general principle has been to lean, again, toward accuracy when possible and render strings of epithets merely as strings of epithets. But in those cases where participles clearly connect together conceptually, or when a participle governs an object or indirect object, I have rendered them as subordinate or independent clauses. I have not followed a formula in doing so but instead relied on intuition and my felt sense of the hymns' effects. I have always kept my grip firmly on the Greek, however, to prevent getting carried away.

I have chosen a simple meter for the poems in English, one that does not require me to bend or contort the translation to fit the poetic form. I felt it was important to have some sort of metrical element to the translation, since meter is essential to the original. However, an attempt at dactylic hexameter in English would require excessive violence upon the original. I have settled therefore on a simple syllable-based meter of ten-syllable lines, without much regard for the location of primary and secondary stresses. I suspect that readers will find this easy to read and fairly transparent while still giving a sense of poetic form. The general result is a loose and conversational iambic pentameter for many lines, dropping to a tetrameter for some, and raising to a hexameter for others. If the metrical scheme required me to distort the translation, I dropped it, something I have not had to do often.

I have transliterated the names of deities using the accurate transliteration recommended by the United States Library of Congress, without marking long vowels with macrons unless it seemed prudent to avoid confusion (such as with **Mēn**, which might otherwise be misread as the English word "men"), because the original Greek spelling is readily available in the Concordance and the macrons would make for an unsightly text. I have used the standard English transliteration of Greek place names in most instances, however, as being more familiar and easier to use than the Greek names, which are nevertheless included in the Concordance.

Because ancient Greek is a more concise language than English, the translations tend to be longer than the original poems. Often one or two words must be translated with several phrases in English. Therefore, this translation is not strictly parallel; lines do not strictly coincidence between the translation and the original. This difference in concision between the two languages also leads to some translations taking multiple pages where the original fits on a single pain, resulting in a few blank pages in order to maintain the useful facing-page structure of the text. This situation was deemed preferable to other options, such as having the originals in a separate section of the book, because parallel texts facilitates comparison between the originals and translations.

I have refrained from imposing my own philosophical perspectives (a nearly incoherent blend of skeptical postmodern Stoical Neoplatonism, more or less) or my own religious perspectives on the poems as a whole. Obviously, however, any translation is a product of its times and its translator. No uninterpreted text can exist, let alone be translated, from one language to another.

VOCABULARY

Certain important words show up with some frequency, often as part of a specialized technical vocabulary. I have not made an effort to translate these words with exactly the same English word each time, but I *have* made an effort to choose words that encompass the variety of meanings for these terms, as appears suitable in context.

For example, the word τέλος (*telos*) occurs in a large number of the hymns. I have usually translated this word as "end," as in "a noble end to life." But the word τέλος is polysemic, having many definitions, and "end" is only one of them. I have preferred "end" because this word, in English, is similarly polysemic, meaning both "conclusion" and "goal" (as in "means and ends"). These definitions also apply to τέλος. A τέλος can also refer to an offering given to a god, a power or magistracy, or even the consummation of marriage. Given the variety of possible meanings for this word, one should not read the repeated calls for an "end of life" as an obsession with death. "A noble end to life" could just as well refer to a life's purpose.

There are particular terms referencing specific initiatory and ritual roles. The most commonly referenced role is that of μύστης (*mustēs*), which I have translated as "initiate" or "worshipper." Another role, referenced several times, is that of βουκόλος (*boukolos*), "oxherd," which was apparently a particular office in the Orphic cult, about which we know nothing. Since the word "pastor" in Christianity means "shepherd," similar metaphors survived into contemporary times, although one would not want to read too much into that similarity without archeological evidence.

The word λόγος (*logos*) occurs several times and is also polysemous. It may mean "word," but also "computation" or "reason" or "story," among many other related possibilities. Among the Stoics, the word was used to denote the underlying reason of providence, a usage echoed in the New Testament, particularly in John 1:1.

The word διφυής (*diphuēs*) means "two-natured" or "two-formed." It's often, but not exclusively, applied to Dionysos, probably in reference to his dual nature as the son of a god (Zeus) and a mortal (Semele). It seems a particularly significant word in the light of the Orphic mystery, viz., that a mortal human can become immortal through initiation and thus partake of two natures.

The mention of Necessity or need often refers to the cosmic goddess Ἀνάγκη (*Ananke*). Less a goddess than a force of nature, Necessity is the ultimate origin of fate. The classical Greek playwright Aischylos says that even Zeus must follow the dictates of Necessity, but in the Orphic Hymns, Hymn 70 for the Eumenides claims that they are placed above or over Necessity itself. In the Orphic cosmology, it is Time (Chronos) and Necessity (Ananke) who form the cosmic egg from which Light (Phanes) and thus all creation hatches.

Dionysos is twice described in these hymns as a "sprout," ἔρνος (*ernos*). Adonis is called a "sprout" once. The word ἔρνος is used in Ancient Greek as a metaphor for a child. These are both vegetative deities, so "sprout" here is an appropriate metaphor. It also recalls the Orphic emphasis of rebirth.

I have translated the titles of the hymns extremely literally. These titles mostly consist of the name of a god in the genitive case. I have translated these as "For So-and-So." A few have the name of the god in the accusative, with the preposition ἐις (*eis*) "to" preceding it, and I have translated these accordingly. Some others identify themselves specifically as hymns for so-and-so, and are thus translated.

Rather than littering the text with footnotes, the Concordance in the appendices lists proper names with definitions and background information as well as which hymns the terms appear in. You can also find the original Greek spelling with Greek a pronunciation guide and notes on English pronunciation in the Concordance. Individual issues with the translations of particular hymns or interesting notes about the Greek occasionally appear in notes after the translations of individual hymns.

WHAT MAKES AN
ORPHIC HYMN ORPHIC?

We sometimes think of ancient Greek religion as a monolithic thing, but in fact there was no one single "ancient Greek religion." Nor is myth the same thing as religion, and neither is there a single mythology that can be called "Greek mythology." There was a set of shared myths and practices with quite a bit of overlap and replacement. Our perception of Greek myth as a single set of stories is erroneous. In fact, there were many competing and conflicting myths. For example, there are several different competing genealogies of the gods, not just Hesiod's. For example, Hesiod calls Chaos the first god, while Orphics declare that Phanes was the first. Believers did not for the most part fight about differences, as far as we can tell; they were simply accepted as the way other people saw things. There were no pagan Councils of Nicea or Diets of Worms, no charges of heresy. Of course, sometimes a mythological view of the world might conflict with the culture, and then such fighting could occur—we see this when Christianity was introduced into Rome, and we also see it in Rome's reaction to some of the rituals worshipping Dionysos, which were seen as subversive.

The theogony of the Orphics, the story of the gods' origins, differs from the standard theogony. The Orphics regarded the first god, Protogonos, to be Phanes. He hatched from an egg nurtured by Chronos (Time) or Aion and Ananke. He either creates or is in himself Eros, the god of sexual attraction, who brings together the disparate matter of Chaos and mixes it into multiple things. The wife of Phanes, Nyx (Night), gives birth to the Titans, among them Ouranos (Heaven), and

Gaia (Earth). This differs from Hesiod's theogony, although from this point on they begin to converge. Ouranos and Gaia give birth to Kronos and Rhea, who give birth to Zeus and his brothers and sisters.

The more vital myth for the Orphics is that of Dionysos, who is himself Phanes. There are actually multiple myths about him, and some efforts to unite them into one coherent narrative have obscured the variety.

In the Orphic tradition, Zeus names Dionysos, who is his son with either Persephone or Demeter (depending on the version of the myth), as his heir. Enraged at Zeus's infidelity, Hera incites the Titans to destroy Dionysos. The Titans trick him with toys and a mirror, then dismember and eat him. Zeus strikes them with a thunderbolt, reducing them to ashes. Athena rescues his heart and gives it to Zeus, who then impregnates Semele with the reborn Dionysos. After incinerating the Titans, Zeus forms humanity from the ashes thus giving humanity both natures, divine and monstrous.

But Hera, jealous of Zeus's philandering, convinces Semele to demand that her divine lover reveal his true form. A god's true form will destroy a mortal on sight, but Zeus had rashly promised Semele whatever she might desire. She asks this boon, and having sworn his word, he cannot deny her. He manifests himself in all his glory and she is incinerated. But Zeus takes the unborn child and sews him into his thigh, where he grows up and is born as Dionysos, god of wine and savior of humanity.

As coherently as these myths are presented (which is not very coherently), there is no single source that lays them all out in this way. In fact, the sources are fragmentary and disjointed, and some ideas—such as the idea that Zeus created humanity from the ashes of Titans—occur only in late sources. It may be that Orphics believed only a portion of this, or (as I think most likely) that different Orphics had different myths, believing none of them as absolute truth but seeing them as elucidating particular important ideas in their religion. Myth is not scripture in the Judeo-Christian sense; it is not infallible or—contrary to some notions of the purpose of myth—explanatory of natural phenomena.

Not only were myths complex and fluid, but so were religious practices themselves. Arguably religious practice is much more important to ancient religion than its mythology, which receives excessive attention in modern times. There were a set of shared practices but again with quite a bit of variation. Central to all Greek religion was the idea of sacrifice or offering, whether of animals or grains or incense or liquids. Particular gods may prefer particular sacrifices, and some local areas may have their own customs. Every region had not only its holidays, but often its own calendars.

It may even be that each region may have had their own versions of the gods. The Zeus of Dodona had different characteristics than the Zeus worshipped in Athens, and the Artemis of Ephesia was more than just a hunting goddess as she might have been elsewhere in Greece. When we say Apollon, we think of one god glued together from his many regional variations and end up with a musician, healer, prophet, and god of plague all at once. The ancients would have seen Apollon at Delphi as being a little different from Apollon in his temple at Delos. They were the same god, but just as we are different people in different places—I am not the same at home as I am at work—so too did the gods' characters change by location. At Delphi, Apollon may have preferred people behave one way, give him certain offerings and so on, yet behave in a completely different way at Delos.

In addition to practices, there was a set of basic beliefs, but here indeed is more than quite a bit of variation. Take the concept of the soul's eventual destination, for example. Some might believe, with Plato and apparently the Orphics, in reincarnation. Others may believe in a place of rather dull postmortem storage. Others expect punishment or reward after death, and some whom we would certainly classify as Pagan expect nothing at all after death but extinction.

When we look at the wide variety of practices, beliefs, stories, and ethics, it is strange to claim an entity such as "ancient Greek religion" existed. By today's standards, we would regard ancient Greeks as having many religions with the same or similar sets of gods, just as many people now regard Islam, Christianity, and Judaism as being three different religions with the same God.

The religions of the book—Islam, Christianity, Judaism—are exclusionary, while the various religions of Greek and Roman cultures were inclusionary. You could be an Orphic and also an initiate in the cult of

Isis, or in the mysteries of Eleusis, or in the cult of Mithris, or in all of the above and more. You could worship Zeus and Hera, but you could also worship Adonis and Serapis. You could honor Abraxas next to Dionysos. You could belong to any of these religions, or all.

Orphism was one of these religions, one among many. It was, as many of these religions were, a mystery cult. In other words, it required initiation and some degree of secrecy. Unlike the cult of Eleusis, we know a bit more about these practices, because they were slightly more public, and also because some practices, such as funereal offerings, involved writing formulas down in short grave texts. In these, the worshipper, having died, is confronted by guards at the lake of Mnemosyne, or memory. He is to respond to their questioning according to formula: "I am the son of the earth and of the starry sky. I am parched by thirst and I am perishing, but give me cold water to drink from the lake of Memory." [4] After that, the guards will let him drink.

Essentially, Orphism was a religion about death and the time after death. Orphics believed in reincarnation, that the body was a trap for the soul, and that the myths of descent into the underworld were myths about the redemption of that soul from its body and the wheel of rebirth. In this Orphism strikes a particularly Eastern note: it seems to share some similarity in ultimate goal with some forms of Hinduism (another set of diverse religions with a shared set of gods).

Ultimately, this concept of the body as a prison led to an ascetic rejection of material pleasure, again much as in particular versions of Hinduism. For a religion dedicated to Dionysos, there was remarkably little indulgence in sensual excess.

Strangely, little of what we know of the Orphics appears in the Orphic Hymns. For example, it might be reasonable to expect that the hymn to Mnemosyne, Titan of memory and mother to the Mousai, would reference the idea of the spring of Mnemosyne of which Orphics should drink after death in order to retain their consciousness in the afterlife, rather than drinking from the river Lethe (literally, "oblivion" or "forgetfulness"), which flows near the white cyprus. And yet, no

---

4. Fritz Graf and Sarah Iles Johnston, *Ritual Texts for the Afterlife: Orpheus and the Bacchic Gold Tablets* (London: Routledge, 2013), 4. My translation.

such mention is made. Instead, the hymn asks that the initiates remember the rituals correctly. In other words, an orthopraxic rather than an orthodox concern is paramount. It matters less what one believes than what one does.

This is not to imply, however, that no Orphic theological elements appear. For example, according to the Orphic theogony, the first god to arise was Phanes, from whom came the rest of the gods. Phanes is in fact the first form of Dionysos, who would later go through two additional forms, eventually to be born in human form although not—unlike Jesus Christ—as a human. The Orphic Hymns reference this particular theogony rather than that of Hesiod, which might be regarded as the more standard theology of Greek religions.

Another striking element of the Orphic hymns is that they exhibit a wide syncretism, although not as wide as some other contemporaneous texts. Syrian, Phrygian, and even Egyptian gods are mentioned in the hymns. And as Guthrie points out, this syncretism is "the order of the day."[5] Not only would a worshipper belong to multiple "religions" as mentioned above, but the person might also adhere to particular philosophies, which were seen more as the theology of the practice. The dominant philosophical schools at the time of the composition of the hymns include: Neoplatonism, which taught that the world we perceived was a shadow of a real world of ideas; Stoicism, which taught that we cannot control events but only our reactions to events; Epicureanism, which taught that carefully selected pleasure was the highest good and only the material world existed; and Skepticism, which taught that absolute knowledge was impossible.

In fact, these particular philosophical schools of the ancient world show up in the hymns. There are more than a few hints of Stoic doctrine, including the Stoic cosmology that Zeus was an underlying fire that would eventually consume the universe. Neoplatonic ideas also appear, as might be expected, considering the prevalence of Neoplatonism at the time.

---

5. William Keith Chambers Guthrie, *Orpheus and Greek Religion* (London: Mehtuen, 1935), 255.

Thomas Taylor, who translated these hymns for the first time into English in the late eighteenth century, was an avowed Neoplatonist, and in his voluminous notes and introduction to his translation, made an argument that the Orphic hymns were essentially allegorical and symbolic arguments for his own particular Neoplatonism. The fact that he was able to make this probably inaccurate argument—and do so convincingly—shows the degree to which these hymns are richly woven syncretic tapestries.

I think it likely that the original cult that used these texts as their liturgy had a more complete and coherent theology external to the hymns themselves. None of these hymns is a credo or a philosophical argument such as one finds in Proclus or Plotinus. And no one should expect them to be: they are hymns, designed for effect, not for catechism.

So, returning to the initial question of this section, what makes these hymns Orphic? The glib answer is that they say they are written by Orpheus, both in the introductory comment to Mousaios and in the hymn to the Fates. Orpheus, the singer of mythology, whose music was inspired directly by the gods, is a paramount Pagan prophet, suitable to any sect or group that wishes to claim divine authority.

A less glib answer is that the hymns reference ideas, albeit with a light touch, that appear in the Orphic theology. Phanes, for example, is given two hymns…but then again, only two. On the other hand, there are fourteen hymns that mention Dionysos or Bakchos. The goddess Night or Nyx, one of the central deities in the Orphic cosmology, is also referenced repeatedly. Yet other gods also appear, including Hera, whose relatively villainous role in the myths is never touched upon. And even stranger deities like Hipta and Melinoe make their appearances here and almost nowhere else. Maybe what makes these hymns Orphic is that they borrow from everything around them. Maybe that's the essence of Orphism, as it is of most of the syncretic ancient Greek mystery cults.

THE USE OF THE HYMNS

I am convinced that the hymns are a liturgy of a particular religious tradition, and that their order represents the progression of an all-night initiatory vigil interspersed with ritual actions, meditations, and rites that are not recorded.

However, because the religion was orthopraxic (more concerned with practice than belief), the hymns are well-suited to being taken from their original context and repurposed. There is among some groups a distaste for this kind of syncretism, which is understandable. However, the original hymns themselves are syncretic as were many of the religious practices of the time. Those who wish to use these hymns as devotional resources divorced from magical practice have my respect and can feel free to use the hymns only for religious devotion. Those of us who find magical practices spiritually fulfilling and efficacious may enjoy considering how to use these hymns for such purposes as well. Ultimately, it would be a hard case to defend that the hymns belong to anyone exclusively or to any exclusive purpose.

Religious Devotion

The most historically accurate use of the hymns, and probably closest to their original purpose, is devotion to the gods they represent. If you wish to use these hymns in worship, then you may wish to know how an ancient Greek sacrifice was done. Here is a simple outline you can follow. A full-fledged sacrifice of cattle would involve an entire community and a large public meal to follow, but by late antiquity it was extremely common to make small offerings of grain or bread. With that in mind, I suggest you focus on bread or fruit, and if you are creative and have some talent baking, you can make your bread in the shape of cattle, which would be appropriately symbolic.

You will need only a few tools. First, you need a dagger or knife that is only used to conduct sacrifice. This should be hidden or covered with a cloth. You will also need a container of water and a source of fire. Finally, you will want a cup of wine or juice or water, and a dish to pour some into, unless you are doing this outside, in which case you can pour it on the ground.

Start by purifying yourself. Take the water and light a small twig (a sprig of rosemary works nicely) in the fire. Throw the twig into the water so that it is extinguished. This makes the water into holy water, *chernips* (χέρνιψ), or literally "hand-washing." Use it to wash your hands and face, knowing that you are purifying yourself. Also sprinkle some over the offering, just a couple drops. Sprinkle a few drops on the ground and altar as well.

Invoke the god by reciting or reading the hymn aloud.

When you finish, light the incense—which can be an offering in its own right—or cut a small piece of the bread off and burn it. You may also pour the libation of wine at this point, pouring out just a small amount from the cup into the dish or onto the ground. You can offer only incense, incense and bread, incense and bread and a libation, *or* just a libation—but something must be offered.

Say a prayer to the god or gods, telling them why you are conducting the sacrifice. This can be a practical request, but it is also important to offer praise and thanks.

When you finish the prayer, cut the bread in two with the knife. Lay out half for the god, and eat the other half. Also drink the remaining wine or juice, if you have it. Let the incense burn down, and then dispose of the god's portion of the bread by leaving it outside in a clean place (so, under a tree for the animals to take, not in a junk heap or on top of a sewer grate or something).

To summarize for simplicity's sake:

1. Clean yourself and the environment with chernips.

2. Read an appropriate hymn (or several).

3. Light incense, pour libation, or cut a small piece of bread off and burn it, or any combination of the three.

4. Pray, telling the gods what is on your mind.

5. Cut the bread if you are using it and eat your portion, leaving the rest for the god. Drink the wine or juice, and let the incense burn down.

6. Dispose of the god's portion.

This can be a quick and simple ritual or an elaborate one depending on your particular desires. I can perform it in ten minutes at my home altar, making a quick offering of incense...or it can take an hour or more.

For more about the religious elements of this kind of work, you can read my book *The Practical Art of Divine Magic.*

Obviously, if you are Wiccan or some other Pagan persuasion and wish to use these hymns, you can find ways to incorporate them into your own work. I am not a purist about the use of these hymns, because I doubt that the original composers of these works were purists. They clearly had a syncretic streak as wide as the Aegean, so I have no doubt that they might have done something similar with any religious tradition coming into contact with them. If you are a purist and wish to reconstruct exactly what ancient Greco-Roman Pagans did, you may be stymied by the Orphic Hymns and the lack of clear archeological information; however, the above formula is probably fairly close to how they might have conducted a sacrifice.

Spell-Crafting with the Orphic Hymns

Although the hymns are religious in nature, it is also clear that they have a practical bent. For example, hymn 5, to Aither, is clearly designed not just to worship the god of the air, but to call upon him to create pleasant weather. Most of the hymns have a clearly defined purpose that we might call "practical," although I doubt that the original authors of the hymns thought in terms that separated the practical and the religious.

How the ancients used these hymns, for practical or religious reasons, is difficult to reconstruct and may be lost forever. But we do have some living magical traditions that make use of similar hymns, and we can take a page from those traditions for our own practice.

I have always had a bit of "holy envy" for the use of the Hebrew Psalms in magic. I remember being a teenager and reading a slender pamphlet that laid out the use of hymns for particular purposes. I no longer have that pamphlet, and I've since discovered that there are many such publications for the folk practitioner of magic. At the time, however, I remember feeling disappointment. Here was a virtual treasure trove of magical incantation, none of which I could really use, since I didn't belong to the Judeo-Christian tradition. That wouldn't stop some magicians, of course, and later I went on to study Cabala and call upon the Hebrew archangels without much problem (and some success). Still, I never used the psalms because while I admire their poetry, they do not speak to my religious experience as it is.

The Orphic Hymns, on the other hand, are a Pagan collection of psalms. Like most Pagan texts of antiquity, they may not always mesh perfectly with our experiences of the gods. There may be a hodgepodge of ideas or even some strange notions. But for the most part, we polytheists may find ourselves more drawn to hymns of this nature.

Moreover, even traditional magicians may—and do—find these hymns useful. Unlike the Homeric Hymns, the Orphic hymns are short. They are easy to read in a single sitting and make constant reference to epithets and identifiers of the god in question. These are all qualities that make them perfect for magic, if not always as poetically moving as their Homeric siblings.

A Katadesmos of the Hymns

There's a tradition in American folk magic known as the Himmelsletter, or "heaven letter." The heaven letter is a talismanic object in the form of a letter that promises the bearer protection in the name of divine forces, in the case of American folk magic, usually Jesus Christ. A longer tradition of written spells, *katadesmoi* (singular katadesmos, κατάδεσμος) in Greek and *defixiones* in Latin, stretches all the way back to antiquity. We find these letters scratched in lead sheets and nailed together in great numbers. Most of them, if not all of them, are curses, and they're often called curse tablets for this reason. Even the love spells are heavy-handed and not very friendly.

But we can use the Orphic Hymns to write our own katadesmoi without cursing people. There's a chance this is not exactly how this was done in the ancient world; we know very little about how to construct a katadesmos. We know that some were probably written by professionals, nailed together with iron, perhaps enlivened by a sacrifice, and buried or placed in a suitable location: a well, a tomb, a fresh grave. The following therefore is an innovation, not a reconstruction.

Begin by deciding what you want. Make your goal positive and express it in direct terms. Not "I want to get rich" but "I will be rich"—or better yet "I am rich." Be specific as well. Even working class Americans are rich by the standards of some people in the world. How about: "I make enough money to pay all my bills and go on a vacation once in a year."

Once you have an idea what you want, take a stack of blank paper and draw your desire. How would it look for you to be in that situation? Feel free to use stick-figures and symbols. Perhaps you can draw yourself holding out your hand with a big dollar bill in it. Now turn over a blank sheet and draw that same image again, all in one line. Do it again and again until you end up with a flowing symbol that does not resemble your original drawing at all.

Now get a clean sheet of paper. Light some incense appropriate to the god. Run the paper through the smoke so that it is smoked on both sides. Draw your symbol on one side of the paper. Turn the paper over. Now, open this book to an appropriate hymn (see Appendix III for a list of purposes and hymns related to them), and carefully copy either the English or if you prefer, the Greek in your best handwriting, very slowly, saying each word and visualizing it as you do. Do not think about your desire. Think about the words you are writing and speaking, and the images you are visualizing.

When you finish, you must dispose of the paper. If the god dedicated to the hymn is a god of water, placing it in a river or stream is a possibility. If the god of the hymn is chthonic, or a god of earth, then you might dispose of it in a hole in the ground or in a hollow in a tree. Best, though, and suitable to all gods, is to burn it along with an offering of incense to the god in question. Again, do not think about your desire, but let it go up in smoke. (Do make sure that you don't set off the smoke alarm in the process; that can be very jarring. I know from experience.)

A Simple Magical Use of the Hymns

Candle magic as practiced in American folk magic, Hoodoo, and other traditions is fairly simple and was predominately popularized by the early twentieth-century writings of Mikhail Strabo.[6]

Candle magic is not authentic to late antiquity, but I include it here to show how flexible these incantations can be. Many practitioners of folk magic do candle magic with the psalms of the Hebrew Bible, and candle magic is no more authentic to the period in which those psalms were written. We do know that lamp magic was commonly practiced by Pagans of late antiquity because the Greek Magical Papyri are filled with lamp spells, mostly to see the future or create a vision of a god in a dream. But I will describe some basic candle magic as practiced by folk magicians from several traditions of American popular magic. I do not want to erase the contribution made to American folk magic by black Hoodoo practitioners, who developed and refined these techniques in their own tradition. Considering that this kind of candle magic is practiced by Wiccans of all stripes and not just folk magicians, I hope my description is not seen as appropriative or disrespectful toward the original American practitioners of Hoodoo candle magic.

Your first step is to choose your goal, and I'd suggest you do this with a pen and a pad of paper. Write out what it is you want, in perfect detail. Spare nothing. For example, "I want to meet a tall, handsome man who respects me and treats me well." Now, revise that statement of desire, casting it in the present tense and removing anything like "I want…" or "I wish to…." In our example, this yields "I meet a tall, handsome man who respects me and treats me well." Books on writing always suggest specific telling details, so now try to figure out how you could more succinctly express this desire. If you think, in your heart of hearts, that tall and handsome go together, you don't need both: "I

6. Catherine Yronwode, "Mikhail Strabo: A Pseudonym of Sydney J. Rosenfeld Steiner" Lucky Mojo Curio Company website. Accessed June 30, 2017. www.luckymojo .com / strabo.html.

meet a handsome man who respects me and treats me well." But respect is similar to treating well: "I meet a handsome man who respects me." Wait—look at your verb! Do you *just* want to meet that man? No! "I love a handsome man who respects me." But few people want to love someone who only respects them. "I love a handsome man who respects me and loves me." Doesn't love include respect for you? (If not, why not? Maybe that's something you need to work on, if you think the two are different.) Try again: "I love a handsome man who loves me." We can make that more concise: "A handsome lover loves me." And we can make it more concise still: "A handsome lover."

Once you have your goal boiled down, you know what category it falls into. You need to select one (or more) hymns to fit under that goal. Here you might select hymn 55, to Aphrodite, the goddess of love.

Your next step is to choose your candle according to the desired goal. There are many different lists of candle colors and goals. Essentially, it comes down to what fits for your tradition. Here's a partial list of possible colors to give you an idea:

- Pink for love
- Green for money (if you're from the United States—otherwise, gold may work better)
- Blue for harmony and peace
- Yellow for enlightenment and happiness
- Red for lust
- Black for protection and harm

And so on. You can obviously come up with your own list, and probably should, by asking yourself what color you see behind your eyes when you think about this or that magical goal. If pink for love doesn't work for you (it doesn't for me at all; to me, pink is healing), pick a color that does.

Once you have selected your candle, you also should select your oil. If you're part of a tradition of magic like Hoodoo, this is easy. The names of the oils are evocative of their use. "Come to Me" works nicely for love magic. It is a good idea to research their particular uses.

If you buy pre-made oils, try to find oil that contains actual bits of herbs in it. I like the Lucky Mojo Curio Company, located just north of San Francisco, which is certainly worth the trip but also has an extensive online catalog and ships to anywhere in the United States and most places internationally. Some places sell Hoodoo oils that smell like carburetor fluid, but the Lucky Mojo folks create delightful smelling oils and source their herbs very carefully. I am not a Hoodoo practitioner, but I do like their oils and use them.

If you don't want to buy Hoodoo oils or can't get them, you can certainly make do. One way is to macerate a dried herb in olive oil for a few weeks and use the result. It won't be strongly tinted and it may not smell good. But it'll be magically effective (though not edible! Wet herbs soaking in oil is a recipe for bacteria growth). Alternately, you can use pure olive oil. But do not forgo oil completely; the oil is a carrier of intent.

Take your candle and inscribe the desire you designed earlier with a pin or—my favorite choice—a ballpoint pen that has run out of ink. If you can't fit the desire in its entirety, aim for a single word. Here, "love" would work just fine (and you might wonder why you went through the rigmarole of writing out the intent if you were going to boil it down to love, but the idea is to arrive at what "love" means to you before you ask for it). Write the intent from the base to the wick if pushing something out and from the wick to the base if drawing in. Here, I'd write "love" from the wick to the base, because I'm drawing love to me. Now anoint the candle with the oil. Put a drop on your finger, and rub the whole candle with it. Start from the middle outwards if getting rid of something, from the tip and base inward to the middle if drawing something in. Again, here I'd start at the tip and the base, and work my way around the candle, anointing the whole thing.

While you do this, keep your mind not just on your desire but also every sensory impression of the process. Here's where it's good to have a scented oil because you can breathe in its scent and let it fill your mind. But also make sure you feel the candle, the smoothness of its wax, the roughness of your inscription, and all other sounds and sensations in your sacred space.

When it's time to light the candle, take a few moments to calm yourself and clear your mind. Recite your statement of intent, and then immediately start the first hymn, starting with the line "Zeus, the king..." As you recite or read each phrase, clearly see in your mind the images described. Don't think about your desire—just see the gods and their attributes as laid out in the poem. When finished, read the hymn you selected for your goal. Again let your mind dwell not on your desire but on the images in the hymn.

When finished, look deeply into the flame for a few moments but do not think about your goal. When your mind comes to your goal, gently bring it back to the flame. Relax and trust the light, an offering to the gods, to handle your goal.

Then back away, turn around, and leave the room. You can come right back again if you need to (I do most of my magic in the study, where I often work on other things, so that's usually the case for me). Let the candle burn out completely, but don't leave it unattended. If you must snuff it, do so with your fingers or a candle snuffer, not by blowing on it. When you relight it, spend a few moments again contemplating the flame without considering your goal. Try to push your goal entirely out of your mind. Worrying about it will not accomplish it. Let the magic work.

Uses of the Hymns in Ceremonial Magic

By "ceremonial" magic I am speaking of the more formal, theatrical magical traditions, such as those of the Golden Dawn and other similar groups. This is the sort of magic that is concerned with planetary forces, timing, and ritual actions. The aim of ceremonial magic is to achieve a particular state of mind through theatre: by saying and doing certain things, taking on certain roles, and so on, the magician can shift his or her mind into a desired state to accomplish some goal.

There are two ways to use the hymns in ceremonial magic. You can use the hymns as pre-made invocations, often suitable at the beginning of a ceremony, or as the foundation of an entire ritual.

The hymns work, out of the box, as a liturgy of invocations for the ceremonial magician. For example, Hymn 1 to Hekate is useful in evocation work, regardless of the aim of the ceremony. You can also use other hymns as invocations of planetary forces. For example, Hymn 8 to Helios can be used to invoke solar force to charge a talisman or invoke solar powers for other ritual work.

A simple opening and balancing ritual can be constructed as follows:

I. Light the incense suitable to the rite and raise your arms. Recite the first hymn, "Orpheus to Mousaios," omitting the first two lines.

II. Face east of the place of working. Inscribe an appropriate symbol in the air, such as the alchemical symbol for air, an upward-pointing triangle with a horizontal line through the middle. Recite hymn 78, "For Eos."

III. Turn to face south. Inscribe an appropriate symbol, such as the upward-pointing triangle that represents fire. Recite hymn 82, "For Notos."

IV. Turn west. Inscribe a symbol, such as the downward-pointing triangle that represents water. Recite hymn 81, "For Zephyros."

V. Turn north. Inscribe a symbol, such as the downward-pointing triangle with a horizontal line through the middle, representing earth. Recite hymn 80, "For Boreas."

VI. Return to the center and recite the hymn of the god appropriate to the rite.

VII. Perform the ritual (i.e., making a talisman, evocation of a spirit, et cetera)

Hymns can be associated with particular sephiroth and planetary or elemental forces, such as the following:

Sephira	Association	Hymn
Malkuth	Earth	26 Gaia
Malkuth	Water	17 Poseidon, 22 The Sea, 23 Nereus
Malkuth	Air	5 Aither, 16 Hera
Malkuth	Fire	66 Hephaistos
Yesod	Moon	9 Selene
Hod	Mercury	28 Hermes
Netzach	Venus	55 Aphrodite

Sephira	Association	Hymn
Tiphareth	Sol	8 Helios
Giburah	Mars	65 Ares
Chesed	Jupiter	15 Zeus
Binah	Saturn	13 Kronos
Chokmah	Fixed Stars	7 Stars
Kether	First Mover	4 Ouranos, 6 Protogonos

Contemplation

The hymns can also be used as a source of contemplative meditation or prayer. Contemplative prayer is a Christian practice but has roots stretching back to the Neoplatonists, some of whose philosophy informs the Orphic hymns. This practice consists of focusing the mind gently upon an idea or an image, and following that image, returning the mind to it when it strays.

This practice is tied to *Lectio divina,* a practice of divine reading used by some Christian groups, but again with roots in earlier, non-Christian philosophy. This practice involves reading a passage slowly, allowing images to build up and accrue without judgment.

For example, in reading 67, "For Asklepios," one might proceed as follows:

I. Begin by looking up any unfamiliar names or references in the glossary and concordance of names and epithets included in Appendix I.

II. Read the hymn all the way through a couple times.

III. Now read slowly, stopping at each phrase to hold the idea in mind. This might look something like this:

Healer of all, [imagine a force that heals the entire universe; what would that be like? Hold it in your mind a few moments.] Asklepios, Paian [why these two names? What do they mean?]

the lord, [this implies power: how is healing a kind of power?] who touches [how is touch healing?] humans with magic [how is healing magic? Is all healing magic? Is all magic healing?]

IV. If thoughts drift, bring them back gently to the text.

V. Finish by reading the hymn again a couple times.

The benefits of this practice are both physical and spiritual. Such meditation can focus the mind, teach thought control, and give a closer relationship to the divine. It can also have physical benefits, such as reduced stress and better health.

Scents

Most of the hymns begin with a scent. These suggestions as to incense are often straight-forward, but not always. Frankincense, myrrh, and storax are obvious enough. Frankincense is the gum of one of several plants in the genus *Boswellia*. Similarly, myrrh is the gum from plants in the genus *Comiphorra*. Storax is a bit more complex. Morand identifies it as *Styrax officianalis*, which is also called benzoin.[7] However, what is now sold as storax often comes from one of the plants in the genus *Liquidambar*.

Two words are used to refer to Frankincense: λίβανος (*libanos*), and λιβανομάννα (*libanomanna*). The first simply means "frankincense," while the second is commonly used to refer to powdered frankincense.

Morand suggests, and Athanassakis agrees, that a third word, μάννα (*manna*), also refers to frankincense. The meaning of this word is, as Morand admits, not entirely clear.[8] It literally means "powder." But since a word for powdered frankincense already appears in the hymns—λιβανομάννα—it is hard to understand why a third distinction might be made. The word itself is not Greek but a borrowing from Hebrew, where it can refer to frankincense or to the gum of the tamarisk tree, *Acacia senegal*. This latter substance is currently available as gum arabic or acacia gum. It is unclear without further context which of these incenses μάννα is meant to denote.

The word ἀρώματα (*arōmata*) simply means "aromatic things." It is not clear, as Morand points out, which specific aromatic substance is meant. The term is used, as she explains, in medicine to describe various therapeutic fumigations that are identified, according to ancient theories of medicine, as "chaude, sèche et imputrescible" (hot, dry, and

---

7. Anne-France Morand, *Études sur les Hymnes Orphiques* (Leiden: Brill, 2001), 125.

8. Ibid., 120.

incorruptible).[9] Since fragrant woods are not mentioned elsewhere, I think it is possible that ἀρώματα are fragrant woods such as sandalwood. It may also refer to fragrant herbs such as rosemary.

The hymn for Aither (5) assigns κρόκος (*krokos*) as the incense. This refers to the crocus plant, *Crocus sativas*, from which we get saffron. Saffron was often used in medicine and a dye, as well as offerings for deities and spicing in food.

Several myths prescribe unusual fumigations such as torch smoke (3), all grains except aromatics and beans (26), and all incenses except frankincense (53). Hymn 53, "For the God of Yearly Feasts," also prescribes a libation of milk. And hymn 85 for Hypnos, the god of sleep prescribes a fumigation μετά μήκωνος (*meta mēkōnos*), meaning "with poppy." The resin of *Papaver somniferum* is the origin of opium.

Finally, two hymns—For Pan (11) and For the Mother of the Gods (27)—prescribe mixed or various incenses.

Ten of the hymns have no suggested fumigation at all.

Attempting to recreate these scents in modern practice is both easier (because of wider availability of scents), and more difficult (because of the uncertainty of the significance of some words or even the identity of ancient plants). There are, for example, artificially scented incenses that smell ostensibly like opium, which can be used for the hymn to Hypnos. There is also saffron-scented incenses. Frankincense and myrrh are easy to find even now, in convenient stick and cone forms, as well as the original powdered form burned on charcoal disks.

I suggest the following substitutions, although it should be borne in mind that these are my personal suggestions, not necessarily claims to historical accuracy. Strict reconstructionists should of course do further research on the history of scent, a history that is both fascinating and far beyond the scope of this book.

Incense can be found in several forms. The most historically accurate (and undoubtedly what the Orphics would have used) would be a container of small hot coals onto which granular or powdered incense is added. If you decide to use this method, make sure you pack the bottom of the container with sand. Small charcoal disks are readily available

---

9. Morand, Études, 120.

online and in occult stores. Also be sure you leave a window open or run an exhaust fan, especially for all-night vigils and similar long rituals if you will be burning a lot of incense this way. Some people prefer the convenience of sticks or cones, as I myself do. This limits some of your choices in some ways, and if you are a purist either in the historical reconstruction or avoidance of artificial materials sense, you will do best to employ the charcoal method.

Frankincense and myrrh: There are bewildering number of brands of incense available, and they all offer frankincense and myrrh. My personal preference is Morning Star, incense produced by Nippon Kodo in Japan that is easily found in the United States. I find that their incense does not irritate my eyes, as other brands do. The distinction between frankincense and powdered frankincense is one I ignore in practice, opting for the stick form out of convenience. Of course, a purist would not wish to cut that corner.

Aromatics: Morning Star offers pine, sandalwood, and cedar, all of which I have used. I prefer sandalwood for aromatics.

Torch smoke: Morning Star's pine scent resembles, to my mind, the scent of a freshly lit torch with its resin-like undertones.

Storax: Morning Star does not offer storax as a scent, but other companies do. You will want to do some research and experimentation if, like me, you prefer to eschew fillers and perfumes that irritate your eyes and nose.

Saffron: There is simply no way to avoid artificial perfumes in stick incense with saffron. Or, at least, I have not found one. Actually burning threads of saffron does not produce a particularly pleasant odor and is pretty expensive.

Poppy: As mentioned before, there are a variety of companies that produce an opium-scented (or so they say) incense. You can also grind poppy seeds fine and place the powder on coals. Whole seeds may pop and crackle, an effect that might distract from the ritual.

Another option is to rely instead on myth to guide our choices of scent. For example, we know from mythology that the bay laurel is sacred to Apollon, so we might burn bay leaves as an incense in worshipping him.

Finally, we can abandon the original tradition entirely and make use of Hermetic methods to select appropriate scents based on correspondences (Cabalistic, planetary, or other). This method is less of an abandonment of tradition than it may seem. For example, it would tell us that frankincense, an incense with solar associations, is a good one to burn for Helios. But we find that very suggestion in the hymns themselves: the fumigation for Helios (8) is powdered frankincense.

In practice, I use all of the above, depending on context and purpose.

THE

HYMNS

OF

ORPHEUS

ΟΡΦΕΥΣ ΠΡΟΣ ΜΟΥΣΑΙΟΝ.
Εὐτυχῶς χρῶ, ἑταῖρε.

Μάνθανε δή, Μουσαῖε, θυηπολίην περισέμνην,
εὐχήν, ἣ δή τοι προφερεστέρη ἐστὶν ἁπασέων.
Ζεῦ βασιλεῦ καὶ Γαῖα καὶ οὐράνιαι φλόγες ἁγναὶ
Ἡελίου, Μήνης θ᾽ ἱερὸν σέλας Ἄστρα τε πάντα·
καὶ σύ, Ποσείδαον γαιήοχε, κυανοχαῖτα,
Φερσεφόνη θ᾽ ἁγνὴ Δημήτηρ τ᾽ ἀγλαόκαρπε
Ἄρτεμί <τ᾽> ἰοχέαιρα, κόρη, καὶ ἤιε Φοῖβε,
ὃς Δελφῶν ναίεις ἱερὸν πέδον· ὅς τε μεγίστας
τιμὰς ἐν μακάρεσσιν ἔχεις, Διόνυσε χορευτά·
Ἄρές τ᾽ ὀμβριμόθυμε καὶ Ἡφαίστου μένος ἁγνὸν
ἀφρογενής τε θεά, μεγαλώνυμα δῶρα λαχοῦσα·
καὶ σύ, καταχθονίων βασιλεῦ, μέγ᾽ ὑπείροχε δαῖμον,
Ἥβη τ᾽ Εἰλείθυια καὶ Ἡρακλέος μένος ἠύ·
καὶ τὸ Δικαιοσύνης τε καὶ Εὐσεβίης μέγ᾽ ὄνειαρ
κικλήσκω Νύμφας τε κλυτὰς καὶ Πᾶνα μέγιστον
Ἥρην τ᾽, αἰγιόχοιο Διὸς θαλερὴν παράκοιτιν·
Μνημοσύνην τ᾽ ἐρατὴν Μούσας τ᾽ ἐπικέκλουμαι ἁγνὰς
ἐννέα καὶ Χάριτάς τε καὶ Ὥρας ἠδ᾽ Ἐνιαυτὸν
Λητώ τ᾽ εὐπλόκαμον, Θείην σεμνήν τε Διώνην
Κουρῆτάς τ᾽ ἐνόπλους Κορύβαντάς τ᾽ ἠδὲ Καβείρους
καὶ μεγάλους Σωτῆρας ὁμοῦ, Διὸς ἄφθιτα τέκνα,
Ἰδαίους τε θεοὺς ἠδ᾽ ἄγγελον Οὐρανιώνων,
Ἑρμείαν κήρυκα, Θέμιν θ᾽, ἱεροσκόπον ἀνδρῶν,
Νύκτα τε πρεσβίστην καλέω καὶ φωσφόρον Ἦμαρ,
Πίστιν τ᾽ ἠδὲ Δίκην καὶ ἀμύμονα θεσμοδότειραν,
Ῥείαν τ᾽ ἠδὲ Κρόνον καὶ Τηθὺν κυανόπεπλον
Ὠκεανόν τε μέγαν, σύν τ᾽ Ὠκεανοῖο θύγατρας
Ἄτλαντός τε καὶ Αἰῶνος μέγ᾽ ὑπείροχον ἰσχὺν
καὶ Χρόνον ἀέναον καὶ τὸ Στυγὸς ἀγλαὸν ὕδωρ
μειλιχίους τε θεούς, ἀγαθήν τ᾽ ἐπὶ τοῖσι Πρόνοιαν
Δαίμονά τ᾽ ἠγάθεον καὶ Δαίμονα πήμονα θνητῶν,

ORPHEUS TO MOUSAIOS
Use it fortunately, friend

Now learn, Mousaios, this most sacred rite,
a prayer, surpassing every other prayer:
Zeus, the king, and Gaia too: the holy
heavenly flames of Helios and Mene's
holy light, all stars, and you, Poseidon,
who fold around the earth with your dark hair;
holy Persephone, and Demeter,
giver of goodly fruit, and Artemis,
the maiden who pours arrows, and Eios
Phoebos, you who dwell in Delphi's sacred
plain; Dionysos, you, who bear greatest
honor among gods in the sacred dance.
And passionate Ares, and the sacred
strength of Hephaistos; and the goddess born
from foam, who won the gifts of greatest grace;
and you, chthonic king, strong and eminent
daimon. And Hebe, and Eileithyia,
and the noble strength of Herakles, and
the great help of justice and piety;
I invoke splendid nymphs, and greatest Pan,
and Hera, the round-bosomed wife of Zeus,
Aigis-bearing; lovely Mnemosyne
and the nine sacred Mousai, the Graces
and the Seasons and the Year, and sweetly
tressed Leto; divine, honored Dione;
the Kouretes armed for war, Kabeiroi,
Korybantes, great saviors and timeless
sons of Zeus, and the Idaian gods; and
the messenger of heaven, great herald
Hermes; and Themis, haruspex for men;
and I call on Night, the oldest, and Day,

ΟΡΦΕΥΣ ΠΡΟΣ ΜΟΥΣΑΙΟΝ.
Εὐτυχῶς χρῶ, ἑταῖρε.

Δαίμονας οὐρανίους καὶ ἠερίους καὶ ἐνύδρους
καὶ χθονίους καὶ ὑποχθονίους ἠδ' ἐμπυριφοίτους,
καὶ Σεμέλην Βάκχου τε συνευαστῆρας ἅπαντας,
Ἰνὼ Λευκοθέην τε Παλαίμονά τ' ὀλβιοδώτην
Νίκην θ' ἡδυέπειαν ἰδ' Ἀδρήστειαν ἄνασσαν
καὶ βασιλῆα μέγαν Ἀσκληπιὸν ἠπιοδώτην
Παλλάδα τ' ἐγρεμάχην κούρην, Ἀνέμους τε πρόπαντας
καὶ Βροντὰς Κόσμου τε μέρη τετρακίονος αὐδῶ·
Μητέρα τ' ἀθανάτων, Ἄττιν καὶ Μῆνα κικλήσκω
Οὐρανίαν τε θεάν, σύν τ' ἄμβροτον ἁγνὸν Ἄδωνιν
Ἀρχήν τ' ἠδὲ Πέρας—τὸ γὰρ ἔπλετο πᾶσι μέγιστον—
εὐμενέας ἐλθεῖν κεχαρημένον ἦτορ ἔχοντας
τήνδε θυηπολίην ἱερὴν σπονδήν τ' ἐπὶ σεμνήν.

ORPHEUS TO MOUSAIOS
Use it fortunately, friend

who brings the light, and on Faith, and Dike,
on noble Thesmodoteira, Rhea,
and Kronos, black veiled Tethys, the mighty
Ocean, with Ocean's daughters; the perfect
strength of Atlas and of Aeon, Chronos
the ever-flowing; the shining waters
of Styx: gentle gods; and good Pronoia;
the most holy daimon, and the daimon
baneful to mortals too, and the daimons
of heaven, of the air, in the water
and earth, under the earth, and coursing through
fire, and Semele of Bakchos, and each
Bacchanal; and Ino Leukothea,
and Palaimon, bringer of happiness.
Sweetly speaking Nike and lady
Adresteia; and the powerful king
Asklepios, who bears the soothing balm,
and maiden Pallas, who rouses battle;
to all winds, and the thunder, and the limbs
of four-pillared Kosmos, I cry. I call
the Mother of the Gods, and on Attis,
and Mēn, and divine Ourania, with
holy, immortal Adonis, and on
the Beginning and the Ending as well—
for in everything, these are the greatest—
gracious ones, to come, with hearts full of joy,
to this sacred rite and holy libation.

Notes: Mousaios is either the son or the student of Orpheus. Here he
is called a "friend" or "companion" or Orpheus. This is an all-purpose
hymn, covering nearly all important gods and a few obscure ones. In
making use of this hymn, I leave off the first two lines and accompany
it with a libation, a pouring out of liquid offerings.

1. <Ἑκάτης>.

Εἰνοδίαν Ἑκάτην κλήιζω, τριοδῖτιν, ἐραννήν,
οὐρανίαν χθονίαν τε καὶ εἰναλίαν, κροκόπεπλον,
τυμβιδίαν, ψυχαῖς νεκύων μέτα βακχεύουσαν,
Περσείαν, φιλέρημον, ἀγαλλομένην ἐλάφοισι,
νυκτερίαν, σκυλακῖτιν, ἀμαιμάκετον βασίλειαν,
θηρόβρομον, ἄζωστον, ἀπρόσμαχον εἶδος ἔχουσαν,
ταυροπόλον, παντὸς κόσμου κληιδοῦχον ἄνασσαν,
ἡγεμόνην, νύμφην, κουροτρόφον, οὐρεσιφοῖτιν,
λισσόμενος κούρην τελεταῖς ὁσίαισι παρεῖναι
βουκόλωι εὐμενέουσαν ἀεὶ κεχαρηότι θυμῶι.

1. For Hekate

I call the beloved goddess of the roads
and places where three ways meet. Heavenly,
earthly, and in the sea, the saffron-cloaked
goddess of graves, performing the Bacchic
rites with the souls of the dead. The daughter
of Perses, lover of solitude, who
delights in deer, the nocturnal goddess,
protector of dogs, implacable queen
roaring like a beast, with image ungirt
and irresistible. Bull-herding queen
and key-bearer to all the universe,
ruler, nymph, and nursemaid who haunts the hills.
I pray you, maiden, to attend these rites,
always with a kind heart to your oxherd.

Notes: Proclus in his hymn to Hekate and Janus, the Roman god of doorways, equates the two. The idea that she rules the heavens, earth, and sea comes from Hesiod, who says that unlike other gods, she gets a share of all three realms. The "oxherd" here is probably the reference to a particular ritual role in the cult of Orpheus.

2 Προθυραίας, θυμίαμα στύρακα.

Κλῦθί μοι, ὦ πολύσεμνε θεά, πολυώνυμε δαῖμον,
ὠδίνων ἐπαρωγέ, λεχῶν ἡδεῖα πρόσοψι,
θηλειῶν σώτειρα μόνη, φιλόπαις, ἀγανόφρον,
ὠκυλόχεια, παροῦσα νέαις θνητῶν, Προθυραία,
κλειδοῦχ᾽, εὐάντητε, φιλοτρόφε, πᾶσι προσηνής,
ἢ κατέχεις οἴκους πάντων θαλίαις τε γέγηθας,
λυσίζων᾽, ἀφανής, ἔργοισι δὲ φαίνηι ἅπασι,
συμπάσχεις ὠδῖσι καὶ εὐτοκίηισι γέγηθας,
Εἰλείθυια, λύουσα πόνους δειναῖς ἐν ἀνάγκαις·
μούνην γὰρ σὲ καλοῦσι λεχοὶ ψυχῆς ἀνάπαυμα·
ἐν γὰρ σοὶ τοκετῶν λυσιπήμονές εἰσιν ἀνῖαι
Ἄρτεμις Εἰλείθυια καὶ ἡ σεμνή, Προθυραία.
κλῦθι, μάκαιρα, δίδου δὲ γονὰς ἐπαρωγὸς ἐοῦσα
καὶ σῶζ᾽, ὥσπερ ἔφυς αἰει σώτειρα προπάντων.

2. For Prothyraia

Incense: storax

Hear me, much honored goddess, many named
spirit and helper of those in labor,
sweet sight to those who give birth, and only
savior of women, gentle-minded one
who loves children. You give quick birth, and guard
mortal young, Prothyraia, the gracious
key holder, delighting in child-rearing.
Kindly to all, you occupy every
household, and take great glee in festivals.
You untie the belts, invisible but
apparent in every action you take.
You share the pains of labor, and rejoice
in every healthy birth. You loosen pains,
Eileithyia, of all those who suffer
in terrible necessity; to you
alone, as a rest for the soul, women
in childbed cry out, for in you the pains
and trouble of childbirth end, Artemis
Eileithyia, and the most honored
Prothyraia, blessed helper, hear me:
deliver and preserve offspring: you are
alway by nature the savior of all.

Notes: Thomas Taylor points out that the sequence of hymns begin with childbirth and end in death, but he includes the previous hymn to Hekate in the introductory hymn to Mousaios.[10] However, his point that this indicates that we have a complete text, with a deliberate order, still holds, because Hekate is also sometimes called Prothyraia.

---

10 Thomas Taylor, "The Hymns of Orpheus" via Sacred Texts Archive. Accessed 29 June 2017. http://www.sacred-texts.com/cla/hoo/index.htm.

3 Νυκτός, θυμίαμα δαλούς.

Νύκτα θεῶν γενέτειραν ἀείσομαι ἠδὲ καὶ ἀδρῶν.
{Νὺξ γένεσις πάντων, ἣν καὶ Κύπριν καλέσωμεν}
κλῦθι, μάκαιρα θεά, κυαναυγής, ἀστεροφεγγής,
ἡσυχίηι χαίρουσα καὶ ἠρεμίηι πολυύπνωι,
εὐφροσύνη, τερπνή, φιλοπάννυχε, μῆτερ ὀνείρων,
ληθομέριμν᾽ ἀγαθή τε, πόνων ἀνάπαυσιν ἔχουσα,
ὑπνοδότειρα, φίλη πάντων, ἐλάσιππε, νυχαυγής,
ἡμιτελής, χθονία ἠδ᾽ οὐρανία πάλιν αὐτή,
ἐγκυκλία, πλάγκτειρα διώγμασιν ἠεροφοίτοις,
ἣ φάος ἐκπέμπεις ὑπὸ νέρτερα καὶ πάλι φεύγεις
εἰς Ἀίδην· δεινὴ γὰρ ἀνάγκη πάντα κρατύνει.
νῦν σε, μάκαιρα, <καλ>ῶ, πολυόλβιε, πᾶσι ποθεινή,
εὐάντητε, κλύουσα ἱκετηρίδα φωνὴν
ἔλθοις εὐμενέουσα, φόβους δ᾽ ἀπόπεμπε νυχαυγεῖς.

3. For Nyx

fumigation with torch smoke
I will sing of Night, the mother of gods
and of humans. Nyx, the source of all things,
whom we may also call Kypris, hear me,
blessed goddess shining in the dark sky,
filled with bright stars, rejoicing in silent
nights of sleeping peace; mirthful and happy,
you love all-night vigils, mother of dreams.
You banish care, gently push away pains;
giver of sleep, friend to all, night shining
you lead your horses forth, and half the time,
you wander the earth; and then, the heavens,
wheeling about in your air-haunting hunt.
You send forth light into the depths, then flee
to Hades; for dreadful necessity
governs all. Now I call on you, happy,
much beloved, hearing my supplicating voice,
kindly come, and drive back the fears of night.

Notes: It's interesting that Kypris, an epithet usually given to Aphrodite the goddess of love in reference to her mythological birth in Cyprus, is appended to Nyx, the goddess of night. I follow Morand in reading παίκτειρα (one who plays) as πλάγκτειρα (one who wanders).[11]

---

11. Morand, *Études*, 3 n.2.

4 Οὐρανοῦ, θυμίαμα λίβανον.

Οὐρανὲ παγγενέτωρ, κόσμου μέρος αἰὲν ἀτειρές,
πρεσβυγένεθλ᾽, ἀρχὴ πάντων πάντων τε τελευτή,
κόσμε πατήρ, σφαιρηδὸν ἑλισσόμενος περὶ γαῖαν,
οἶκε θεῶν μακάρων, ῥόμβου δίναισιν ὁδεύων,
οὐράνιος χθόνιός τε φύλαξ πάντων περιβληθείς,
ἐν στέρνοισιν ἔχων φύσεως ἄτλητον ἀνάγκην,
κυανόχρως, ἀδάμαστε, παναίολε, αἰολόμορφε,
πανδερκές, Κρονότεκνε, μάκαρ, πανυπέρτατε δαῖμον,
κλῦθ᾽ ἐπάγων ζωὴν ὁσίαν μύστηι νεοφάντηι.

4. For Ouranos

Incense: frankincense

Ouranos, source of all, eternal share
of the cosmos, and first born. Origin
of all, and of all the end, o cosmic
father, your turning sphere pivots around
the earth, home of the blessed gods, whirling
like a bull-roarer, spinning, wrapped around
everything, the guardian of heaven
and earth, who holds in his bosom nature's
irresistible necessity. Blue
skinned, the unbending, sparkling, changeable.
You see all things, blessed father of Kronos,
highest daimon, hear and bring to the new
initiate a life of holiness.

Notes: A bull-roarer is a device on a string that when spun, produces a
loud whirring noise. It was an ancient toy as well as a cult instrument.

5 Αἰθέρος, θυμίαμα κρόκον.

Ὦ Διὸς ὑψιμέλαθρον ἔχων κράτος αἰὲν ἀτειρές,
ἄστρων ἡελίου τε σεληναίης τε μέρισμα,
πανδαμάτωρ, πυρίπνου, πᾶσι ζωοῖσιν ἔναυσμα,
ὑψιφανὴς Αἰθήρ, κόσμου στοιχεῖον ἄριστον,
ἀγλαὸν ὦ βλάστημα, σελασφόρον, ἀστεροφεγγές,
κικλήσκων λίτομαί σε κεκραμένον εὔδιον εἶναι.

5. For Aither

Incense: crocus

Holding Zeus's high-built and eternal,
indelible power, you have a share
of the sun and the stars and the moon; all
subduing, flame breathing, to all the beasts
a spark: high-shining Aither, the finest
element of the cosmos, o shining
offspring, who brings light and shines with the stars,
I call and ask you for fair, clear weather.

Note: Thomas Taylor calls this hymn "Fire." [12] Aither refers to the upper air.

---

12. Taylor, *Hymns*.

6 Πρωτογόνου, θυμίαμα σμύρναν.

Πρωτόγονον καλέω διφυῆ, μέγαν, αἰθερόπλαγκτον,
ὠιογενῆ, χρυσέαισιν ἀγαλλόμενον πτερύγεσσι,
ταυροβόαν, γένεσιν μακάρων θνητῶν τ' ἀνθρώπων,
σπέρμα πολύμνηστον, πολυόργιον, Ἡρικεπαῖον,
ἄρρητον, κρύφιον ῥοιζήτορα, παμφαὲς ἔρνος,
ὅσσων ὃς σκοτόεσσαν ἀπημαύρωσας ὁμίχλην
πάντη δινηθεὶς πτερύγων ῥιπαῖς κατὰ κόσμον
λαμπρὸν ἄγων φάος ἁγνόν, ἀφ' οὗ σε Φάνητα κικλήσκω
ἠδὲ Πρίηπον ἄνακτα καὶ Ἀνταύγην ἑλίκωπον.
ἀλλά, μάκαρ, πολύμητι, πολύσπορε, βαῖνε γεγηθὼς
ἐς τελετὴν ἁγίαν πολυποίκιλον ὀργιοφάνταις.

6. For Protogonos

Incense: myrrh
I call Protogonos, two-natured, great
wind-striding, egg-born, fluttering golden
wings in delight, bull roaring. Begetter
of blessed ones and of mortal humans:
much remembered, often celebrated
seed—Erikepaios, ineffable
hidden whirling bright scion. You scattered
the dim mist that confounded sight, and spun
about with your wings on all sides, and to
the universe you brought bright and holy
light, and so I call you Phanes and Lord
Priapos, and the bright-eyed Antauges.
Blessed, wise, and fecund divinity,
come with joy to the initiators
of this most intricate and holy rite.

Notes: The word *protogonos* simply means "firstborn." Phanes is a primal deity in the Orphic cosmology, and this poem is particularly Orphic in tone. The mention of Priapos puts me in mind of the Egyptian myth of Atum, who in some accounts created the universe through masturbation.

7 Ἄστρων, θυμίαμα ἀρώματα.

Ἄστρων οὐρανίων ἱερὸν σέλας ἐκπροκαλοῦμαι
εὐιέροις φωναῖσι κικλήσκων δαίμονας ἁγ[ν]ούς.
Ἀστέρες οὐράνιοι, Νυκτὸς φίλα τέκνα μελαίνης,
ἐγκυκλίοις δίναισι περιθρόνια κυκλέοντες.
ἀνταυγεῖς, πυρόεντες, ἀεὶ γενετῆρες ἁπάντων,
μοιρίδιοι, πάσης μοίρης σημάντορες ὄντες,
θνητῶν ἀνθρώπων θείαν διέποντες ἀταρπόν,
ἑπταφαεῖς ζώνας ἐφορώμενοι, ἠερόπλαγκτοι,
οὐράνιοι χθόνιοί τε, πυρίδρομοι, αἰὲν ἀτειρεῖς,
αὐγάζοντες ἀεὶ νυκτὸς ζοφοειδέα πέπλον,
μαρμαρυγαῖς στίλβοντες, εὔφρονες ἐννύχιοί τε·
ἔλθετ᾽ ἐπ᾽ εὐιέρου τελετῆς πολυΐστορας ἄθλους
ἐσθλὸν ἐπ᾽ εὐδόξοις ἔργοις δρόμον ἐκτελέοντες.

7. For the Stars

Incense: aromatics
I call for the holy light of the stars
in heaven, and with very holy words,
I invoke the sacred daimons. The stars
of heaven, dear children of the black night,
whirling in circles round about the throne,
flame reflecting parents of all that is.
Destinies: you are signals of all fates.
You lay out the divine path for mortals,
overseeing the seven shining spheres.
You wander in the middle air. On earth,
in heaven, trailing fire, ever-flowing,
indestructible, always discerning
the dark hued tapestry of night. Brilliant,
sparkling, and gentle in the night, come now
to learned contests of the holy rite,
and accomplish for these glorious works
the finish of an honorable course.

Notes: The belief in astrology was extremely widespread throughout all of antiquity, and the course of the stars was regarded as determining or indicating destiny. It is interesting that the rites here are described as a kind of contest or task. Presumably the initiate was required to accomplish some goal as part of the initiation. There are seven visible "planets," or wandering stars, in Hellenistic astrology: Luna, Mercury, Venus, Sol, Mars, Jupiter, Saturn. These were associated with Greek gods early on, in order: Selene, Hermes, Aphrodite, Helios, Ares, Zeus, Kronos. They were also given individual names, sometimes personified, such as Stilbon for Mercury.

8 Εἰς Ἥλιον, θυμίαμα λιβανομάνναν.

Κλῦθι μάκαρ, πανδερκὲς ἔχων αἰώνιον ὄμμα,
Τιτὰν χρυσαυγής, Ὑπερίων, οὐράνιον φῶς,
αὐτοφυής, ἀκάμα<ς>, ζώιων ἡδεῖα πρόσοψι,
δεξιὲ μὲν γενέτωρ ἠοῦς, εὐώνυμε νυκτός,
κρᾶσιν ἔχων ὡρῶν, τετραβάμοσι ποσσὶ χορεύων,
εὔδρομε, ῥοιζήτωρ, πυρόεις, φαιδρωπέ, διφρευτά,
ῥόμβου ἀπειρεσίου δινεύμασιν οἶμον ἐλαύνων,
εὐσεβέσιν καθοδηγὲ καλῶν, ζαμενὴς ἀσεβοῦσι,
χρυσολύρη, κόσμου τὸν ἐναρμόνιον δρόμον ἕλκων,
ἔργων σημάντωρ ἀγαθῶν, ὡροτρόφε κοῦρε,
κοσμοκράτωρ, συρικτά, πυρίδρομε, κυκλοέλικτε,
φωσφόρε, αἰολόδικτε, φερέσβιε, κάρπιμε Παιάν,
αἰθαλής, ἀμίαντε, χρόνου πάτερ, ἀθάνατε Ζεῦ,
εὔδιε, πασιφαής, κόσμου τὸ περίδρομον ὄμμα,
σβεννύμενε λάμπων τε καλαῖς ἀκτῖσι φαειναῖς,
δεῖκτα δικαιοσύνης, φιλονάματε, δέσποτα κόσμου,
πιστοφύλαξ, αἰεὶ πανυπέρτατε, πᾶσιν ἀρωγέ,
ὄμμα δικαιοσύνης, ζωῆς φῶς· ὦ ἐλάσιππε,
μάστιγι λιγυρῆι τετράορον ἅρμα διώκων·
κλῦθι λόγων, ἡδὺν δὲ βίον μύστηισι πρόφαινε.

8. To Helios

Incense: powdered frankincense
Hear me, blessed god with the eternal
eye, all-seeing; golden shining Titan;
Hyperion, heavenly light; natural,
enduring, sweet sight to all living things:
on the right hand, the father of the dawn;
on the left, the night. You hold the mixture
of the seasons, and your four-hoofed steeds dance
swift of foot, with a rushing noise. Fiery,
cheerful charioteer, you ceaselessly
drive the endless, turning path through the sky.
You guide the worshipful ones to goodness,
and give your rage to evil. Your golden
lyre holds up the harmonic cosmic course.
Leader of good works, youthful attendant
to the seasons' turning, the world's ruler,
you play the pipes, trailing fire in your wake,
revolving in a circle, bringing light,
all-shining, life-bringing, fruitful Paian.
Always young, undefiled, father of time,
deathless Zeus, clear, shining on all, the eye
that runs around the world, quenching the light,
and then shining forth your beautiful rays.
You guide us to justice, water-loving
lord of the world, guardian of the truth,
ever the very highest aid of all.
Eye of justice, light of life, o horseman,
with cracking whip your drive the four horses
of your chariot. Hear my words and show
a pleasant life to the initiates.

Note: The fact that the hymn to the stars is followed by Helios and then
Selene, is more evidence that these hymns were carefully arranged. Helios here is conflated to some degree with Apollon, not at all unusual in
late antiquity.

9 Εἰς Σελήνην, θυμίαμα ἀρώματα.

Κλῦθι, θεὰ βασίλεια, φαεσφόρε, δῖα Σελήνη,
ταυρόκερως Μήνη, νυκτιδρόμε, ἠεροφοῖτι,
ἐννυχία, δαιδοῦχε, κόρη, εὐάστερε, Μήνη,
αὐξομένη καὶ λειπομένη, θῆλύς τε καὶ ἄρσην,
αὐγάστειρα, φίλιππε, χρόνου μῆτερ, φερέκαρπε,
ἠλεκτρίς, βαρύθυμε, καταυγάστειρα, νυχία,
πανδερκής, φιλάγρυπνε, καλοῖς ἄστροισι βρύουσα,
ἡσυχίηι χαίρουσα καὶ εὐφρόνηι ὀλβιομοίρωι,
λαμπετίη, χαριδῶτι, τελεσφόρε, νυκτὸς ἄγαλμα,
ἀστράρχη, τανύπεπλ᾽, ἑλικοδρόμε, πάνσοφε κούρη,
ἐλθέ, μάκαιρ᾽, εὔφρων, εὐάστερε, φέγγεϊ τρισσῶι
λαμπομένη, σώζουσα νέους ἱκέτας σέο, κούρη.

9. To Selene

Incense: aromatics
Hear, royal goddess, light-bearing, divine
Selene, bull-horned Mene, night-runner,
roamer through the nightly air, torch bearing
fair-starred maiden, Mene, you wax and wane
both male and female, a shining lover
of horses, mother of time, fruit-bearing,
amber, somber, shining down in the night,
all-seeing, wakeful, full of lovely stars,
rejoicing in silence and the blessed
peace of the night, bright giver of good grace
and bringer of completion, a holy
image of the night, you lead out the stars,
your long cloak streaming, running in spirals.
All-wise maiden, come, blessed kind goddess
of beautiful stars, and shine with threefold
light, maid, redeeming your new supplicants.

Note: Taylor suggests, based on an Orphic fragment and a passage by Proclus, that Mene is the mortal name of the moon, while Selene is the name the gods gave it.[13]

---

13. Taylor, *Hymns.*

10 Φύσεως, θυμίαμα ἀρώματα.

Ὦ Φύσι, παμμήτειρα θεά, πολυμήχανε μῆτερ,
οὐρανία, πρέσβειρα, πολύκτιτε δαῖμον, ἄνασσα,
πανδαμάτωρ, ἀδάμαστε, κυβερνήτειρα, παναυγής,
παντοκράτειρα, τιτιμενέα πανυπέρτατε πᾶσιν
ἄφθιτε, πρωτογένεια, παλαίφατε, κυδιάνειρα,
ἐννυχία, πολύτειρε, σελασφόρε, δεινοκάθεκτι,
ἄψοφον ἀστραγάλοισι ποδῶν ἴχνος εἰλίσσουσα,
ἁγνή, κοσμήτειρα θεῶν ἀτελής τε τελευτή,
κοινὴ μὲν πάντεσσιν, ἀκοινώνητε δὲ μούνη,
αὐτοπάτωρ, ἀπάτωρ, ἐρατή, πολύγηθε, μεγίστη,
εὐάνθεια, πλοκή, φιλία, πολύμικτε, δαῆμον
ἡγεμόνη, κράντειρα, φερέσβιε, παντρόφε κούρη,
αὐτάρκεια, δίκη, Χαρίτων πολυώνυμε πειθώ,
αἰθερία, χθονία καὶ εἰναλία μεδέουσα,
πικρὰ μέν φαύλοισι, γλυκεῖα δὲ πειθομένοισι,
πάνσοφε, πανδώτειρα, κομίστρια, παμβασίλεια,
αὐξιτρόφος, πίειρα πεπαινομένων τε λύτειρα.
πάντων μὲν σὺ πατήρ, μήτηρ, τροφὸς ἠδὲ τιθηνός,
ὠκυλόχεια, μάκαιρα, πολύσπορος, ὡριὰς ὁρμή,
παντοτεχνές, πλάστειρα, πολύκτιτε, ποντία δαῖμον,
αἰδία, κινησιφόρε, πολύπειρε, περίφρων,
ἀενάωι στροφάλιγγι θοὸν ῥύμα δινεύουσα,
πάνρυτε, κυκλοτερής, ἀλλοτριομορφοδίαιτε,
εὔθρονε, τιμήεσσα, μόνη τὸ κριθὲν τελέουσα,
σκηπτούχων ἐφύπερθε βαρυβρεμέτειρα κρατίστη,
ἄτρομε, πανδαμάτειρα, πεπρωμένη, αἶσα, πυρίπνους,
ἀίδιος ζωὴ ἠδ' ἀθανάτη τε πρόνοια·
πάντα σύ ἐσσι, ἄνασσα· σὺ γὰρ μούνη τάδε τεύχεις.
ἀλλά, θεά, λίτομαί σε σὺν εὐόλβοισιν ἐν ὥραις
εἰρήνην ὑγίειαν ἄγειν, αὔξησιν ἁπάντων.

10. For Physis

Incense: aromatics
O Physis, all-mother goddess, mother
of infinite means, heavenly, ancient,
ever-making daimon, almighty queen,
unbending tamer and shining pilot,
honored above all others, immortal,
first-born, legendary glorifier:
in the night you bring forth light, full of stars,
and invincible. You turn the ankles
of your feet in a silent dance. Awesome
divine ruler, the end, and the endless,
shared by all, but without peer—self-fathered,
and fatherless—lovely, cheerful, and great.
You mingle life, beloved, into a web;
flowery and full of knowledge, you lead
and rule, giving life, maiden nurse of all,
self-sufficient. Dike, the many-named
Peitho of the Graces. You guard the air,
the earth, the sea. You are bitter to fools
but sweet to those who obey. All-giving,
all-wise, queen and nurse of all. You make fruit
grow fat, then melt away. Indeed, you are
father, mother, nurse, nursemaid of all things.
You bring quick birth, blessed one, of many seeds,
and the onrush of seasons. You are deft,
shaping and building, daimon of the sea.
O eternal, skilled and thoughtful mover,
you spin the swift stream into a turning
eddy, fluid and swirling round; you are
ever changing forms on your beautiful
throne; precious, you alone bring the judgment
to fruition. Roaring with thunder, you
stand mighty above the staff-bearers. You,

dauntless, all-taming, fated and Fate, breath
flaming, eternal life, deathless forethought;
you yourself are everything, queen, for you
alone fashion all. So, Goddess, I pray
that you in your season, with wealth, bring peace
as well as health and growth to everyone.

Note: Peitho is sometimes an epithet of Aphrodite, who is often considered a goddess of nature due to the role of sexual reproduction in
natural growth.

11 Πανός, θυμίαμα ποικίλα.

Πᾶνα καλῶ κρατερόν, νόμιον, κόσμοιο τὸ σύμπαν,
οὐρανὸν ἠδὲ θάλασσαν ἰδὲ χθόνα παμβασίλειαν
καὶ πῦρ ἀθάνατον· τάδε γὰρ μέλη ἐστὶ τὰ Πανός.
ἐλθέ, μάκαρ, σκιρτητά, περίδρομε, σύνθρονε Ὥραις,
αἰγομελές, βακχευτά, φιλένθεε, ἀστροδίαιτε,
ἁρμονίαν κόσμοιο κρέκων φιλοπαίγμονι μολπῆι,
φαντασιῶν ἐπαρωγέ, φόβων ἔκπαγλε βροτείων,
αἰγονόμοις χαίρων ἀνὰ πίδακας ἠδέ τε βούταις,
εὔσκοπε, θηρητήρ, Ἠχοῦς φίλε, σύγχορε νυμφῶν,
παντοφυής, γενέτωρ πάντων, πολυώνυμε δαῖμον,
κοσμοκράτωρ, αὐξητά, φαεσφόρε, κάρπιμε Παιάν,
ἀντροχαρές, βαρύμηνις, ἀληθὴς Ζεὺς ὁ κεράστης.
σοὶ γὰρ ἀπειρέσιον γαίης πέδον ἐστήρικται,
εἴκει δ᾽ ἀκαμάτου πόντου τὸ βαθύρροον ὕδωρ
Ὠκεανός τε πέριξ ἐν ὕδασι γαῖαν ἑλίσσων,
ἀέριόν τε μέρισμα τροφῆς, ζωοῖσιν ἔναυσμα,
καὶ κορυφῆς ἐφύπερθεν ἐλαφροτάτου πυρὸς ὄμμα.
βαίνει γὰρ τάδε θεῖα πολύκριτα σαῖσιν ἐφετμαῖς·
ἀλλάσσεις δὲ φύσεις πάντων ταῖς σαῖσι προνοίαις
βόσκων ἀνθρώπων γενεὴν κατ᾽ ἀπείρονα κόσμον.
ἀλλά, μάκαρ, βακχευτά, φιλένθεε, βαῖν᾽ ἐπὶ λοιβαῖς
εὐιέροις, ἀγαθὴν δ᾽ ὄπασον βιότοιο τελευτὴν
Πανικὸν ἐκπέμπων οἶστρον ἐπὶ τέρματα γαίης.

11. For Pan

Incense: mixed
I call mighty Pan, the god of shepherds
and the whole universe together; sky
and sea, the all-regal earth, and deathless
fire: for these are the limbs of Pan himself.
Come, blessed, spinning, cavorting, enthroned
with the Seasons, goat-limbed, Bacchic, frenzy
of gods' inspiration under the stars.
You strike cosmic harmony with playful
song. You, the aid of imagination
and bringer of terrible images
to mortal fears, delighting in shepherds
and herdsmen among the fountains. Sharp-eyed
hunter, the lover of Echo, you dance
with the nymphs. All-growing god, the father
of all, many-named daimon, the ruler
of the cosmos, increaser, light-bringer,
fruitful Paian, cave-haunting god, heavy
with wrath, truly the horned Zeus, for through you
the boundless plain of the Earth lies firm, but
deeply flowing waters of the tireless
seas yield, and Ocean, surrounding the earth
with waters, and the air that we share for
nourishment, the spark of all life, the eye
of most nimble fire high above: For these
holy things stand apart by your command;
you change the natures of all by your wise
will, nourishing the human race throughout
the boundless world. So come, blessed one, frenzied
with divine inspiration to this most
holy libation: give life a good end
and send out Pan's passion to the earth's ends.

Note: Pan's name is the origin of the English word "panic." He was said to inspire frenzy in those lost in the wilderness. His name's similarity to the Greek word for "all" has led some later writers to regard him as a universal deity.

12 Ἡρακλέος, θυμίαμα λίβανον.

Ἥρακλες ὀμβριμόθυμε, μεγασθενές, ἄλκιμε Τιτάν,
καρτερόχειρ, ἀδάμαστε, βρύων ἄθλοισι κραταιοῖς,
αἰολόμορφε, χρόνου πάτερ, ἀίδιέ τε εὔφρων,
ἄρρητ', ἀγριόθυμε, πολύλλιτε, παντοδυνάστα,
παγκρατὲς ἦτορ ἔχων, κάρτος μέγα, τοξότα, μάντι,
παμφάγε, παγγενέτωρ, πανυπέρτατε, πᾶσιν ἀρωγέ,
ὃς θνητοῖς κατέπαυσας ἀνήμερα φῦλα διώξας,
εἰρήνην ποθέων κουροτρόφον, ἀγλαότιμ[ον],
αὐτοφυής, ἀκάμας, γαίης βλάστημα φέριστον,
πρωτογόνοις στράψας βολίσιν, μεγαλώνυμε Παιών,
ὃς περὶ κρατὶ φορεῖς ἠῶ καὶ νύκτα μέλαιναν,
δώδεκ' ἀπ' ἀντολιῶν ἄχρι δυσμῶν ἆθλα διέρπων,
ἀθάνατος, πολύπειρος, ἀπείριτος, ἀστυφέλικτος·
ἐλθέ, μάκαρ, νούσων θελκτήρια πάντα κομίζων,
ἐξέλασον δὲ κακὰς ἄτας κλάδον ἐν χερὶ πάλλων,
πτηνοῖς τ' ἰοβόλοις κῆρας χαλεπὰς ἐπίπεμπε.

12. For Herakles

Incense: frankincense

Herakles, strong in mind and mighty, stout
Titan, your powerful hand is filled
with brave victories. You change form, father
of time, eternal, kind, ineffable.
Your passion is fierce, you to whom we pray—
All powerful, with a ruling heart,
strong archer, prophet. Devouring father,
higher than all, and aid to everyone.
For mortals, you chased and tamed the wild races
because you yearned for peace, the splendidly
honored nurturer of the young. Self-raised,
tireless, the unmatched offspring of the Earth,
you flash the lightning of your ancient spears,
famous Paian, and dawn and dark night whirl
around your head. Your twelve brave deeds spread east
to west. Undying and practiced, immense
and unshaken—come, blessed one, and bring
all your charms against diseases. Shaking
your club in hand, drive off foul confusion,
and with feathered bolts, send away hard death.

13 Κρόνου, θυμίαμα στύρακα.

Ἀιθαλής, μακάρων τε θεῶν πάτερ ἠδὲ καὶ ἀνδρῶν,
ποικιλόβουλ', ἀμίαντε, μεγασθενές, ἄλκιμε Τιτάν,
ὃς δαπαναῖς μὲν ἄπαντα καὶ αὔξεις ἔμπαλιν αὐτός,
δεσμοὺς ἀρρήκτους ὃς ἔχεις κατ' ἀπείρονα κόσμον,
αἰῶνος Κρόνε παγγενέτωρ, Κρόνε ποικιλόμυθε,
Γαίης τε βλάστημα καὶ Οὐρανοῦ ἀστερόεντος,
γέννα, φυή, μείωσι, Ῥέας πόσι, σεμνὲ Προμηθεῦ,
ὃς ναίεις κατὰ πάντα μέρη κόσμοιο, γενάρχα,
ἀγκυλομῆτα, φέριστε· κλύων ἱκετηρίδα φωνὴν
πέμποις εὔολβον βιότου τέλος αἰὲν ἄμεμπτον.

13. For Kronos

Incense: storax

Ever-young father of the blessed gods
and men, clever, pure, all-mighty Titan:
you exhaust all things, and then restore them.
Adamant are the chains you wind about
the boundless universe; Kronos, father
of aeon, Kronos, sung in many myths.
You are the child of Gaia and star-filled
Ouranos. Birth, growth, and withering,
Rhea's husband, o honored Prometheus
who lives in every part of the cosmos:
wily, brave creator, hear the request
in my voice: send always a prosperous
and a blameless conclusion to my life.

Note: Prometheus is the Titan who benefited humanity by bringing us
fire. Here Kronos is associated with that Titan. There is a hint of confla-
tion with Chronus as well, the god of time. This was a common association due to the similarity of names.

14 Ῥέας, θυμίαμα ἀρώματα.

Πότνα Ῥέα, θύγατερ πολυμόρφου Πρωτογόνοιο,
ἥτ' ἐπὶ ταυροφόρον ἱερότροχον ἄρμα τιταίνεις,
τυμπανόδουπε, φιλοιστρομανές, χαλκόκροτε κούρη,
μῆτερ Ζηνὸς ἄνακτος Ὀλυμπίου, αἰγιόχοιο,
πάντιμ', ἀγλαόμορφε, Κρόνου σύλλεκτρε μάκαιρα,
οὔρεσιν ἣ χαίρεις θνητῶν τ' ὀλολύγμασι φρικτοῖς,
παμβασίλεια Ῥέα, πολεμόκλονε, ὀμβριμόθυμε,
ψευδομένη, σώτειρα, λυτηριάς, ἀρχιγένεθλε,
μήτηρ μέν τε θεῶν ἠδὲ θνητῶν ἀνθρώπων·
ἐκ σοῦ γὰρ καὶ γαῖα καὶ οὐρανὸς εὐρὺς ὕπερθεν
καὶ πόντος πνοιαί τε· φιλόδρομε, ἀερόμορφε·
ἐλθέ, μάκαιρα θεά, σωτήριος εὔφρονι βουλῆι
εἰρήνην κατάγουσα σὺν εὐόλβοις κτεάτεσσι,
λύματα καὶ κῆρας πέμπουσ' ἐπὶ τέρματα γαίης.

14. For Rhea

Incense: aromatics

Lady Rhea, daughter of many-shaped
Protogonos. Bull-slaying beasts pull
your holy chariot. Frenzy-loving
maiden, the roaring brass and sounding drum
surround you, mother of Zeus, holy lord
of Olympos, who carries the Aigis.
Much honored, lovely and blessed consort
of Kronos, you rejoice in the mountains
and thrilling ritual howls of mortals.
Rhea, queen of all, you raise shouts of war.
The strong-minded and first born, you deceive
and release, savior, mother of the gods
and of mortals, for from you come the earth,
the wide sky, the rivers, the sea, and winds.
Ethereal and ever in motion, come
blessed goddess, a savior with gentle
will. Bring down peace and rich possessions too.
Send death and pollution to the earth's ends.

Note: Rhea here is said to "deceive and release" as part of her role in saving the gods from Kronos.

15 Διός, θυμίαμα στύρακα.

Ζεῦ πολυτίμητε, Ζεῦ ἄφθιτε, τήνδε τοι ἡμεῖς
μαρτυρίαν τιθέμεσθα λυτήριον ἠδὲ πρόσευξιν.
ὦ βασιλεῦ, διὰ σὴν κεφαλὴν ἐφάνη τάδε θεῖα,
γαῖα θεὰ μήτηρ ὀρέων θ' ὑψηχέες ὄχθοι,
καὶ πόντος καὶ πάνθ', ὁπόσ' οὐρανὸς ἐντὸς ἔταξε·
Ζεῦ Κρόνιε, σκηπτοῦχε, καταιβάτα, ὀμβριμόθυμε,
παντογένεθλ', ἀρχὴ πάντων, πάντων τε τελευτή,
σεισίχθων, αὐξητά, καθάρσιε, παντοτινάκτα,
ἀστραπαῖε, βρονταῖε, κεραύνιε, φυτάλιε Ζεῦ·
κλῦθί μου, αἰολόμορφε, δίδου δ' ὑγίειαν ἀμεμφῆ
εἰρήνην τε θεὰν καὶ πλούτου δόξαν ἄμεμπτον.

15. For Zeus

Incense: storax

Much honored Zeus, immortal Zeus, we bear
this freeing testimony and this prayer.
O king, these divine things shine through your head:
the holy mother earth, and loud sounding
slopes of mountains; the sea, and all things, as
many as the heavens array within.
Kronian Zeus, holding your scepter, you
send down thunder, fierce in spirit, father
of all, the first and the end of everything.
Earth-quaker, increaser, purifier,
the vibration of all things. The lightning,
thunder, and the bolt, o nourishing Zeus.
Hear me, the god of many forms, and give
unto us faultless health, and divine peace,
glorious prosperity without blame.

16 Ἥρης, θυμίαμα ἀρώματα.

Κυανέοις κόλποισιν ἐνημένη, ἀερόμορφε,
Ἥρη παμβασίλεια, Διὸς σύλλεκτρε μάκαιρα,
ψυχοτρόφους αὔρας θνητοῖς παρέχουσα προσηνεῖς,
ὄμβρων μὲν μήτηρ, ἀνέμων τροφέ, παντογένεθλε·
χωρὶς γὰρ σέθεν οὐδὲν ὅλως ζωῆς φύσιν ἔγνω·
κοινωνεῖς γὰρ ἅπασι κεκραμένη ἠέρι σεμνῶι·
πάντων γὰρ κρατέεις μούνη πάντεσσί τ' ἀνάσσεις
ἠερίοις ῥοίζοισι τινασσομένη κατὰ χεῦμα.
ἀλλά, μάκαιρα θεά, πολυώνυμε, παμβασίλεια,
ἔλθοις εὐμενέουσα καλῶι γήθοντι προσώπωι.

16. For Hera

Incense: aromatics

You enthrone yourself in dark vales, wind-shaped
Hera, queen of all, the blessed consort
of Zeus. You give sweet breezes to nourish
the souls of mortals. Mother of rains, nurse
of the winds, from you all things have their births.
For without you, nothing at all would know
the nature of life. For you share in all,
mingled in the sacred air. Of all things,
you are the ruler, and of all, the queen.
You tremble in the flows of the whistling
wind. So blessed goddess of many names,
queen of all, may you come kindly minded
and with a beautifully smiling face.

Note: In myth, Hera often takes the part of the vindictive and wronged wife against her husband Zeus and more often his paramours or victims. In religious practice, however, she was treated with respect as the patron of women and here as a goddess of the air.

17 Ποσειδῶνος, θυμίαμα σμύρναν.

Κλῦθι, Ποσείδαον γαιήοχε, κυανοχαῖτα,
ἵππιε, χαλκοτόρευτον ἔχων χείρεσσι τρίαιναν,
ὃς ναίεις πόντοιο βαθυστέρνοιο θέμεθλα,
ποντομέδων, ἁλίδουπε, βαρύκτυπε, ἐννοσίγαιε,
κυμοθαλής, χαριδῶτα, τετράορον ἅρμα διώκων,
εἰναλίοις ῥοίζοισι τινάσσων ἁλμυρὸν ὕδωρ,
ὃς τριτάτης ἔλαχες μοίρης βαθὺ χεῦμα θαλάσσης,
κύμασι τερπόμενος θηρσίν θ' ἅμα, πόντιε δαῖμον·
ἔδρανα γῆς σώζοις καὶ νηῶν εὔδρομον ὁρμήν,
εἰρήνην, ὑγίειαν ἄγων ἠδ' ὄλβον ἀμεμφῆ.

17. For Poseidon

Incense: myrrh

Hear me, Poseidon, who protects the earth,
the dark-haired horseman, bearing in your hand
a bronze trident, you who dwell in the low
foundations of the deep-chested ocean.
Loud-thundering lord of the briny sea,
earth-shaker and joy-giver, blossoming
in the waves, through which you drive your four-horsed
chariot, splashing through the salty sea.
You won the third share, the deepest currents
of the sea. You delight in waves and beasts
of the water, daimon of the deep. Save
the foundations of the earth, and the ships,
running fast in their advance. Bring us peace,
health, and wealthy happiness without blame.

18 Εἰς Πλούτωνα.

Ὦ τὸν ὑποχθόνιον ναίων δόμον, ὀμβριμόθυμε,
Ταρτάριον λειμῶνα βαθύσκιον ἠδὲ λιπαυγῆ,
Ζεῦ χθόνιε, σκηπτοῦχε, τάδ᾽ ἱερὰ δέξο προθύμως,
Πλούτων, ὃς κατέχεις γαίης κληῖδας ἁπάσης,
πλουτοδοτῶν γενεὴν βροτέην καρποῖς ἐνιαυτῶν·
ὃς τριτάνης μοίρης ἔλαχες χθόνα παμβασίλειαν,
ἕδρανον ἀθανάτων, θνητῶν στήριγμα κραταιόν·
ὃς θρόνον ἐστήριξας ὑπὸ ζοφοειδέα χῶρον
τηλέπορον {τ᾽}, ἀκάμαντα, λιπόπνοον, ἄκριτον Ἄιδην
κυάνεόν τ᾽ Ἀχέρονθ᾽, ὃς ἔχει ῥιζώματα γαίης·
ὃς κρατέεις θνητῶν θανάτου χάριν, ὦ πολυδέγμων
Εὔβουλ᾽, ἁγνοπόλου Δημήτερος ὅς ποτε παῖδα
νυμφεύσας λειμῶνος ἀποσπαδίην διὰ πόντου
τετρώροις ἵπποισιν ὑπ᾽ Ἀτθίδος ἤγαγες ἄντρον
δήμου Ἐλευσῖνος, τόθι περ πύλαι εἰσ᾽ Ἀίδαο.
μοῦνος ἔφυς ἀφανῶν ἔργων φανερῶν τε βραβευτής,
ἔνθεε, παντοκράτωρ, ἱερώτατε, ἀγλαότιμε,
σεμνοῖς μυστιπόλοις χαίρων ὁσίοις τε σεβασμοῖς·
ἵλαον ἀγκαλέω σε μολεῖν κεχαρηότα μύσταις.

18. To Plouton

Mighty spirit, you have your home under
the earth, a grassy mead in Tartaros,
deep shadowed and sunless, Chthonian Zeus
holding a scepter, kindness in your heart.
Accept these holy offerings, Plouton,
you who hold fast the bars that bind the whole
earth, and give yearly fruit to mortal kind.
You who won the third share: earth, queen of all,
foundation of the deathless gods, and strong
support to mortal kind. You established
your throne beneath a shadowy, distant
realm; never-tiring and never breathing,
indiscriminate Hades, and blue-black
Acheron, who holds the roots of the Earth.
You who governs the grace of mortal death,
O host of many, Euboulos, who once
tore the daughter of holy Demeter
from her meadow as a bride; with your four
yoked steeds, you dragged her through the ocean, down
to an Attic cavern in the region
of Eleusis, that very place where lie
the gates to Hades. You alone came forth
to be the judge of deeds, obscure and known.
The inspired ruler of all, most holy,
most highly honored, rejoicing in rites
majestic, revered, and pious, I call
you, come with kind joy to the worshippers.

Note: Zeus, Poseidon, and Hades divided up the cosmos after over-
throwing the Titans. Hades received the share of the earth. The myth
mentioned here is the kidnapping of Persephone, daughter of Demeter. This legend is central to the mystery religion of Eleusis. Here Hades is called Plouton, a common euphemism, meaning "wealthy."

19 Κεραυνοῦ Διός, θυμίαμα στύρακα.

Ζεῦ πάτερ, ὑψίδρομον πυραυγέα κόσμον ἐλαύνων,
στράπτων αἰθερίου στεροπῆς πανυπέρτατον αἴγλην,
παμμακάρων ἕδρανον θείαις βρονταῖσι τινάσσων,
νάμασι παννεφέλοις στεροπὴν φλεγέθουσαν ἀναίθων,
λαίλαπας, ὄμβρους, πρηστῆρας κρατερούς τε κεραυνούς,
βάλλων ἐς ῥοθίους φλογερούς, βελέεσσι καλύπτων
παμφλέκτους, κρατερούς, φρικώδεας, ὀμβριμοθύμους,
πτηνὸν ὅπλον δεινόν, κλονοκάρδιον, ὀρθοέθειρον,
αἰφνίδιον, βρονταῖον, ἀνίκητον βέλος ἁγνόν,
ῥοίζου ἀπειρεσίου δινεύμασι παμφάγον ὁρμήν,
ἄρρηκτον, βαρύθυμον, ἀμαιμάκετον πρηστῆρα
οὐράνιον βέλος ὀξὺ καταιβάτου αἰθαλόεντος,
ὃν καὶ γαῖα πέφρικε θάλασσά τε παμφανόωντα,
καὶ θῆρες πτήσσουσιν, ὅταν κτύπος οὖας ἐσέλθηι·
μαρμαίρει δὲ πρόσωπ᾽ αὐγαῖς, σμαραγεῖ δὲ κεραυνὸς
αἰθέρος ἐν γυάλοισι· διαρρήξας δὲ χιτῶνα
οὐράνιον προκάλυμμα βάλλεις ἀργῆτα κεραυνόν.
ἀλλά, μάκαρ, θυμὸν [βαρὺν ἔμβαλε] κύμασι πόντου
ἠδ᾽ ὀρέων κορυφαῖσι· τὸ σὸν κράτος ἴσμεν ἅπαντες.
ἀλλὰ χαρεὶς λοιβαῖσι δίδου φρεσὶν αἴσιμα πάντα
ζωήν τ᾽ ὀλβιόθυμον, ὁμοῦ θ᾽ ὑγίειαν ἄνασσαν
εἰρήνην τε θεόν, κουροτρόφον, ἀγλαότιμον,
καὶ βίον εὐθύμοισιν ἀεὶ θάλλοντα λογισμοῖς.

19. For Zeus the Thunderbolt

Incense: storax

Father Zeus, racing through the high flame-bright
course of the cosmos, casting from the air
the highest flashes of lightning, shaking
the most blessed foundations with divine
thunder bolts, setting the swells of storm clouds
aflame with scorching forks of lightning—you
throw cyclones, storms, wild rain, mighty lightning.
In red riots, blanketing with arrows
blazing, all-mighty, horrid, strong-hearted,
the feathered, terrible weapon makes hearts
shake and hair stand in sudden thunder,
unvanquished awful arrows, in cyclones
of endless whistling, all-consuming rage,
the heavy, unstoppable, adamant
sharp bolts of the heavens you throw down from
the sooty hurricane, which has made earth
and the sea tremble in fear at the flash.
And the beasts cower when the crash pierces
their ears; the lightning dazzles their faces
in beams, crashes from hollows in the air.
You've torn the chiton of heaven, its veil,
and you throw bright lightning; but blessed one
[throw down heavy] rage to the waves of the sea
and the peaks of the mountains; we all know
your might. You rejoice in the libations.
Give all things the gods endorse to the heart—
a life of happiness, together with
royal health, and divine peace, nurturing
the youth, and shining honor and a life
always growing with kindly reasoning.

Note: The thunderbolt is Zeus's chief weapon, the tool he used to kill the Titans who were consuming the body of Dionysos.

There is a lacuna in the text. Quandt offers βαρὺν ἔμβαλε, which fits both the meter and the sense and which I have translated as "throw down heavy." [14]

---

14. Orpheus and Wilhelm Quandt, *Orphei Hymni*. Berolini: Weidmann, 1955, 19.

20 Διὸς Ἀστραπαίου, θυμίαμα λιβανομάνναν.

Κικλήσκω μέγαν, ἁγνόν, ἐρισμάραγον, περίφαντον,
ἀέριον, φλογόεντα, πυρίδρομον, ἀεροφεγγῆ,
ἀστράπτοντα σέλας νεφέων παταγοδρόμωι αὐδῆι,
φρικώδη, βαρύμηνιν, ἀνίκητον θεὸν ἁγνόν,
ἀστραπαῖον Δία, παγγενέτην, βασιλῆα μέγιστον,
εὐμενέοντα φέρειν γλυκερὴν βιότοιο τελευτήν.

20. For Zeus, Throwing Lightning

Incense: powdered frankincense

I call on the great, pure, loud-thundering,
bright in flame, airy and fiery god, who
runs in a burning track, and who enflames
the air, sets the clouds alight with lightning,
and who makes us tremble with his loud voice,
his deep wrath, the unconquered holy god,
lightning-throwing Zeus, all father, mighty
gracious king, to bring a sweet end to life.

Note: These two hymns, numbers 19 and 20, seem to offer two aspects
of the same Zeus: the thunderer and the wielder of lightning bolts.

21 Νεφῶν, θυμίαμα σμύρναν.

Ἀέριοι νεφέλαι, καρποτρόφοι, οὐρανόπλαγκτοι,
ὀμβροτόκοι, πνοιαῖσιν ἐλαυνόμεναι κατὰ κόσμον,
βρονταῖαι, πυρόεσσαι, ἐρίβρομοι, ὑγροκέλευθοι,
ἀέρος ἐν κόλπωι πάταγον φρικώδη ἔχουσαι,
πνεύμασιν ἀντίσπαστοι ἐπιδρομάδην παταγεῦσαι,
ὑμᾶς νῦν λίτομαι, δροσοείμονες, εὔπνοοι αὔραις,
πέμπειν καρποτρόφους ὄμβρους ἐπὶ μητέρα γαῖαν.

21. For the Clouds

Incense: myrrh

The ethereal Clouds who nourish fruit
wandering through the skies, bringing the rains—
you are driven throughout the universe
by gusts of wind, flaming and thunderous,
loudly shouting, you leave a trail behind
of wet earth. In the folds of air you make
a terrible crash, yanked apart by gusts
of rapid and roaring wind. I pray now
to you, clad in dew and sweetly breathing
in breezes, send us the nourishing rains
to water fruit upon the mother earth.

A play by the same name, *The Clouds*, was written by Aristophanes in 423 BCE. Socrates, a contemporary of Aristophanes, was featured as a character. In the play, the character Socrates teaches that the clouds are new gods that people should worship, something that according to Plato and Xenophon, he never did in reality. A few years later, Socrates would be sentenced to death by the Athenian courts on charges of corrupting youth and introducing new gods. The clouds in that play tell the audience that they exist to confound the impious and lead them astray from worship of the true gods. It is interesting to see them make an appearance, many hundreds of years later, in this hymn.

22 Θαλάσσης, θυμίαμα λιβανομάνναν.

Ὠκεανοῦ καλέω νύμφην, γλαυκώπιδα Τηθύν,
κυανόπεπλον ἄνασσαν, εὔτροχα κυμαίνουσαν,
αὔραις ἡδυπνόοισι πατασσομένην περὶ γαῖαν.
θραύουσ᾽ αἰγιαλοῖσι πέτρηισί τε κύματα μακρά,
εὐδίνοις ἁπαλοῖσι γαληνιόωσα δρόμοισι,
ναυσὶν ἀγαλλομένη, θηροτρόφε, ὑγροκέλευθε,
μήτηρ μὲν Κύπριδος, μήτηρ νεφέων ἐρεβεννῶν
καὶ πάσης πηγῆς νυμφῶν νασμοῖσι βρυούσης·
κλῦθί μου, ὦ πολύσεμνε, καὶ εὐμενέουσ᾽ ἐπαρήγοις,
εὐθυδρόμοις οὖρον ναυσὶν πέμπουσα, μάκαιρα.

22. For the Sea

Incense: powdered frankincense

I call you, bride of the ocean, gray-eyed
Tethys, dark shrouded lady of turning,
rising waves that, driven by sweet breezes,
lap against the earth. You shatter in great
waves on the rocky beaches, calm yourself
in peaceful, sweetly sheltered strands. You take
joy in ships, nourish beasts, and leave wet sand
behind. Mother of Kypris, and mother
of gloomy Clouds, and every spring of Nymphs
bursting forth with streams; hear me, o much-praised
goddess: may you give gracious help, and send
fair winds to ships on their courses, blessed one.

Note: Kypris here refers to Aphrodite, who was by some accounts born
out of ocean foam.

23 Νηρέως, θυμίαμα σμύρναν.

Ὦ κατέχων πόντου ῥίζας, κυαναυγέτιν ἕδρην,
πεντήκοντα κόραισιν ἀγαλλόμενος κατὰ κῦμα
καλλιτέκνοισι χοροῖς, Νηρεῦ, μεγαλώνυμε δαῖμον,
πυθμὴν μὲν πόντου, γαίης πέρας, ἀρχὴ ἁπάντων,
ὃς κλονέεις Δηοῦς ἱερὸν βάθρον, ἡνίκα πνοιὰς
ἐν μυχίοις κευθμῶσιν ἐλαυνομένας ἀποκλείῃς·
ἀλλά, μάκαρ, σεισμοὺς μὲν ἀπότρεπε, πέμπε δὲ μύσταις
ὄλβον τ᾽ εἰρήνην τε καὶ ἠπιόχειρον ὑγείην.

23. For Nereus

Incense: myrrh
You who guard the roots of the sea, the dark
gleaming throne, delighting in your fifty
daughters as they dance below the waves, your
lovely children. Nereus, the famous
daimon, yours is the bottom of the sea
and the limits of the earth, beginning
of all, you who shake the sacred bedrock
of Deo, when you shut up the driven
wind within hidden hollows. Blessed one,
turn away earthquakes and send wealth and peace
to worshippers, and soothing-handed health.

Note: Nereus shares many similarities with Proteus—a shape-changing, wise sea god who will prophesy and counsel whoever can keep him in one form long enough. He is the father of sea nymphs or Nereids, for which see the next hymn.

24 Νηρηίδων, θυμίαμα ἀρώματα.

Νηρέος εἰναλίου νύμφαι καλυκώπιδες, ἁγναί,
σφράγιαι βύθιαι, χοροπαίγμονες, ὑγροκέλευθοι,
πεντήκοντα κόραι περὶ κύμασι βακχεύουσαι,
Τριτώνων ἐπ' ὄχοισιν ἀγαλλόμεναι περὶ νῶτα
θηροτύποις μορφαῖς, ὧν βόσκει σώματα πόντος,
ἄλλοις θ' οἳ ναίουσι βυθόν, Τριτώνιον οἶδμα,
ὑδρόδομοι, σκιρτηταί, ἑλισσόμενοι περὶ κῦμα,
ποντοπλάνοι δελφῖνες, ἁλιρρόθιοι, κυαναυγεῖς.
ὑμᾶς κικλήσκω πέμπειν μύσταις πολὺν ὄλβον·
ὑμεῖς γὰρ πρῶται τελετὴν ἀνεδείξατε σεμνὴν
εὐιέρου Βάκχοιο καὶ ἁγνῆς Φερσεφονείης,
Καλλιόπηι σὺν μητρὶ καὶ Ἀπόλλωνι ἄνακτι.

24. For the Nereids

Incense: aromatics

Flower-faced nymphs, pure daughters of Nereus
of the briny sea, in the deep you print
wet tracks in the dance, fifty girls among
the waves celebrating the rituals
of Bakchos, you ride the backs of Tritones
and rejoice in the shapes of beasts, bodies
nourished by the sea; and like the other
dwellers of the deep, the swell of Tritones,
you swim, leaping and spinning on the waves,
dolphins roaming and dashing over dark
gleaming seas. I invoke you to send great
prosperity to the initiates,
for you were the first to reveal the august
rituals of most holy Bakchos and
sacred Persephone, with the mother
Kalliope, and the lord Apollon.

Note: Here the Nereids are depicted as fifty sea nymphs, revealing mysteries. Kalliope is not their mother, but the mother of Orpheus. Their mother is Doris. One of the Nereids, Thetis, is the mother of Achilles, the hero of the *Iliad*. Hesiod lists all fifty Nereids in lines 240–265 of the *Theogony*.

25 Πρωτέως, θυμίαμα στύρακα.

Πρωτέα κικλήσκω, πόντου κληῖδας ἔχοντα,
πρωτογενῆ, πάσης φύσεως ἀρχὰς ὃς ἔφηνεν
ὕλην ἀλλάσσων ἱερὴν ἰδέαις πολυμόρφοις,
πάντιμος, πολύβουλος, ἐπιστάμενος τά τ᾽ ἐόντα
ὅσσα τε πρόσθεν ἔην ὅσα τ᾽ ἔσσεται ὕστερον αὖτις·
πάντα γὰρ αὐτὸς ἔχων μεταβάλλεται οὐδέ τις ἄλλος
ἀθανάτων, οἳ ἔχουσιν ἕδος νιφόεντος Ὀλύμπου
καὶ πόντον καὶ γαῖαν ἐνηέριοί τε ποτῶνται·
πάντα γὰρ Πρωτεῖ πρώτη φύσις ἐγκατέθηκε.
ἀλλά, πάτερ, μόλε μυστιπόλοις ὁσίαισι προνοίαις
πέμπων εὐόλβου βιότου τέλος ἐσθλὸν ἐπ᾽ ἔργοις.

25. For Proteus

Incense: storax

I call Proteus, keeper of the keys
of the sea, the first born, who has revealed
the origin of all nature, changing
holy matter into many different
forms. All-honored, great counselor, who knows
what is, what was, and what will be hereafter.
For he holds everything himself; and he
can change himself, unlike some other gods,
who have their thrones on snowy Olympos
and fly through the air, over land and sea.
For nature first placed everything in him,
Proteus; Father, come to these mystic
rites with your holy foresight; send a good
end to a life rich in accomplishments.

Note: There is a hint of Neoplatonic philosophy here, in that the word
used for "form" (ἰδέα, *idea*) is the same used in Platonism for the underlying pattern or reality of existence.

26 Γῆς, θυμίαμα πᾶν σπέρμα πλὴν κυάμων καὶ ἀρωμάτων.

Γαῖα θεά, μῆτερ μακάρων θνητῶν τ' ἀνθρώπων,
παντρόφε, πανδώτειρα, τελεσφόρε, παντολέτειρα,
αὐξιθαλής, φερέκαρπε, καλαῖς ὥραισι βρύουσα,
ἕδρανον ἀθανάτου κόσμου, πολυποίκιλε κούρη,
ἣ λοχίαις ὠδῖσι κύεις καρπὸν πολυειδῆ,
αἰδία, πολύσεπτε, βαθύστερν', ὀλβιόμοιρε,
ἡδυπνόοις χαίρουσα χλόαις πολυανθέσι δαῖμον,
ὀμβροχαρής, περὶ ἣν κόσμος πολυδαίδαλος ἄστρων
εἰλεῖται φύσει ἀενάωι καὶ ῥεύμασι δεινοῖς.
ἀλλά, μάκαιρα θεά, καρποὺς αὔξοις πολυγηθεῖς
εὐμενὲς ἦτορ ἔχουσα, σὺν ὀλβίοισιν ἐν ὥραις.

26. For Gaia

Incense: every grain excepts beans or aromatics
Divine Gaia, mother of blessed ones
and mortal humans, nourisher of all
and the giver of everything, the nurse
of endings and destroyer of all things—
you bring forth growth in the lovely seasons
bearing fruit and full to bursting. You are
the seat of the deathless cosmos, brightly
decorated maiden. You through the pangs
of labor bear varieties of fruits.
Eternal, the most revered, deep-chested
with a blessed portion, you rejoice in sweet
breaths of the newly sprung plants, flower-decked
daimon. You delight in rain, and around
you spins the brightly wrought cosmos of stars,
in its eternally flowing nature
and awesome streams. And now holy goddess
may you swell the fruits that bring great delight.
Kind hearted, be with the blessed in season.

27 Μητρὸς θεῶν, θυμίαμα ποικίλα.

Ἀθανάτων θεότιμε θεῶν μῆτερ, τροφὲ πάντων,
τῆιδε μόλοις, κράντειρα θεά, σέο, πότνι', ἐπ' εὐχαῖς,
ταυροφόνων ζεύξασα ταχυδρόμον ἅρμα λεόντων,
σκηπτοῦχε κλεινοῖο πόλου, πολυώνυμε, σεμνή,
ἣ κατέχεις κόσμοιο μέσον θρόνον, οὕνεκεν αὐτὴ
γαῖαν ἔχεις θνητοῖσι τροφὰς παρέχουσα προσηνεῖς.
ἐκ σέο δ' ἀθανάτων τε γένος θνητῶν τ' ἐλοχεύθη,
σοὶ ποταμοὶ κρατέονται ἀεὶ καὶ πᾶσα θάλασσα,
Ἑστία αὐδαχθεῖσα· σὲ δ' ὀλβοδότιν καλέουσι,
παντοίων ἀγαθῶν θνητοῖς ὅτι δῶρα χαρίζηι,
ἔρχεο πρὸς τελετήν, ὦ πότνια, τυμπανοτερπή<ς>,
πανδαμάτωρ, Φρυγίη{ς}, σώτειρα, Κρόνου συνόμευνε,
Οὐρανόπαι, πρέσβειρα, βιοθρέπτειρα, φίλοιστρε·
ἔρχεο γηθόσυνος, κεχαρημένη εὐσεβίηισιν.

27. For the Mother of the Gods

Incense: various

Divinely praised mother of the deathless
gods, nourisher of all things, by our prayers
come to this place, queen and mighty goddess.
Yoke your swiftly running chariot to
the bull-devouring lions. Many-named,
sacred, holding a scepter, the goddess
of the great axis of the sky, you sit
on the throne in the middle of the world;
you hold the earth and bring sweet nourishment
to mortal creatures. And from you the race
of mortals, and the gods as well, came forth.
By you, the rivers take strength, and the sea.
You are invoked as Hestia, called upon
as the giver of bliss, of all good things
to mortals, since you give generously.
Come to the ritual, queen delighting
in drums: tamer of all, the Phrygian
savior, and bed companion of Kronos,
child of heaven, most honored, you support
life and love the frenzy-causing gadfly;
come in joy, who graced us with piety.

Note: The cult of the Magna Mater, the Great Mother, was widespread
throughout Rome. It began with a Phrygian mother deity, Kybele, who
is not named in these hymns but was often associated with Rhea, Gaia,
Demeter, and here Hestia. The mention of a gadfly brings to mind the
role of the Platonic Socrates: a gadfly to sting Athens into thought. The
authors of the hymns could hardly be unaware of that association.

28 Ἑρμοῦ, θυμίαμα λίβανον.

Κλῦθί μου, Ἑρμεία, Διὸς ἄγγελε, Μαιάδος υἱέ,
παγκρατὲς ἦτορ ἔχων, ἐναγώνιε, κοίρανε θνητῶν,
εὔφρων, ποικιλόβουλε, διάκτορε ἀργειφόντα,
πτηνοπέδιλε, φίλανδρε, λόγου θνητοῖσι προφῆτα,
γυμνάσιν ὃς χαίρεις δολίαις τ᾽ ἀπάταις, τροφιοῦχε,
ἑρμηνεῦ πάντων, κερδέμπορε, λυσιμέριμνε,
ὃς χείρεσσιν ἔχεις εἰρήνης ὅπλον ἀμεμφές,
Κωρυκιῶτα, μάκαρ, ἐριούνιε, ποικιλόμυθε,
ἐργασίαις ἐπαρωγέ, φίλε θνητοῖς ἐν ἀνάγκαις,
γλώσσης δεινὸν ὅπλον τὸ σεβάσμιον ἀνθρώποισι·
κλῦθί μου εὐχομένου, βιότου τέλος ἐσθλὸν ὀπάζων
ἐργασίαισι, λόγου χάρισιν, καὶ μνημοσύνηισιν.

28. For Hermes

Incense: frankincense
Hear me, Hermes, herald of Zeus and son
of Maia, having an all-mighty heart.
The lord of contests and guide of mortals,
kind and clever messenger of the gods
and slayer of Argos. With your winged
feet, you are a friend to humans, and you
are a prophet of the word to mortals.
You delight in exercise, in deceit
and trickery, and you wear the sacred
band. Interpreter of all, you preside
over the profits of business, driving
off all our cares, you who hold in your hands
the blameless weapon of peace. Blessed
god of Korykos, bringer of good luck,
with many stories, helper in business
and friend to mortals in need, you possess
the venerable and dreadful weapon
of language. Hear me in my prayers and bring
a noble end to life in deeds, and graceful
remembrances of reputation.

Note: The term used for "word" above (λόγος, *logos*) can also mean reason, logic, ratio, story, and account, among other things. In Stoic philosophy, it describes the underlying order of the universe. It is unclear what the "sacred band" refers to; perhaps a ritual blindfold.

29 Ὕμνος Περσεφόνης.

Φερσεφόνη, θύγατερ μεγάλου Διός, ἐλθέ, μάκαιρα,
μουνογένεια θεά, κεχαρισμένα δ' ἱερὰ δέξαι,
Πλούτωνος πολύτιμε δάμαρ, κεδνή, βιοδῶτι,
ἣ κατέχεις Ἀίδαο πύλας ὑπὸ κεύθεα γαίης,
Πραξιδίκη, ἐρατοπλόκαμε, Δηοῦς θάλος ἁγνόν,
Εὐμενίδων γενέτειρα, ὑποχθονίων βασίλεια,
ἣν Ζεὺς ἀρρήτοισι γοναῖς τεκνώσατο κούρην,
μῆτερ ἐριβρεμέτου πολυμόρφου Εὐβουλῆος,
Ὡρῶν συμπαίκτειρα φαεσφόρε, ἀγλαόμορφε,
σεμνή, παντοκράτειρα, κόρη καρποῖσι βρύουσα,
εὐφεγγής, κερόεσσα, μόνη θνητοῖσι ποθεινή,
εἰαρινή, λειμωνιάσιν χαίρουσα πνοῆισιν,
ἱερὸν ἐκφαίνουσα δέμας βλαστοῖς χλοοκάρποις,
ἁρπαγιμαῖα λέχη μετοπωρινὰ νυμφευθεῖσα,
ζωὴ καὶ θάνατος μούνη θνητοῖς πολυμόχθοις,
Φερσεφόνη· φέρβεις γὰρ ἀεὶ καὶ πάντα φονεύεις.
κλῦθι, μάκαιρα θεά, καρποὺς δ' ἀνάπεμπ' ἀπὸ γαίης
εἰρήνηι θάλλουσα καὶ ἠπιοχείρωι ὑγείαι
καὶ βίωι εὐόλβωι λιπαρὸν γῆρας κατάγοντι
πρὸς σὸν χῶρον, ἄνασσα, καὶ εὐδύνατον Πλούτωνα.

29. Hymn for Persephone

Come, Persephone, daughter of great Zeus,
blessed one, only begotten goddess.
Accept these gracious offerings to you.
Many-honored wife of Plouton, you give
life diligently, and control the gates
of Hades, beneath the depths of the Earth.
Praxidike, with lovely locks of hair:
Holy child of Deo, and the mother
of the Furies, queen of the Underworld,
maiden whom Zeus sired with ineffable
seed—you are the mother of loud-roaring
and many-formed Eubouleus. The shining
and luminous playmate of the seasons,
honored and mighty, maid bursting with fruit.
Mortals long for you alone, bright, horned,
spring time goddess, who is delighted with
meadow breezes, revealing your holy
body in the green and yellow new shoots.
In autumn, you were seized and forced to wed.
Now you, Persephone, alone are life
and death to toiling mortals, for you feed
us always, and also kill everything.
Hear, blessed goddess, and send up the fruits
from the earth, blossoming in peace and with
the soothing hand of health, and a rich life
that leads old age, sleek and shining, downward,
queen, to your kingdom, to mighty Plouton.

30 Διονύσου, θυμίαμα στύρακα.

Κικλήσκω Διόνυσον ἐρίβρομον, εὐαστῆρα,
πρωτόγονον, διφυῆ, τρίγονον, Βακχεῖον ἄνακτα,
ἄγριον, ἄρρητον, κρύφιον, δικέρωτα, δίμορφον,
κισσόβρυον, ταυρωπόν, Ἀρήιον, εὔιον, ἀγνόν,
ὠμάδιον, τριετῆ, βοτρυηφόρον, ἐρνεσίπεπλον.
Εὐβουλεῦ, πολύβουλε, Διὸς καὶ Περσεφονείης
ἀρρήτοις λέκτροισι τεκνωθείς, ἄμβροτε δαῖμον·
κλῦθι, μάκαρ, φωνῆς, ἡδὺς δ' ἐπίπνευσον ἀμεμ[φ]ής
εὐμενὲς ἦτορ ἔχων, σὺν ἐυζώνοισι τιθήναις.

30. For Dionysos

Incense: storax

I invoke Dionysos, the roaring
god of the Bacchanal, first made, double
natured and thrice born, the Bacchic lord, wild,
ineffable, hidden, two-horned, two-formed
teaming with ivy, bull-faced like Ares,
crying "evoe," holy and savage.
You hold triennial feasts where you are
clothed in ivy, bearing clusters of grapes.
Clever Eubouleus, you were born from Zeus
and Persephone when he lay with her
in her bed, which is not to be spoken.
Immortal daimon, sweet and blameless, hear
my voice, and, with a kind heart, inspire us,
together with your finely dressed nurses.

Note: Dionysos was of course the god of wine, but to the ascetic Orphics he was regarded much more strongly as a god of resurrection.

31 Ὕμνος Κουρήτων.

Σκιρτηταὶ Κουρῆτες, ἐνόπλια βήματα θέντες,
ποσσίκροτοι, ῥομβηταί, ὀρέστεροι, εὐαστῆρες,
κρουσιλύραι, παράρυθμοι, ἐπεμβάται, ἴχνεσι κοῦφοι,
ὁπλοφόροι, φύλακες, κοσμήτορες, ἀγλαόφημοι,
μητρὸς ὀρειομανοῦς συνοπάονες, ὀργιοφάνται·
ἔλθοιτ᾽ εὐμενέοντες ἐπ᾽ εὐφήμοισι λόγοισι,
βουκόλωι εὐάντητοι ἀεὶ κεχαρηότι θυμῶι.

31. Hymn for the Kouretes

Bounding Kouretes, marching to the beat,
you whirl and howl, dancing in the mountains.
You strike your lyres in strange rhythm, and ride
your horses with nimble feet. Shining famed
soldiers, guards, commanders, comrades in arms,
you reveal the rites of your mountain-mad
mother. Come, pleased by these well-omened words;
with gracious hearts, be kind to the oxherd.

32 Ἀθηνᾶς, θυμίαμα ἀρώματα.

Παλλὰς μουνογενή<ς>, μεγάλου Διὸς ἔκγονε σεμνή,
δῖα, μάκαιρα θεά, πολεμόκλονε, ὀμβριμόθυμε,
ἄρρητε, ῥητή, μεγαλώνυμε, ἀντροδίαιτε,
ἣ διέπεις ὄχθους ὑψαύχενας ἀκρωρείους
ἠδ' ὄρεα σκιόεντα, νάπαισί τε σὴν φρένα τέρπεις,
ὁπλοχαρής, οἰστροῦσα βροτῶν ψυχὰς μανίαισι,
γυμνάζουσα κόρη, φρικώδη θυμὸν ἔχουσα,
Γοργοφόνη, φυγόλεκτρε, τεχνῶν μῆτερ πολύολβε,
ὁρμάστειρα, φίλοιστρε κακοῖς, ἀγαθοῖς δὲ φρόνησις·
ἄρσην μὲν καὶ θῆλυς ἔφυς, πολεματόκε, μῆτι,
αἰολόμορφε, δράκαινα, φιλένθεε, ἀγλαότιμε,
Φλεγραίων ὀλέτειρα Γιγάντων, ἱππελάτειρα,
Τριτογένεια, λύτειρα κακῶν, νικηφόρε δαῖμον,
ἤματα καὶ νύκτας αἰεὶ νεάταισιν ἐν ὥραις,
κλῦθί μου εὐχομένου, δὸς δ' εἰρήνην πολύολβον
καὶ κόρον ἠδ' ὑγίειαν ἐπ' εὐόλβοισιν ἐν ὥραις,
γλαυκῶφ', εὑρεσίτεχνε, πολυλλίστη βασίλεια.

32. For Athena

Incense: aromatics
August Pallas, who sprang from Zeus alone,
divine, blessed goddess, with a powerful
heart, who stirs the turmoil of war, your name
is mighty, spoken and unspeakable.
Dwelling in caves, you rule the hills, valleys,
high flowing streams, and shadowy mountains
and you gladden your breast in shady vales.
Delighting in weapons you sting the souls
of mortals to madness, exhausting them.
Maiden, having a horrible anger,
Gorgon-slaying, shunning the marriage bed,
yet the abundant mother of the arts.
Loving frenzy, you urge on the wicked
to madness, but give wisdom to the good.
You are both male and female in nature,
the wise mother of war. Ever changing
dragon, filled with divine power, splendid
in honors, you destroyed the Phlegraian
giants. Horse-driving Tritogeneia,
you deliver from evils, o daimon
bearing victory always day and night,
and even in the smallest of the hours.
Hear my prayer, and give us a rich measure
of peace and health, in prosperous seasons,
grey-eyed, creative queen to whom all pray.

Note: The mention of the Phlegrain giants refers to the Gigantomachy, the war between the giants and the gods. This should not be confused with the Titanomachy, as giants and titans were different beings. Athena is said to bear victory here, as her statue in the Parthenon was said to have her holding a smaller statue of Nike, goddess of victory, in her hand.

33 Νίκης, θυμίαμα μάνναν.

Εὐδύνατον καλέω Νίκην, θνητοῖσι ποθεινήν,
ἣ μούνη λύει θνητῶν ἐναγώνιον ὁρμὴν
καὶ στάσιν ἀλγινόεσσαν ἐπ' ἀντιπάλοισι μάχαισιν,
ἐν πολέμοις κρίνουσα τροπαιούχοισιν ἐπ' ἔργοις,
οἷς ἂν ἐφορμαίνουσα φέροις γλυκερώτατον εὖχος·
πάντων γὰρ κρατέεις, πάσης δ' ἔριδος κλέος ἐσθλὸν
Νίκηι ἐπ' εὐδόξωι κεῖται θαλίαισι βρυάζον.
ἀλλά, μάκαιρ', ἔλθοις πεποθημένη ὄμματι φαιδρῶι
αἰεὶ ἐπ' εὐδόξοις ἔργοις κλέος ἐσθλὸν ἄγουσα.

33. For Nike

Incense: manna

I call truly mighty Nike, longed for
by mortals, the only one who frees us
from the assault of contention, the pain
of standing and fighting when battle comes.
You judge us in battles, in trophy-winning
deeds, for which, rushing forth, you grant our sweet
prayer. For you rule over all. In every
strife, noble fame swells with festivities,
which are set up for glorious Nike.
So come, yearned for and blessed one, bright-eyed:
always bring fine glory to famous works.

Note: Nike is sometimes considered a companion of Athena, whose hymn she follows here.

34 Ἀπόλλωνος, θυμίαμα μάνναν

Ἐλθέ, μάκαρ, Παιάν, Τιτυοκτόνε, Φοῖβε Λυκωρεῦ,
Μεμφῖτ', ἀγλαότιμε, ἰήιε, ὀλβιοδῶτα,
χρυσολύρη, σπερμεῖε, ἀρότριε, Πύθιε, Τιτάν.
Γρύνειε, Σμινθεῦ, Πυθοκτόνε, Δελφικέ, μάντι,
ἄγριε, φωσφόρε δαῖμον, ἐράσμιε, κύδιμε κοῦρε,
μουσαγέτα, χοροποιέ, ἑκηβόλε, τοξοβέλεμνε,
Βράγχιε καὶ Διδυμεῦ, ἑκάεργε, Λοξία, ἁγνέ,
Δήλι' ἄναξ, πανδερκὲς ἔχων φαεσίμβροτον ὄμμα,
χρυσοκόμα, καθαρὰς φήμας χρησμούς τ' ἀναφαίνων·
κλῦθί μου εὐχομένου λαῶν ὕπερ εὔφρονι θυμῶι·
τόνδε σὺ γὰρ λεύσσεις τὸν ἀπείριτον αἰθέρα πάντα
γαῖαν δ' ὀλβιόμοιρον ὕπερθέ τε καὶ δι' ἀμολγοῦ
νυκτὸς ἐν ἡσυχίαισιν ὑπ' ἀστεροόμματον ὄρφνην
ῥίζας νέρθε δέδορκας, ἔχεις δέ τε πείρατα κόσμου
παντός· σοὶ δ' ἀρχή τε τελευτή τ' ἐστὶ μέλουσα,
παντοθαλής, σὺ δὲ πάντα πόλον κιθάρηι πολυκρέκτωι
ἁρμόζεις, ὁτὲ μὲν νεάτης ἐπὶ τέρματα βαίνων,
ἄλλοτε δ' αὖθ' ὑπάτης, ποτὲ Δώριον εἰς διάκοσμον
πάντα πόλον κιρνὰς κρίνεις βιοθρέμμονα φῦλα,
ἁρμονίηι κεράσας {τὴν} παγκόσμιον ἀνδράσι μοῖραν,
μίξας χειμῶνος θέρεός τ' ἴσον ἀμφοτέροισιν,
ταῖς ὑπάταις χειμῶνα, θέρος νεάταις διακρίνας,
Δώριον εἰς ἔαρος πολυηράτου ὥριον ἄνθος.
ἔνθεν ἐπωνυμίην σε βροτοὶ κλήιζουσιν ἄνακτα,
Πᾶνα, θεὸν δικέρωτ', ἀνέμων συρίγμαθ' ἱέντα·
οὕνεκα παντὸς ἔχεις κόσμου σφραγῖδα τυπῶτιν.
κλῦθι, μάκαρ, σώζων μύστας ἱκετηρίδι φωνῆι.

34. For Apollon

Incense: manna

Come, blessed Paian, slayer of Tityos;
O Phoibos, Lykoreus, god of Memphis,
bright famed giver of wealth, crying "ie!"
With a golden lyre, herdsman, lord of seeds,
Pythios, Titan, Gryneios, Smintheus,
slayer of Python, and Delphic prophet.
Wild, lovely, light-bringing daimon, renowned
youth, you lead the Mousai in choral dance,
flinging far arrows from a bow, holy
finned-one, Didymeus, Loxias working
from afar, Lord of Delos. Your eye sees
all and brings light to mortals. Gold haired, you
reveal accurate oracular words.
Hear me praying for the people and have
a kindly heart. For you see the boundless
Aither, and the rich earth from up above;
and through the dead of night, in still silence,
under starry-eyed darkness, you perceive
the roots below. You hold the cosmic bounds.
You have concern for the first and the last.
Decked with flowers, you harmonize the poles
with your quick-striking lyre, arriving now
at the highest string, then turning downward
to the lowest ones, in the Doric mode;
balancing the poles you draw distinctions
between living nations. In harmony
you measure a common share to people,
an equal mix of winter and summer
for each of them; and you pick out the notes:
the lowest with winter, and the highest
for summer. In the Doric mode you play
for spring's much loved and flowery season.

For this, mortals celebrate you in song,
and call you Lord and Pan, the two-horned god
who sends forth the whistling songs of the winds.
Wherefore you hold the seal of the cosmos—
hear, blessed one, the initiates' cry,
supplicants, for you to be their savior.

Note: While there are mythological references, most of the hymn focuses on Apollon's lyre, a gift from Hermes, with which he controls the seasons. The Doric mode, in modern music, is a minor scale with a major sixth. But ancient Greek music interpreted the modes differently, according to a complex system of genera and scales. The diatonic Greek Doric corresponds to the modern Phrygian mode, which is a minor scale with a minor second. The word βράγχιε, which Quandt prefers to Βάκχιε (*Bakchos*), and which I have translated here as "finned one," is probably a reference to Apollo's role as god of dolphins.

35 Λητοῦς, θυμίαμα σμύρναν.

Λητὼ κυανόπεπλε, θεὰ διδυματόκε, σεμνή,
Κοιαντίς, μεγάθυμε, πολυλλίστη βασίλεια,
εὔτεκνον Ζηνὸς γονίμην ὠδῖνα λαχοῦσα,
γειναμένη Φοῖβόν τε καὶ Ἄρτεμιν ἰοχέαιραν,
τὴν μὲν ἐν Ὀρτυγίηι, τὸν δὲ κραναῆι ἐνὶ Δήλωι,
κλῦθι, θεὰ δέσποινα, καὶ ἵλαον ἦτορ ἔχουσα
Βαῖν' ἐπὶ πάνθειον τελετὴν τέλος ἡδὺ φέρουσα.

35. For Leto

Incense: myrrh
Holy Leto, dark clothed divine mother
of twins, daughter of Koios, great hearted
queen to whom we pray: The lot fell to you
to endure the birth pains and to be blessed
with the children of Zeus. You bore Phoibos
and Artemis who pours arrows as well,
her in Ortygia; him on rugged
Delos. Hear, o divine mistress, and come,
with a gracious heart, to our holy rite
honoring all gods, and bring a sweet end.

Note: In the version of the myth recounted here, bearing the twins of
Zeus, Leto must seek a place to give birth, because Hera has made all
lands shun her. She gives birth to Artemis on Ortygia, and then travels
on to Delos, where the newly born Artemis assists her in her labor with
Apollon.

36 Ἀρτέμιδος, θυμίαμα μάνναν.

Κλῦθί μου, ὦ βασίλεια, Διὸς πολυώνυμε κούρη,
Τιτανίς, βρομία, μεγαλώνυμε, τοξότι, σεμνή,
πασιφαής, δαιδοῦχε θεά, Δίκτυννα, λοχεία,
ὠδίνων ἐπαρωγὲ καὶ ὠδίνων ἀμύητε,
λυσίζωνε, φίλοιστρε, κυνηγέτι, λυσιμέριμνε,
εὔδρομε, ἰοχέαιρα, φιλαγρότι, νυκτερόφοιτε,
κληισία, εὐάντητε, λυτηρία, ἀρσενόμορφε,
Ὀρθία, ὠκυλόχεια, βροτῶν κουροτρόφε δαῖμον,
ἀμβροτέρα, χθονία, θηροκτόνε, ὀλβιόμοιρε,
ἣ κατέχεις ὀρέων δρυμούς, ἐλαφηβόλε, σεμνή,
πότνια, παμβασίλεια, καλὸν θάλος, αἰὲν ἐοῦσα,
δρυμονία, σκυλακῖτι, Κυδωνιάς, αἰολόμορφε·
ἐλθέ, θεὰ σώτειρα, φίλη, μύστηισιν ἅπασιν
εὐάντητος, ἄγουσα καλοὺς καρποὺς ἀπὸ γαίης
εἰρήνην τ’ ἐρατὴν καλλιπλόκαμόν θ’ ὑγίειαν·
πέμποις δ’ εἰς ὀρέων κεφαλὰς νούσους τε καὶ ἄλγη.

36. For Artemis

Incense: manna
Hear me, Queen, many-named daughter of Zeus,
Titanis, boisterous and great-named holy
archer, divine Diktynna, with a torch
shining on all, attending birth. You help
women in childbirth, although you are not
initiated in childbirth yourself.
Frenzy-loving hunter who loosens bonds
and chases cares away, you love the hunt,
running, roaming the night, pouring arrows.
You bind up and you loosen, kind hearted
with a masculine nature. Orthia,
granter of quick birth, daimon who nurtures
mortals, you are most divine, though earthly,
slaying beasts, richly blessed: You, who governs
the mountain copses of oak, who shoots deer,
blessed lady, queen of all, beautiful
child forever. Many shaped, wood haunting
protector of dogs, Kydonian goddess:
Come, divine and beloved savior, gracious
to all initiates, bringing fair fruits
from the earth, with lovely peace, and Health, too,
with her beautiful hair. And send away
pain and disease to the peaks of mountains.

Note: Artemis is one of the virginal goddesses, but she is also regarded
as patron of childbirth.

37 Τιτάνων, θυμίαμα λίβανον.

Τιτῆνες, Γαίης τε καὶ Οὐρανοῦ ἀγλαὰ τέκνα,
ἡμετέρων πρόγονοι πατέρων, γαίης, ὑπένερθεν
οἴκοις Ταρταρίοισι μυχῶι χθονὸς ἐνναίοντες,
ἀρχαὶ καὶ πηγαὶ πάντων θνητῶν πολυμόχθων,
εἰναλίων πτηνῶν τε καὶ οἳ χθόνα ναιετάουσιν·
ἐξ ὑμέων γὰρ πᾶσα πέλει γενεὰ κατὰ κόσμον.
ὑμᾶς κικλήσκω μῆνιν χαλεπὴν ἀποπέμπειν,
εἴ τις ἀπὸ χθονίων προγόνων οἴκοις ἐπελάσθη.

37. For the Titans

Incense: frankincense

Titans, the shining children of Gaia
and Ouranos, our fathers' ancestors,
you dwell below the earth, in hollow caves
with homes in Tartaros, the beginning
and spring of every mortal who struggles,
and the fishes of the sea, and winged
creatures, and all those that dwell on the earth,
for every species is derived from you,
according to cosmic order. I call
upon you to send away the cruel
anger of any primal being who
approaches the homes from below the earth.

Note: This appears to be an appeasement of angry spirits. Titans are not inherently evil, and not all Titans took place in the Titanomachy which led to them being bound below the earth in Tartaros.

38 Κουρήτων, θυμίαμα λίβανον.

Χαλκόκροτοι Κουρῆτες, Ἀρήια τεύχε᾽ ἔχοντες,
οὐράνιοι χθόνιοί τε καὶ εἰνάλιοι, πολύολβοι,
ζωιογόνοι πνοιαί, κόσμου σωτῆρες ἀγαυοί,
οἵτε Σαμοθράικην, ἱερὴν χθόνα, ναιετάοντες
κινδύνους θνητῶν ἀπερύκετε ποντοπλανήτων·
ὑμεῖς καὶ τελετὴν πρῶτοι μερόπεσσιν ἔθεσθε,
ἀθάνατοι Κουρῆτες, Ἀρήια τεύχε᾽ ἔχοντες·
νωμᾶτ᾽ Ὠκεανόν, νωμᾶθ᾽ ἅλα δένδρεά θ᾽ αὔτως·
ἐρχόμενοι γαῖαν κοναβίζετε ποσσὶν ἐλαφροῖς,
μαρμαίροντες ὅπλοις· πτήσσουσι δὲ θῆρες ἅπαντες
ὁρμώντων, θόρυβος δὲ βοή τ᾽ εἰς οὐρανὸν ἵκει
εἰλιγμοῖς τε ποδῶν κονίη νεφέλας ἀφικάνει
ἐρχομένων· τότε δή ῥα καὶ ἄνθεα πάντα τέθηλε.
δαίμονες ἀθάνατοι, τροφέες καὶ αὖτ᾽ ὀλετῆρες,
ἡνίκ᾽ ἂν ὁρμαίνητε χολούμενοι ἀνθρώποισιν
ὀλλύντες βίοτον καὶ κτήματα ἠδὲ καὶ αὐτοὺς
πιμπλάντες, στοναχεῖ δὲ μέγας πόντος βαθυδίνης,
δένδρη δ᾽ ὑψικάρην᾽ ἐκ ῥιζῶν ἐς χθόνα πίπτει,
ἠκὼ δ᾽ οὐρανία κελαδεῖ ῥοιζήμασι φύλλων.
Κουρῆτες Κορύβαντες, ἀνάκτορες εὐδύνατοί τε
ἐν Σαμοθράικηι ἄνακτες, ὁμοῦ <δὲ> Διόσκοροι αὐτοί,
πνοιαὶ ἀέναοι, ψυχοτρόφοι, ἀεροειδεῖς,
οἵτε καὶ οὐράνιοι δίδυμοι κλήιζεσθ᾽ ἐν Ὀλύμπωι,
εὔπνοοι, εὔδιοι, σωτήριοι ἠδὲ προσηνεῖς,
ὡροτρόφοι, φερέκαρποι ἐπιπνείοιτε ἄνακτες.

38. For the Kouretes

Incense: frankincense

Kouretes, beating bronze with the weapons
of Ares, dwelling in sky, sea and earth,
much blessed life-giving breath and glorious
saviors of the world, dwelling in the land
of holy Samothrace, ward off danger
to the mortals who roam the sea. And you
were the first to set up the rituals
for articulate humans. Immortal
Kouretes, with the weapons of Ares,
you rule the ocean, and you rule the sea,
and the forests as well. When you advance,
your nimble footsteps resound on the earth,
in flashing armor, and all the wild beasts
flee in fear, and the noise and battlecries
reach to the heavens, and when you come
by the twirling of your feet, dust rises up
to the clouds. And then, every flower blooms.
Deathless daimons, who nurture and destroy,
whenever you grow angry at mankind,
you destroy life, wealth, and people themselves
by burning. The great, deep-swirling sea groans,
and high trees fall, uprooted, to the earth,
and the whirling rush of their leaves reaches
the heavens. Kouretes, Korybantes,
truly mighty lords, lords of Samothrace,
the same as the Dioskouroi themselves,
ever-blowing cloudy winds, nourishing
the soul. And on Olympos, you are called
the celestial twins, sweet breathed and kind
saviors who make calm weather, nourishing
the seasons, bringing fruits, inspire us, lords.

Note: I read the participle, πιμπράντες for πιμπλάντες, "burning" rather than "filling." The association with the Dioskouroi, Castor and Pollux, is unusual; this is not a classical correspondence. There are two hymns to the Kouretes, this and Hymn 31. It appears that these seemingly minor figures were important to the Orphic cult, perhaps due to some ritual dance that recalled their noise-making in order to drown out the cries of the infant Zeus.

39 Κορύβαντος, θυμίαμα λίβανον.

Κικλήσκω χθονὸς ἀενάου βασιλῆα μέγιστον,
Κύρβαντ᾽ ὀλβιόμοιρον, Ἀρήιον, ἀπροσόρατον,
νυκτερινὸν Κουρῆτα, φόβων ἀποπαύστορα δεινῶν,
φαντασιῶν ἐπαρωγόν, ἐρημοπλάνον Κορύβαντα,
αἰολόμορφον ἄνακτα, θεὸν διφυῆ, πολύμορφον,
φοίνιον, αἱμαχθέντα κασιγνήτων ὑπὸ δισσῶν,
Δηοῦς ὃς γνώμαισιν ἐνήλλαξας δέμας ἁγνόν,
θηρότυπον θέμενος μορφὴν δνοφεροῖο δράκοντος·
κλῦθι, μάκαρ, φωνῶν, χαλεπὴν δ᾽ ἀποπέμπεο μῆνιν,
παύων φαντασίας, ψυχῆς ἐκπλήκτου ἀνάγκας.

39. For Korybas

Incense: frankincense
I call the greatest king of eternal
earth, richly blessed Korybas, like Ares,
whose face is terrible to look upon:
Korybas, who dwells in night and who quells
terrible fear. He assists by bringing
visions—Korybas, wandering alone,
two-natured god, lord, of many changing
forms. When stained blood-red by the two brothers
you followed the plan of Deo, exchanged
your holy body with a savage beast,
a dark and murky dragon. Hear my voice,
blessed one, and banish severe anger,
ceasing figments in a soul struck by need.

Note: Korybas is said to be the leader of the Korybantes. He may also refer to a particular role in the rituals of initiation of the cult of Eleusis, which would fit thematically with the next hymn in sequence. The myth about turning into a dragon is obscure; we do not seem to have any other reference to it. Evidently, Korybas transforms himself into a dragon in order to avenge or perhaps atone for the death of brothers, though whether these were his brothers (Boötes and Ploutos) is unknown. The word translated "figments" here is φαντασία, (*fantasia*), which is also used to mean the imagination in general, as well as appearances, illusions, and figments of the imagination.

40 Δήμητρος Ἐλευσινίας, θυμίαμα στύρακα.

Δηώ, παμμήτειρα θεά, πολυώνυμε δαῖμον,
σεμνὴ Δήμητερ, κουροτρόφε, ὀλβιοδῶτι,
πλουτοδότειρα θεά, σταχυοτρόφε, παντοδότειρα,
εἰρήνηι χαίρουσα καὶ ἐργασίαις πολυμόχθοις,
σπερμεία, σωρῖτι, ἀλωαία, χλοόκαρπε,
ἢ ναίεις ἁγνοῖσιν Ἐλευσῖνος γυάλοισιν,
ἱμερόεσσ᾽, ἐρατή, θνητῶν θρέπτειρα προπάντων,
ἡ πρώτη ζεύξασα βοῶν ἀροτῆρα τένοντα
καὶ βίον ἱμερόεντα βροτοῖς πολύολβον ἀνεῖσα,
αὐξιθαλής, Βρομίοιο συνέστιος, ἀγλαότιμος,
λαμπαδόεσσ᾽, ἁγνή, δρεπάνοις χαίρουσα θερείοις·
σὺ χθονία, σὺ δὲ φαινομένη, σὺ δε πᾶσι προσηνής·
εὔτεκνε, παιδοφίλη, σεμνή, κουροτρόφε κούρα,
ἅρμα δρακοντείοισιν ὑποζεύξασα χαλινοῖς
ἐγκυκλίοις δίναις περὶ σὸν θρόνον εὐάζουσα,
μουνογενής, πολύτεκνε θεά, πολυπότνια θνητοῖς,
ἧς πολλαὶ μορφαί, πολυάνθεμοι, ἱεροθαλεῖς.
ἐλθέ, μάκαιρ᾽, ἁγνή, καρποῖς βρίθουσα θερείοις,
εἰρήνην κατάγουσα καὶ εὐνομίην ἐρατεινὴν
καὶ πλοῦτον πολύολβον, ὁμοῦ δ᾽ ὑγίειαν ἄνασσαν.

40. For Eleusinian Demeter

Incense: storax

Deo, divine mother of all, daimon
with many names, Demeter, nourisher
of the young and bestower of blessings,
wealth-granting goddess and giver of all,
nourisher of ears of grain, who delights
in peace and in hard work too, the sower,
thresher, who heaps up grain, and brings green fruit,
you dwell in Eleusis, in holy vales;
charming, lovely, who feeds all mortal things,
who first yoked cattle with sinew to plough,
and produced a lovely, prosperous life
for mortals, causing things to grow: Bright-famed,
you share your hearth with Bromios. Bearing
light, you rejoice in the scythes of summer.
You are terrestrial, you show yourself,
and you are kind to all. Blessed with child,
you love and nourish children, o holy
youth. And to bridled dragons, you yoke up
your chariot, and in whirls you conduct
them in frenzied circles around your throne.
Divine only daughter, but with many
children; to mortals, a mighty lady
of many forms, flowery and blooming.
Come, blessed and holy, heavy with the fruits
of summer, leading down peace and lovely
order, rich wealth, as well as queenly health.

For Demeter's role in the rituals and myths of Eleusis, see the notes to
Hymn 29.

41 Μητρὸς Ἀνταίας, θυμίαμα ἀρώματα.

Ἀνταία βασίλεια, θεά, πολυώνυμε μῆτερ
ἀθανάτων τε θεῶν ἠδὲ θνητῶν ἀνθρώπων,
ἥ ποτε μαστεύουσα πολυπλάγκτωι ἐν ἀνίηι
νηστείαν κατέπαυσας Ἐλευσῖνος {ἐν} γυάλοισιν
ἦλθές τ᾽ εἰς Ἀίδην πρὸς ἀγαυὴν Περσεφόνειαν
ἁγνὸν παῖδα Δυσαύλου ὁδηγητῆρα λαβοῦσα,
μηνυτῆρ᾽ ἁγίων λέκτρων χθονίου Διὸς ἁγνοῦ
Εὔβουλον τεύξασα θεὸν θνητῆς ἀπ᾽ ἀνάγκης.
ἀλλά, θεά, λίτομαί σε, πολυλλίστη βασίλεια,
ἐλθεῖν εὐάντητον ἐπ᾽ εὐιέρωι σέο μύστηι.

41. For Mother Antaia

Incense: aromatics

Antaia, the divine queen, many-named
mother of both deathless gods and mortal
humans, you once, wandering and seeking
in sorrow, broke your fast in the valleys
of Eleusis. And you came to Hades
for noble Persephone, and you brought
the holy child of Dysaules as guide,
the one who announced the holy union
of the sacred subterranean Zeus.
Because mortals needed him, you prepared
the divine Euboulos. So I beseech
that you, divine and much-worshipped queen, come
kindly to your pious initiate.

Note: Antaia is an epithet of Demeter. See Hymns 29 and 40.

42 Μίσης, θυμίαμα στύρακα.

Θεσμοφόρον καλέω ναρθηκοφόρον Διόνυσον,
σπέρμα πολύμνηστον, πολυώνυμον Εὐβουλῆα,
ἁγνήν εὐίερόν τε Μίσην ἄρρητον ἄνασσαν,
ἄρσενα καὶ θῆλυν, διφυῆ, λύσειον Ἴακχον·
εἴτ᾽ ἐν Ἐλευσῖνος τέρπηι νηῶι θυόεντι,
εἴτε καὶ ἐν Φρυγίηι σὺν Μητέρι μυστιπολεύεις,
ἢ Κύπρωι τέρπηι σὺν εὐστεφάνωι Κυθερείηι,
ἤ καὶ πυροφόροις πεδίοις ἐπαγάλλεαι ἁγνοῖς
σὺν σῆι μητρὶ θεᾶι μελανηφόρωι Ἴσιδι σεμνῆι,
Αἰγύπτου παρὰ χεῦμα σὺν ἀμφιπόλοισι τιθήναις·
εὐμενέουσ᾽ ἔλθοις ἀγαθοὺς τελετῆς ἐπ᾽ ἀέθλους.

42. For Mise

Incense: storax
I call on law-giving Dionysos,
who bears the fennel wand, much remembered
and many-titled seed of Eubouleus
and on the holy, sacred, queen Mise,
ineffable, with two natures, female
and male, the liberating Iakchos.
Whether you rejoice in your perfumed
temple in Eleusis, or whether you
perform your mysteries in Phrygia
with the Mother, or you enjoy yourself
in Cyprus with sweet-crowned Kythereia,
or you exult in holy wheat-filled fields
with your divine, holy mother Isis
dressed all in black, along Egypt's river
with busy nurses, may you come with grace
to the good contests of this ritual.

Note: Morand calls Mise *un Dionysos féminin,* "a feminine Dionysos." [15] This interpretation helps explain the fact that the poem seems much more focused on Dionysos initially. Again we see the idea that these rituals are a kind of contest. See Hymn 7, For the Stars.

---

15. Morand, *Études,* 169.

43 Ὡρῶν, θυμίαμα ἀρώματα.

Ὧραι θυγατέρες Θέμιδος καὶ Ζηνὸς ἄνακτος,
Εὐνομίη τε Δίκη τε καὶ Εἰρήνη πολύολβε,
εἰαριναί, λειμωνιάδες, πολυάνθεμοι, ἁγναί,
παντόχροοι, πολύοδμοι ἐν ἀνθεμοειδέσι πνοιαῖς,
Ὧραι ἀειθαλέες, περικυκλάδες, ἡδυπρόσωποι,
πέπλους ἑννύμεναι δροσεροὺς ἀνθῶν πολυθρέπτων,
<ἁγνῆς> Περσεφόνης συμπαίκτορες, ἡνίκα Μοῖραι
καὶ Χάριτες κυκλίοισι χοροῖς πρὸς φῶς ἀνάγωσι
Ζηνὶ χαριζόμεναι καὶ μητέρι καρποδοτείρηι·
ἔλθετ' ἐπ' εὐφήμους τελετὰς ὁσίας νεομύστοις
εὐκάρπους καιρῶν γενέσεις ἐπάγουσαι ἀμεμφῶς.

43. For the Horai

Incense: aromatics

Horai, daughters of Themis and Lord Zeus,
Eunomia and Dike and much-blessed
Eirene, many-colored spring meadows,
holy ones, sweet-smelling with flowery
breezes: the ever-blooming, beautiful
Horai, you circle 'round dressed in dewy
clothes of blooming flowers. You are playmates
of holy Persephone, when the Fates
and the Graces lead in a circling dance
to the light, pleasing Zeus and the Mother
who gives fruit. Come, at our propitious sound
of holy rites for new initiates,
and blamelessly bring forth the good fruit
generated in suitable season.

Note: The ancient Greeks had three seasons, not four: winter, spring, and then summer. Thus there are three Horai or deities of the seasons.

44 Σεμέλης, θυμίαμα στύρακα.

Κικλήσκω κούρην Καδμηίδα παμβασίλειαν,
εὐειδῆ Σεμέλην, ἐρατοπλόκαμον, βαθύκολπον,
μητέρα θυρσοφόροιο Διωνύσου πολυγηθοῦς,
ἣ μεγάλας ὠδῖνας ἐλάσσατο τυρφόρωι αὐγῆι
ἀθανάτη τε<υ>χθεῖσα Διὸς βουλαῖς Κρονίοιο
τιμὰς τευξαμένη παρ' ἀγαυῆς Περσεφονείης
ἐν θνητοῖσι βροτοῖσιν ἀνὰ τριετηρίδας ὥρας,
ἡνίκα σοῦ Βάκχου γονίμην ὠδῖνα τελῶσιν
εὐίερόν τε τράπεζαν ἰδὲ μυστήριά θ' ἁγνά.
νῦν σέ, θεά, λίτομαι, κούρη Καδμηίς, ἄνασσα,
πρηύνοον καλέων αἰεὶ μύσταισιν ὑπάρχειν.

44. For Semele

Incense: storax
I call the maiden daughter of Kadmos,
the queen of all, beautiful Semele,
with lovely hair and deep breasts, the mother
of joyful Dionysos, who carries
the thyrsus. She was struck with labor pain,
made immortal by the will of Kronian
Zeus, and brought to honors by the shining
Persephone every third year among
mortals, when they perform rites enacting
the fruitful birth pains for your son Bakchos,
the sacred table and holy secrets.
Now, to you, divine lady, and daughter
of Kadmos, I pray, to place a gentle,
fair mind, always, in the initiates.

45 Ὕμνος Διονύσου Βασσαρέως Τριετηρικοῦ.

Ἐλθέ, μάκαρ Διόνυσε, πυρίσπορε, ταυρομέτωπε,
Βάσσαρε καὶ Βακχεῦ, πολυώνυμε, παντοδυνάστα,
ὃς ξίφεσιν χαίρεις ἠδ᾿ αἵματι Μαινάσι θ᾿ ἁγναῖς,
εὐάζων κατ᾿ Ὄλυμπον, ἐρίβρομε, μανικὲ Βάκχε,
θυρσεγχής, βαρύμηνι, τετιμένε πᾶσι θεοῖσι
καὶ θνητοῖσι βροτοῖσιν, ὅσοι χθόνα ναιετάουσιν·
ἐλθέ, μάκαρ, σκιρτητά, φέρων πολὺ γῆθος ἅπασι.

45. Hymn to the Triennial Dionysos Bassareus

Come, blessed Dionysos, bull-faced god,
seed of fire, Bassareus and Bakchos,
many named and almighty, you delight
in blood and swords and the holy Mainades,
roaring "Evoe" down from Olympos,
frenzied Bakchos, very wrathful, with your
spearlike thyrsus, honored by all the gods,
and mortals who dwell on earth. Come, blessed one,
and, leaping, bring much joy to everyone.

Note: The thyrsus is a fennel stalk tipped with a pinecone, a ritual wand used in worship of Dionysos. A triennial feast is a feast held every other year, as we would now say, rather than every third year as the name implies.

46 Λικνίτου, θυμίαμα μάνναν.

Λικνίτην Διόνυσον ἐπευχαῖς τᾶισδε κικλήσκω,
Νύσιον ἀμφιθαλῆ, πεποθημένον, εὔφρονα Βάκχον,
νυμφῶν ἔρνος ἐραστὸν ἐυστεφάνου τ' Ἀφροδίτης,
ὅς ποτ' ἀνὰ δρυμοὺς κεχορευμένα βήματα πάλλες
σὺν νύμφαις χαρίεσσιν ἐλαυνόμενος μανίηισι,
καὶ βουλαῖσι Διὸς πρὸς ἀγαυὴν Φερσεφόνειαν
ἀχθεὶς ἐξετράφης φίλος ἀθανάτοισι θεοῖσιν.
εὔφρων ἐλθέ, μάκαρ, κεχαρισμένα δ' ἱερὰ δέξαι.

46. For Liknites

Incense: manna
I invoke by these prayers Dionysos
Liknites of Nysa, covered in blooms,
yearned for and kindly Bakchos, beloved
sprout of nymphs and fair-crowned Aphrodite.
who once, dancing in the woods, swayed your steps
with graceful nymphs, leading them to frenzy.
And by the will of Zeus, to glorious
Persephone you were brought and reared up,
a friend to the deathless gods. Blessed one,
come, and accept this offered sacrifice.

Note: This hymn recalls a myth that Dionysos was cradled in a *liknon,* λίκνον, a winnowing fan.

47 Περικιονίου, θυμίαμα ἀρώματα.

Κικλήσκω Βάκχον περικιόνιον, μεθυδώτην,
Καδμείοισι δόμοις ὃς ἑλισσόμενος πέρι πάντη
ἔστησε κρατερῶς βρασμοὺς γαίης ἀποπέμψας,
ἡνίκα πυρφόρος αὐγὴ ἐκίνησε χθόνα πᾶσαν
πρηστῆρος ῥοίζοις· ὃ δ' ἀνέδραμε δεσμὸς ἁπάντων.
ἐλθέ, μάκαρ, βακχευτά, γεγηθυίαις πραπίδεσσιν.

47. For Perikionios

Incense: aromatics
I call Bakchos Perikionios,
giver of wine, who coiled around all
in the houses of Kadmos, and stood firm,
sending away the shaking of the earth,
when the blazing fire bolt and the howling
hurricane set the whole land in motion;
Then everyone's fetters came undone. Come
blessed Bacchanal with joy in your heart.

Note: In one myth of Dionysos, he is mistaken by some pirates for a mortal prince and kidnapped for ransom, but the fetters will not hold him. He slays them, but those who leap off the ship in an attempt to flee are turned into dolphins. This hymn might hint at that myth, although it seems to be alluding to another, unknown myth, one in which he saves the palace of Kadmos from a hurricane by twining himself around the pillars in the form of grape vines.

48 Σαβαζίου, θυμίαμα ἀρώματα.

Κλῦθι, πάτερ, Κρόνου υἱέ, Σαβάζιε, κύδιμε δαῖμον,
ὃς Βάκχον Διόνυσον, ἐρίβρομον, εἰραφιώτην,
μηρῶι ἐγκατέραψας, ὅπως τετελεσμένος ἔλθηι
Τμῶλον ἐς ἠγάθεον παρ<ὰ> Ἵπταν καλλιπάρηιον.
ἀλλά, μάκαρ, Φρυγίης μεδέων, βασιλεύτατε πάντων,
εὐμενέων ἐπαρωγὸς ἐπέλθοις μυστιπόλοισιν.

48. For Sabazios

Incense: aromatics

Listen, father Sabazios, the son
of Cronos, renowned daimon, who stitched up
in your thigh the Bacchic Dionysos,
loud-roaring Eiraphiotes, so that
he might come, completed, to most holy
Tmolos, beside the lovely-cheeked Hipta.
But, blessed ruler of Phrygia, come,
greatest king of all, may you deliver
kind aid to those performing mystic rites.

Note: Sabazios or Sabos was a Phrygian deity identified with Zeus. This
hymn references the myth that Zeus sewed the fetus of Dionysos into
his thigh after destroying Semele.

49 Ἵπτας, θυμίαμα στύρακα.

Ἵπταν κικλήσκω, Βάκχου τροφόν, εὐάδα κούρην,
μυστιπόλοις τελεταῖσιν ἀγαλλομένην Σάβου ἁγνοῦ
νυκτερίοις τε χοροῖσιν ἐριβρεμέταο Ἰάκχου.
κλῦθί μου εὐχομένου, χθονία μῆτηρ, βασίλεια,
εἴτε σύ γ᾽ ἐν Φρυγίηι κατέχεις Ἴδης ὄρος ἁγνὸν
ἢ Τμῶλος τέρπει σε, καλὸν Λυδοῖσι θόασμα·
ἔρχεο πρὸς τελετὰς ἱερῶι γήθουσα προσώπωι.

49. For Hipta

Incense: storax

I invoke Hipta, the nurse of Bakchos,
the maid who cries "Euoi!" and glorifies
the holy one, Sabos, in mystical
rituals, and who dances in the night
in honor of loud-thundering Iacchus.
Hear me praying, chthonic mother and queen,
whether you are on Ide, the sacred
mountain in Phrygia, or if Tmolos
delights you, the beautiful dancing place
of the Lydians: come to the mystic
rites with happiness on your holy face.

50 Λυσίου Ληναίου

Κλῦθι, μάκαρ, Διὸς υἷ᾽, ἐπιλήνιε Βάκχε, διμάτωρ,
σπέρμα πολύμνη<σ>τον, πολυώνυμε, λύσιε δαῖμον,
κρυψίγονον μακάρων ἱερὸν θάλος, εὔιε Βάκχε,
εὐτραφές, εὔκαρπε, πολυγηθέα καρπὸν αέξων,
ῥηξίχθων, ληναῖε, μεγασθενές, αἰολόμορφε,
παυσίπονον θνητοῖσι φανεὶς ἄκος, ἱερὸν ἄνθος
χάρμα βροτοῖς φιλάλυπον, ἐπάφιε, καλλιέθειρε,
λύσιε, θυρσομανές, βρόμι᾽, εὔιε, πᾶσιν ἔυφρων,
οἷς ἐθέλεις θνητῶν ἠδ᾽ ἀθανάτων ἐπιφαύσκων
νῦν σε καλῶ μύσταισι μολεῖν ἡδύν, φερέκαρπον.

50. For the Redeeming God of the Wine-Press

Hear, Bakchos of the wine press, blessed son
of Zeus and two mothers, long-remembered
seed with many names, redeeming daimon.
Holy child of blessed gods, born in secret,
Bakchos Euios, thriving and happy,
fruitful, and increasing fruit, bursting forth
from the earth, Lenaios, the many-shaped
and powerful holy flower who ends
toil and reveals the cure to mortals,
a delight that loves relief for humans,
Epaphios with fair hair, who redeems
and bears the thyrsus that drives to madness.
Roaring Euios, kind to all, you wish
to become manifest to the mortals
and the deathless gods. I call you, now, come
to the initiates, bearing sweet fruit.

51 Νυμφῶν, θυμίαμα ἀρώματα.

Νύμφαι, θυγατέρες μεγαλήτορος Ὠκεανοῖο,
ὑγροπόροις γαίης ὑπὸ κεύθεσιν οἰκί᾽ ἔχουσαι,
κρυψίδρομοι, Βάκχοιο τροφοί, χθόνιαι, πολυγηθεῖς,
καρποτρόφοι, λειμωνιάδες, σκολιοδρόμοι, ἀγναί,
ἀντροχαρεῖς, σπήλυγξι κεχαρμέναι, ἠερόφοιτοι,
πηγαῖαι, δρομάδες, δροσοείμονες, ἴχνεσι κοῦφαι,
φαινόμεναι, ἀφανεῖς, αὐλωνιάδες, πολυανθεῖς,
σὺν Πανὶ σκιρτῶσαι ἀν᾽ οὔρεα, εὐάστειραι
πετρόρυτοι, λιγυραί, βομβήτριαι, οὐρεσίφοιτοι,
ἀγρότεραι κοῦραι, κρουνίτιδες ὑλονόμοι τε,
παρθένοι εὐώδεις, λευχείμονες, εὔπνοοι αὔραις,
αἰπολικαί, νόμιαι, θηρσὶν φίλαι, ἀγλαόκαρποι,
κρυμοχαρεῖς, ἁπαλαί, πολυθρέμμονες αὐξίτροφοί τε,
κοῦραι ἁμαδρυάδες, φιλοπαίγμονες, ὑγροκέλευθοι,
Νύσιαι, μανικαί, παιωνίδες, εἰαροτερπεῖς,
σὺν Βάκχωι Δηοῖ τε χάριν θνητοῖσι φέρουσαι·
ἔλθετ᾽ ἐπ᾽ εὐφήμοις ἱεροῖς κεχαρηότι θυμῶι
νᾶμα χέουσαι ὑγιεινὸν ἀεξιτρόφοισιν ἐν ὥραις.

51. For the Nymphs

Incense: aromatics

Nymphs, the daughters of great-hearted Ocean,
in the damp-trailing depths of the earth, you
have your homes. With hidden courses, chthonic
and joyful nurses of Bakchos, you bear
fruit in meadows and on winding roads. Pure
ones who delight in the caves where you dwell
and in the air and well-springs, you run
dew-clad, with nimble steps. Both visible
and invisible, much-blooming glen nymphs,
you howl and dance with Pan on the mountains,
and flowing down the rocks, you hum sweetly.
Wild maidens of streams and forests, perfumed
virgins all in white, breathing sweet breezes,
you love goatherds and shepherds and bright fruit,
friends to beasts. Delighting in frost, tender,
you spur growth and nourish many. Maidens,
hamadryads, playful with wet footprints,
dwelling on Nysa, and chanting paeans
in a frenzy with Bakchos and Deo,
you bring grace to mortals. Come
with a grateful temper to this holy
sacrifice and pour down a health-giving
stream in the seasons of fecundity.

52 Τριετηρικοῦ, θυμίαμα ἀρώματα.

Κικλήσκω σε, μάκαρ, πολυώνυμε, μανικέ, Βακχεῦ,
ταυρόκερως, ληναῖε, πυρίσπορε, Νύσιε, λυσεῦ,
μηροτρεφής, λικνῖτα, πυριπόλε καὶ τελετάρχα,
νυκτέρι᾽, Εὐβουλεῦ, μιτρηφόρε, θυρσοτινάκτα,
ὄργιον ἄρρητον, τριφυές, κρύφιον Διὸς ἔρνος,
πρωτόγον᾽, Ἡρικεπαῖε, θεῶν πάτερ ἠδὲ καὶ υἱέ,
ὠμάδιε, σκηπτοῦχε, χοροιμανές, ἀγέτα κώμων,
βακχεύων ἁγίας τριετηρίδας ἀμφὶ γαληνάς,
ῥηξίχθων, πυριφεγγές, ἐπάφριε, κοῦρε διμάτωρ,
οὐρεσιφοῖτα, κερώς, νεβριδοστόλε, ἀμφιέτηρε,
Παιὰν χρυσεγχής ὑποκόλπιε, βοτρυόκοσμε,
Βάσσαρε, κισσοχαρής, πολυπάρθενε καὶ διάκοσμε
ἐλθέ, μάκαρ, μύσταισι βρύων κεχαρημένος αἰεί.

52. For the God of Triennial Feasts

Incense: aromatics

I call you, blessed, many-named, Bakchos,
manic god of the wine-press, with the horns
of a bull, redeemer of Nysa born
from flame, nourished in the thigh, then cradled
with a winnowing fan, destroyed by fire,
And then you began the mystery rites.
Nocturnal Eubouleus with a garland,
shaking a thyrsus. Silently growing
mature, three-natured hidden sprout of Zeus,
primal Erikepaios, the father
of the gods, and the son as well, you eat
raw flesh and with a scepter, madly dance,
leader of revels, to stir to frenzy
near the holy, calm triennial feasts.
Epaphrios, you burst out of the earth
in flames, a boy with two mothers. Haunting
the mountains, with your horned head, you are dressed
in the skin of a fawn, celebrating
yearly festivals, Paian with a spear
of gold under the folds of your robe, decked
with grapes, Bassaros, loving ivy vines,
with many girls and in cosmic order,
come, blessed one, to the initiates,
forever abundant and delighted.

Note: As mentioned above, a triennial feast is one held every other year.

53 Ἀμφιετοῦς, θυμίαμα πάντα πλὴν λιβάνου καὶ σπένδε γάλα.

Ἀμφιετῆ καλέω Βάκχον, χθόνιον Διόνυσον,
ἐγρόμενον κούραις ἅμα νύμφαις εὐπλοκάμοισ<ιν>,
ὃς παρὰ Περσεφόνης ἱεροῖσι δόμοισιν ἰαύων
κοιμίζει τριετῆρα χρόνον, Βακχήιον ἁγνόν.
αὐτὸς δ' ἡνίκα τὸν τριετῆ πάλι κῶμον ἐγείρηι,
εἰς ὕμνον τρέπεται σὺν ἐυζώνοισι τιθήναις
εὐνάζων κινῶν τε χρόνους ἐνὶ κυκλάσιν ὥραις.
ἀλλά, μάκαρ, χλοόκαρπε, κερασφόρε, κάρπιμε Βάκχε,
βαῖν' ἐπὶ πάνθειον τελεὴν γανόωντι προσώπωι
εὐιέροις καρποῖσι τελεσσιγόνοισι βρυάζων.

53. For the God of Yearly Feasts

Incense: Everything but frankincense. Give a libation of milk, too.
I call on Bakchos of the yearly feast,
the chthonic Dionysos, wakening
with the young nymphs having beautiful hair,
who, in Persephone's sacred domain,
slumbers and puts to sleep every three years
the time for Bacchic revelry. And when
he himself wakes up the triennial
festival, he spins a hymn with fair-girt
nurses, putting to bed and then rousing
the spans of time in seasonal circles.
But, blessed and horned Bakchos yielding green fruit,
come to this ritual honoring all
gods, with a shining face and abounding
in fully ripe fruit for the sacrifice.

Note: Dionysos is one of the few gods who can bring souls back from the underworld. In his role as a god of immortality and resurrection, he is thus chthonic. He brings Semele to Olympos, thus deifying her. In this hymn he is also seen as a god of time.

54 Σιληνοῦ Σατύρου Βακχῶν, θυμίαμα μάνναν.

Κλῦθί μου, ὦ πολύσεμνε τροφεῦ, Βάκχοιο τιθηνέ,
Σιληνῶν ὄχ' ἄριστε, τετιμένε πᾶσι θεοῖσι
καὶ θνητοῖσι βροτοῖσιν ἐπὶ τριετηρίσιν ὥραις,
ἁγνοτελής, γεραρός, θιάσου νομίου τελετάρχα,
εὐαστής, φιλάγρυπνε σὺν εὐζώνοισι τιθήναις,
Ναῖσι καὶ Βάκχαις ἡγούμενε κισσοφόροισι·
δεῦρ' ἐπὶ πάνθειον τελετὴν Σατύροις ἅμα πᾶσι
θηροτύποις, εὔασμα διδοὺς Βακχείου ἄνακτος,
σὺν Βάκχαις Λήναια τελεσφόρα σεμνὰ προπέμπων,
ὄργια νυκτιφαῆ τελεταῖς ἁγίαις ἀναφαίνων,
εὐάζων, φιλόθυρσε, γαληνιόων θιάσοισιν.

54. For Seilenos the Satyr, and the Bakchai

Incense: manna

Attend me, o much-honored nurturer
and foster father of Bakchos, by far
the best of the Silenoi, and honored
by all of the gods and mortal humans
at the seasons of triennial feasts,
majestic one worshipped in holy rites,
founder of the mystery of shepherds,
marching in procession, and crying out
"evoe!" Watchful, you lead well-girded
nurses, the Naiades and the Bacchantes
with ivy up to the rite in honor
of all the gods, with all the Satyrs, too,
in the forms of beasts, shouting out to praise
the lord Bakchos. With the Bakchai you lead
the Lenean procession, revealing
the secret rites shining in the night, through
holy rituals, crying *evoe!*,
shaking a thyrsus, calm in procession.

55 Εἰς Ἀφροδίτην.

Οὐρανία, πολύυμνε, φιλομμειδὴς Ἀφροδίτη,
ποντογενής, γενέτειρα θεά, φιλοπάννυχε, σεμνή,
νυκτερία ζεύκτειρα, δολοπλόκε μῆτερ Ἀνάγκης·
πάντα γὰρ ἐκ σέθεν ἐστίν, ὑπεζεύξω δέ <τε> κόσμον
καὶ κρατέεις τρισσῶν μοιρῶν, γεννᾷς δὲ τὰ πάντα,
ὅσσα τ' ἐν οὐρανῶι ἐστι καὶ ἐν γαίηι πολυκάρπωι
ἐν πόντου τε βυθῶι {τε}, σεμνὴ Βάκχοιο πάρεδρε,
τερπομένη θαλίαισι, γαμοστόλε μῆτερ Ἐρώτων,
Πειθοῖ λεκτροχαρής, κρυφία, χαριδῶτι,
φαινομένη, {τ'} ἀφανής, ἐρατοπλόκαμ', εὐπατέρεια,
νυμφιδία σύνδαιτι θεῶν, σκηπτοῦχε, λύκαινα,
γεννοδότειρα, φίλανδρε, ποθεινοτάτη, βιοδῶτι,
ἡ ζεύξασα βροτοὺς ἀχαλινώτοισιν ἀνάγκαις
καὶ θηρῶν πολὺ φῦλον ἐρωτομανῶν ὑπὸ φίλτρων·
ἔρχεο, Κυπρογενὲς θεῖον γένος, εἴτ' ἐν Ὀλύμπωι
ἐσσί, θεὰ βασίλεια, καλῶι γήθουσα προσώπωι,
εἴτε καὶ εὐλιβάνου Συρίης ἕδος ἀμφιπολεύεις,
εἴτε σύ γ' ἐν πεδίοισι σὺν ἅρμασι χρυσεοτεύκτοις
Αἰγύπτου κατέχεις ἱερῆς γονιμώδεα λουτρά,
ἢ καὶ κυκνείοισιν ὄχοις ἐπὶ πόντιον οἶδμα
ἐρχομένη χαίρεις κητῶν κυκλίαισι χορείαις,
ἢ νύμφαις τέρπηι κυανώπισιν ἐν χθονὶ Δίηι
θῖνας ἐπ' αἰγιαλοῖς ψαμμώδεσιν ἅλματι κούφωι·
εἴτ' ἐν Κύπρωι, ἄνασσα, τροφῶι σέο, ἔνθα καλαί τε
παρθένοι ἄδμηται νύμφαι τ' ἀνὰ πάντ' ἐνιαυτὸν
ὑμνοῦσιν, σέ, μάκαιρα, καὶ ἄμβροτον ἁγνὸν Ἄδωνιν.
ἐλθέ, μάκαιρα θεά μάλ' ἐπήρατον εἶδος ἔχουσα·
ψυχῆι γάρ σε καλῶ σεμνῆι ἁγίοισι λόγοισιν.

55. To Aphrodite

O heavenly, much hymned Aphrodite,
loving laughter, born from the sea, goddess
of birth, lover of all-night festivals,
holy nocturnal and wily goddess
who binds, and mother of Necessity:
For everything exists because of you,
who yoked together the whole universe
and govern three shares; you gave birth to all,
what's in the sky, upon the fruitful earth,
in the depths of the sea. Revered companion
of Bakchos, taking joy in abundance,
mother of the Erotes, preparing
weddings, Persuasion of the marriage bed,
you give joy in secret, decked with love-locks,
visible and invisible, daughter
of a great father. You join the bridal
feasts of the gods, with a scepter, she-wolf,
giver of birth, lover of men, longed for
giver of life, who yoked mortals with spells
to unbridled needs, and the many kinds
of beasts to an erotic madness. Come,
goddess born in Cyprus, whether you are
on Olympos, divine queen, with gladness
on your lovely face, or in Syria
with fine frankincense, seated on your throne,
or even if, on the plains with golden
chariots, you occupy the fruitful
baths of sacred Egypt, or coming in
swanlike carriages on the ocean waves,
you rejoice, dancing in circles with beasts
of the sea, or if you are delighted
with the dark-eyed nymphs in their holy land
upon the shores of the sandy beaches,

with the nimble salt sea; or in Cyprus,
lady, land of your nursing, where lovely
virgins and the unwed brides all year sing
hymns to you and to immortal, holy
Adonis. Come, blessed goddess, who has
a very beautiful form, for I call you
with a pious soul and these holy words.

Note: While mostly Aphrodite is seen as a goddess of love, in her form
of Aphrodite Ourania, she was sometimes worshipped as a cosmic principle of order and fertility. The Epicurean philosopher Lucretius makes
Venus, her Roman counterpart, the goddess of nature, in his treatise *On
the Nature of Things (De Rerum Natura).*

56 Ἀδώνιδος, θυμίαμα ἀρώματα.

Κλῦθί μου εὐχομένου, πολυώνυμε, δαῖμον ἄριστε,
ἁβροκόμη, φιλέρημε, βρύων ὠιδαῖσι ποθειναῖς,
Εὐβουλεῦ, πολύμορφε, τροφεῦ πάντων ἀρίδηλε,
κούρη καὶ κόρε, σὺ πᾶσιν θάλος αἰέν, Ἄδωνι,
σβεννύμενε λάμπων τε καλαῖς ἐν κυκλάσιν ὥραις,
αὐξιθαλής, δίκερως, πολυήρατε, δακρυότιμε,
ἀγλαόμορφε, κυναγεσίοις χαίρων, βαθυχαῖτα,
ἱμερόνους, Κύπριδος γλυκερὸν θάλος, ἔρνος Ἔρωτος,
Φερσεφόνης ἐρασιπλοκάμου λέκτροισι λοχευθείς,
ὃς ποτὲ μὲν ναίεις ὑπὸ Τάρταρον ἠερόεντα,
ἠδὲ πάλιν πρὸς Ὄλυμπον ἄγεις δέμας ὠριόκαρπον·
ἐλθέ, μάκαρ, μύσταισι φέρων καρποὺς ἀπὸ γαίης.

56. For Adonis

Incense: aromatics

Hear me praying, many-named excellent
daimon, with delicate foliage, and fond
of solitude, swelling with longing songs:
Eubouleus, many formed and manifest
nurturer of all things. Both girl and boy,
you are forever a flower to all,
Adonis, who is quenched and blazes up
in the beautiful circle of seasons.
Two-horned and much loved, you increase the blooms,
honored by tears, bright-formed with deep, thick hair.
You rejoice in packs of dogs. The sweet sprout
of Eros, and the offspring of Cyprus,
with desires you were brought forth from the bed
of Persephone of the lovely hair.
You sometimes dwell in murky Tartaros,
and then again you carry your body
to Olympos with ripe fruit. Come, blessed one,
with fruit from the earth to the worshippers.

57 Ἑρμοῦ Χθονίου, θυμίαμα στύρακα.

Κωκυτοῦ ναίων ἀνυπόστροφον οἶμον ἀνάγκης,
ὃς ψυχὰς θνητῶν κατάγεις ὑπὸ νέρτερα γαίης,
Ἑρμῆ, βακχεχόροιο Διωνύσοιο γένεθλον
καὶ Παφίης κούρης, ἑλικοβλεφάρου Ἀφροδίτης,
ὃς παρὰ Περσεφόνης ἱερὸν δόμον ἀμφιπολεύεις,
αἰνομόροις ψυχαῖς πομπὸς κατὰ γαῖαν ὑπάρχων,
ἃς κατάγεις, ὁπόταν μοίρης χρόνος εἰσαφίκηται
εὐιέρωι ῥάβδωι θέλγων ὑπνοδώτειρα πάντα,
καὶ πάλιν ὑπνώοντας ἐγείρεις· σοὶ γὰρ ἔδωκε {τιμὴν}
τιμὴν Φερσεφόνεια θεὰ κατὰ Τάρταρον εὐρὺν
ψυχαῖς ἀενάοις θνητῶν ὁδὸν ἡγεμονεύειν.
ἀλλά, μάκαρ, πέμποις μύσταις τέλος ἐσθλὸν ἐπ᾽ ἔργοις.

57. For Chthonic Hermes

Incense: storax

Dwelling by the Kokytos, the wailing
river, paths of Necessity from which
no one returns, you lead down to the depths
of the earth the souls of mortals. Hermes,
kin to Dionysos of the Bacchic
dance and winking Aphrodite, the maid
of Paphos, you care for the holy home
beside Persephone. You are the guide
of sad-fated souls, down below the earth,
whom you lead down, whenever their fated
time arrives. You touch with your most holy
wand, now enchanting everything to sleep,
and then rousing them again. For to you
divine Persephone gave the office
to lead the way for the ever-lasting
souls of mortals on the road down to wide
Tartaros. But come, blessed one. May you send
for the worshippers a good end to works.

Note: Hermes is traditionally a psychopomp, or a guide of souls into the afterlife. For another view of Hermes, see Hymn 28.

58 Ἔρωτος, θυμίαμα ἀρώματα.

Κικλήσκω μέγαν, ἁγνόν, ἐράσμιον, ἡδὺν Ἔρωτα,
τοξαλκῆ, πτερόεντα, πυρίδρομον, εὔδρομον ὁρμῆι,
συμπαίζοντα θεοῖς ἡδὲ θνητοῖς ἀνθρώποις,
εὐπάλαμον, διφυῆ, πάντων κληῖδας ἔχοντα,
αἰθέρος οὐρανίου, πόντου, χθονός, ἠδ᾽ ὅσα θνητοῖς
πνεύματα παντογένεθλα θεὰ βόσκει χλοόκαρπος,
ἠδ᾽ ὅσα Τάρταρος εὐρὺς ἔχει πόντος· θ᾽ ἁλίδουπος·
μοῦνος γὰρ τούτων πάντων οἴηκα κρατύνεις.
ἀλλά, μάκαρ, καθαραῖς γνώμαις μύσταισι συνέρχου,
φαύλους δ᾽ ἐκτοπίους θ᾽ ὁρμὰς ἀπὸ τῶνδ᾽ ἀπόπεμπε.

58. For Eros

Incense: aromatics

I call the great, holy, lovely, and sweet
Eros. Winged and mighty archer, you rush
forth swiftly over fiery paths, playing
with the gods and mortal humans. Skillful,
two-natured, holding the keys to all things:
of airy sky, ocean, earth and the winds
that create everything for mortals, fed
by the goddess of green fruit, and all things
wide Tartaros holds, the depths, and the sounding
sea. For you alone command the rudder
of everything. But blessed one, accompany
the purified minds of the worshippers
and drive from them strange and mean desires.

Note: Eros is the god of sexual desire, but in keeping with the ascetic
Orphic way of life, here he is asked to curtail such desires.

59 Μοιρῶν, θυμίαμα ἀρώματα.

Μοῖραι ἀπειρέσιοι, Νυκτὸς φίλα τέκνα μελαίνης,
κλῦτέ μου εὐχομένου, πολυώνυμοι, αἵτ᾽ ἐπὶ λίμνης
οὐρανίας, ἵνα λευκὸν ὕδωρ νυχίας ὑπὸ θέρμης
ῥήγνυται ἐν σκιερῶι λιπαρῶι μυχῶι εὐλίθου ἄντρου,
ναίουσαι πεπότησθε βροτῶν ἐπ᾽ ἀπείρονα γαῖαν·
ἔνθεν ἐπὶ βρότεον δόκιμον γένος ἐλπίδι κοῦφον
στείχετε πορφυρέηισι καλυψάμεναι ὀθόνηισι
μορσίμωι ἐν πεδίωι, ὅθι πάγγεον ἅρμα διώκει
δόξα δίκης παρὰ τέρμα καὶ ἐλπίδος ἠδὲ μεριμνῶν
καὶ νόμου ὠγυγίου καὶ ἀπείρονος εὐνόμου ἀρχῆς·
Μοῖρα γὰρ ἐν βιότωι καθορᾶι μόνη, οὐδέ τις ἄλλος
ἀθανάτων, οἳ ἔχουσι κάρη νιφόεντος Ὀλύμπου,
καὶ Διὸς ὄμμα τέλειον· ἐπεί γ᾽ ὅσα γίγνεται ἡμῖν,
Μοῖρά τε καὶ Διὸς οἶδε νόος διὰ παντὸς ἅπαντα.
ἀλλά μοι εὐκταῖαι, μαλακόφρονες, ἠπιόθυμοι,
Ἄτροπε καὶ Λάχεσι, Κλωθώ, μόλετ᾽, εὐπατέρειαι,
ἀέριοι, ἀφανεῖς, ἀμετάτροποι, αἰὲν ἀτειρεῖς,
παντοδότειραι, ἀφαιρέτιδες, θνητοῖσιν ἀνάγκη·
Μοῖραι, ἀκούσατ᾽ ἐμῶν ὁσίων λοιβῶν τε καὶ εὐχῶν,
ἐρχόμεναι μύσταις λυσιπήμονες εὔφρονι βουλῆι.
{Μοιράων τέλος ἔλλαβ᾽ ἀοιδή, ἣν ὕφαν᾽ Ὀρφεύς}

59. For the Fates

Incense: aromatics

Boundless Fates, beloved children of black Night,
hear me praying, many-named ones, who dwell
on a heavenly lake, where clear water
breaks under hot nights, to rush in a dim
and glistening nook of a finely stoned
cavern, from where you fly to the mortals
upon the boundless earth. From there you walk
wearing purple linen to the esteemed
mortal race, with empty hope, on a doomed
plain, where glory follows the chariot
that holds the earth, beyond the end of hope,
of judgement and worry and primal law,
and the limitless dominion of good
order. For Fate alone looks down on life,
no other gods who hold the snowy top
of Olympos, except the perfect eye
of Zeus. Whatever comes to pass for us,
Fate and the Mind of Zeus know everything
through all time. But come to me, with gentle
hearts and moods, Atropos and Lachesis,
and Klotho I pray, daughters of noble
father, airy, invisible, never
turned from your purpose, never worn away:
Givers of all, the ones who take away,
Necessity to mortals, Fates, attend
my holy libation and prayer. Kind hearts,
come and end pain for the initiates.
(Fate's song, which Orpheus wove, is ended.)

Note: This is one of the only two hymns that mention Orpheus by
name as author (the other being the introductory prayer for Mousaios).

60 Χαρίτων, θυμίαμα στύρακα.

Κλῦτέ μοι, ὦ Χάριτες μεγαλώνυμοι, ἀγλαότιμοι,
θυγατέρες Ζηνός τε καὶ Εὐνομίης βαθυκόλπου,
Ἀγλαΐη Θαλίη τε καὶ Εὐφροσύνη πολύολβε,
χαρμοσύνης γενέτειραι, ἐράσμιαι, εὔφρονες, ἀγναί,
αἰολόμορφοι, ἀειθαλέες, θνητοῖσι ποθειναί·
εὐκταῖαι, κυκλάδες, καλυκώπιδες, ἱμερόεσσαι·
ἔλθοιτ᾽ ὀλβοδότειραι, ἀεὶ μύσταισι προσηνεῖς.

60. For the Graces

Incense: storax
Hear me, O Charites, much famed, brightly
honored daughters of Zeus and deep breasted
Eunomia: Aglaia, Thalia,
and richly blessed Euphrosyne, mothers
of joyfulness; lovely, kind, and holy,
with many forms, ever-blooming, desired
by mortals, invoked by prayer, with faces
like flower buds, dancing in a circle,
sparking love: May you always come kindly
giving rich blessings for your worshippers.

61 Νεμέσεως ὕμνος.

Ὦ Νέμεσι, κλήιζω σε, θεά, βασίλεια μεγίστη,
πανδερκής, ἐσορῶσα βίον θνητῶν πολυφύλων·
ἀιδία, πολύσεμνε, μόνη χαίρουσα δικαίοις,
ἀλλάσσουσα λόγον πολυποίκιλον, ἄστατον αἰεί,
ἣν πάντες δεδίασι βροτοὶ ζυγὸν αὐχένι θέντες·
σοὶ γὰρ ἀεὶ γνώμη πάντων μέλει, οὐδέ σε λήθει
ψυχὴ ὑπερφρονέουσα λόγων ἀδιακρίτωι ὁρμῆι.
πάντ' ἐσορᾶις καὶ πάντ' ἐπακούεις, {καὶ} πάντα βραβεύεις·
ἐν σοὶ δ' εἰσὶ δίκαι θνητῶν, πανυπέρτατε δαῖμον.
ἐλθέ, μάκαιρ', ἁγνή, μύσταις ἐπιτάρροθος αἰεί·
δὸς δ' ἀγαθὴν διάνοιαν ἔχειν, παύουσα πανεχθεῖς
γνώμας οὐχ ὁσίας, πανυπέρφρονας, ἀλλοπροσάλλας.

61. A Hymn of Nemesis

O Nemesis, I exalt you, divine
and mighty queen, all seeing, looking
upon the life of the many races
of mortals, eternal and holy, you
alone take joy in the just, exchanging
manifold words, never resting, whose yoke
all mortals have feared having on their neck.
For you care about the judgment of all,
and no arrogant soul escapes you with
an indiscreet rush of words. You behold
all and hear all, and arbitrate all things.
And the punishment of humanity
is in you, highest daimon. Come, blessed
and holy one, ever a defender
of the initiates, and give a good
understanding, and prevent what you hate:
Unholy thoughts, the arrogant, and those
who fight first on one side, then the other.

Note: The entire last line is the rendering of a single Greek word, ἀλλοπροσάλλας (alloprosallas), which is a compound meaning literally "other to other." It is applied to Ares, who changes sides in the *Iliad* (5.831).

62 Δίκης, θυμίαμα λίβανον.

Ὄμμα Δίκης μέλπω πανδερκέος, ἀγλαομόρφου,
ἣ καὶ Ζηνὸς ἄνακτος ἐπὶ θρόνον ἱερὸν ἵζει
οὐρανόθεν καθορῶσα βίον θνητῶν πολυφύλων,
τοῖς ἀδίκοις τιμωρὸς ἐπιβρίθουσα δικαία,
ἐξ ἰσότητος ἀληθείαι συνάγουσ᾽ ἀνόμοια·
πάντα γάρ, ὅσσα κακαῖς γνώμαις θνητοῖσιν ὀχεῖται
δύσκριτα, βουλομένοις τὸ πλέον βουλαῖς ἀδίκοισι,
μούνη ἐπεμβαίνουσα δίκην ἀδίκοις ἐπεγείρεις·
ἐχθρὰ τῶν ἀδίκων, εὔφρων δὲ σύνεσσι δικαίοις.
ἀλλά, θεά, μόλ᾽ ἐπὶ γνώμαις ἐσθλαῖσι δικαία,
ὡς ἂν ἀεὶ βιοτῆς τὸ πεπρωμένον ἦμαρ ἐπέλθοι.

62. For Dike

Incense: frankincense

I celebrate in song the all-seeing
eye of splendid Dike, who also seats
herself on the holy throne of Lord Zeus,
and looks down from the heavens on the lives
of the many different kinds of mortals,
an avenging, heavy judgement against
the unjust. Out of equality, she
corrects imbalance by means of the truth.
For everything that wicked mortal minds
hold in obscurity, in greedy plans
and unjust desires, you alone step forth
and wake up justice against the unjust.
The enemy of the unjust, you join
yourself kindly with the just. But, come,
fair goddess, to noble minds when the day
that was ever destined for life arrives.

Note: The word used for "life" in the last line is βιοτῆς (*biotēs*) which
more commonly means "livelihood" or "means of living."

63 Δικαιοσύνης, θυμίαμα λίβανον.

Ὦ θνητοῖσι δικαιοτάτη, πολύολβε, ποθεινή,
ἐξ ἰσότητος ἀεὶ θνητοῖς χαίρουσα δικαίοις,
πάντιμ᾽, ὀλβιόμοιρε, Δικαιοσύνη μεγαλαυχής,
ἣ καθαραῖς γνώμαισ<ιν> ἀεὶ τὰ δέοντα βραβεύεις,
ἄθραυστος τὸ συνειδὸς ἀεί·θραύεις γὰρ ἅπαντας,
ὅσσοι μὴ τὸ σὸν ἦλθον ὑπὸ ζυγόν, ἀλλ᾽ ὑπὲρ αὐτοῦ
πλάστιγξι βριαραῖσι παρεγκλίναντες ἀπλήστως·
ἀστασία<σ>τε, φίλη πάντων, φιλόκωμ᾽, ἐρατεινή,
εἰρήνηι χαίρουσα, βίον ζηλοῦσα βέβαιον·
αἰεὶ γὰρ τὸ πλέον στυγέεις, ἰσότητι δὲ χαίρεις·
ἐν σοὶ γὰρ σοφίη ἀρετῆς τέλος ἐσθλὸν ἱκάνει.
κλῦθι, θεά, κακίην θνητῶν θραύουσα δικαίως,
ὡς ἂν ἰσορροπίαισιν ἀεὶ βίος ἐσθλὸς ὁδεύοι
θνητῶν ἀνθρώπων, οἳ ἀρούρης καρπὸν ἔδουσι,
καὶ ζώιων πάντων, ὁπόσ᾽ ἐν κόλποισι τιθηνεῖ
γαῖα θεὰ μήτηρ καὶ πόντιος εἰνάλιος Ζεύς.

63. For Justice

Incense: frankincense

O utmost Justice, blessed and desired
by mortals, rejoicing always in just
people equally, honored by all, the greatly
shining Dikaiosyne of blessed
portion: always unbroken in knowledge,
you determine what is right for pure minds;
for you always shatter every one who
does not come under your yoke but struggles
to take control over it for themselves,
who greedily try to tip the balance
of your stout scales. Taking no sides, a friend
to all, charming one who loves festivals,
you joy in peace, eager for a steady
life, for you always hate excess, but you
rejoice in fairness. For virtue's wisdom
within you hits its noble end. Listen,
goddess, and shatter human evil with
justice, so a noble life might always
travel amid equanimity for
mortal humans, who eat of the fruit of
the tilled fields, and for all the living things
whom the divine mother Gaia nurses
at her breast, and Zeus of the salty sea.

Note: "Zeus of the salty sea" is a reference to Poseidon. Both Poseidon
and Hades are sometimes called the "Zeus" of their respective realms.

64 Ὕμνος Νόμου.

Ἀθανάτων καλέω καὶ θνητῶν ἁγνὸν ἄνακτα,
οὐράνιον Νόμον, ἀστροθέτην, σφραγῖδα δικαίαν
πόντου τ' εἰναλίου καὶ γῆς, φύσεως τὸ βέβαιον
ἀκλινὲς ἀστασίαστον ἀεὶ τηροῦντα νόμοισιν,
οἷσιν ἄνωθε φέρων μέγαν οὐρανὸν αὐτὸς ὁδεύει,
καὶ φθόνον οὐ δίκαιον ῥοίζου τρόπον ἐκτὸς ἐλαύνει·
ὃς καὶ θνητοῖσιν βιοτῆς τέλος ἐσθλὸν ἐγείρει·
αὐτὸς γὰρ μοῦνος ζώιων οἴακα κρατύνει
γνώμαις ὀρθοτάταισι συνών, ἀδιάστροφος αἰεί,
ὠγύγιος, πολύπειρος, ἀβλάπτως πᾶσι συνοικῶν
τοῖς νομίμοις, ἀνόμοις δὲ φέρων κακότητα βαρεῖαν.
ἀλλά, μάκαρ, πάντιμε, φερόλβιε, πᾶσι ποθεινέ,
εὐμενὲς ἦτορ ἔχων μνήμην σέο πέμπε, φέριστε.

64. A Hymn of Nomos

I call the holy lord of deathless gods
and mortals, heavenly Nomos, signet
of justice, and arranger of the stars,
and of the salty sea, and of the earth,
and the steadfast constancy of nature,
not taking sides, always guiding by laws,
which he carries when he comes from above
through mighty heaven: he drives out ill will
with a roar, turning it aside, and he
rouses a noble end to mortal life;
for he alone steers the rudders of life,
sharing presence in righteous minds, always
unbending, primal, much-experienced,
harmlessly dwelling with all lawful ones,
but to the lawless, bearing stern distress.
But blessed one, all-honored, bringing blessings,
beloved of all, with a kind heart send us
the remembrance of you, the bravest one.

Note: Nomos is the personification of law, especially cosmic rather than human law. In this, he is much like Dike as described in hymn 62.

65 Ἄρεος, θυμίαμα λίβανον.

Ἄρρηκτ᾽, ὀμβριμόθυμε, μεγασθενές, ἄλκιμε δαῖμον,
ὁπλοχαρής, ἀδάμαστε, βροτοκτόνε, τειχεσιπλῆτα,
Ἄρες ἄναξ, ὁπλόδουπε, φόνοις πεπαλαγμένος αἰεί,
αἵματι ἀνδροφόνωι χαίρων, πολεμόκλονε, φρικτέ,
ὃς ποθέεις ξίφεσίν τε καὶ ἔγχεσι δῆριν ἄμουσον·
στῆσον ἔριν λυσσῶσαν, ἄνες πόνον ἀλγεσίθυμον,
εἰς δὲ πόθον νεῦσον Κύπριδος κώμους τε Λυαίου
ἀλλάξας ἀλκὴν ὅπλων εἰς ἔργα τὰ Δηοῦς,
εἰρήνην ποθέων κουροτρόφον, ὀλβιοδῶτιν.

65. For Ares

Incense: frankincense

Unbroken, mighty-hearted, very strong,
stout daimon, who takes pleasure in weapons,
untamed man-slaying sacker of cities,
Lord Ares, rattling in armor, always
smeared with slaughter, rejoicing in bloody
murder of men, raising the noise of war,
horrible one, you yearn after the sword
and the unmusical battle of spears:
make raging discord stand still and release
the pain that grieves the heart, and bow your head
to the desire of Kypris and the feasts
of the Deliverer. And craving peace
that gives happiness and nurtures children,
turn strength of arms to the work of Deo.

Note: Ares is a ferocious god, who changed sides in the battle at Troy. Here he is asked to succumb to the wiles of Aphrodite (Kypris). Later in this hymn, Ares is asked to turn himself over to the work of Demeter (Deo), which resembles the prophesy in Isaiah 2:4, that people will beat their swords into plowshares and give up war. The Deliverer is a reference to Dionysos.

66 Ἡφαίστου, θυμίαμα λιβανομάνναν.

Ἥφαιστ' ὀμβριμόθυμε, μεγασθενές, ἀκάματον πῦρ,
λαμπόμενε φλογέαις αὐγαῖς, φαεσίμβροτε δαῖμον,
φωσφόρε, καρτερόχειρ, αἰώνιε, τεχνοδίαιτε,
ἐργαστήρ, κόσμοιο μέρος, στοιχεῖον ἀμεμφές,
παμφάγε, πανδαμάτωρ, πανυπέρτατε, παντοδίαιτε,
αἰθήρ, ἥλιος, ἄστρα, σελήνη, φῶς ἀμίαντον·
ταῦτα γὰρ Ἡφαίστοιο μέλη θνητοῖσι προφαίνει.
πάντα δὲ οἶκον ἔχεις, πᾶσαν πόλιν, ἔθνεα πάντα,
σώματά τε θνητῶν οἰκεῖς, πολύολβε, κραταιέ.
κλῦθι, μάκαρ, κλήιζω <σε> πρὸς εὐιέρους ἐπιλοιβάς,
αἰεὶ ὅπως χαίρουσιν ἐπ' ἔργοις ἥμερος ἔλθοις.
παῦσον λυσσῶσαν μανίαν πυρὸς ἀκαμάτοιο
καῦσιν ἔχων φύσεως ἐν σώμασιν ἡμετέροισιν.

66. For Hephaistos

Incense: powdered frankincense
Hephaistos, strong of spirit, great of heart,
unresting fire, radiant, shining one,
the daimon who illuminates mortals,
bearer of light, strong-handed eternal
one who dwells in art, craftsman and a part
of the cosmos, the blameless element,
all eating, all taming, all consuming,
highest one: the sky, the stars, and the moon,
and the undefiled light: for all these things
show the limbs of Hephaistos to mortals.
And you hold every home, every city,
every nation; you dwell in the bodies
of mortals, much blessed and mighty. Listen,
blessed one, I call you to libations
fit for offering, as you always come
gentle to the welcoming works, and cease
the raging madness of the untamed fire,
keeping nature's burning in our bodies.

Note: Again, we see a hint of the asceticism of Orphic practice, perhaps, in the last couple lines. For the most part, though, this is a hymn of praise to fire.

67 Ἀσκληπιοῦ, θυμίαμα μάνναν.

Ἰητὴρ πάντων, Ἀσκληπιέ, δέσποτα Παιάν,
θέλγων ἀνθρώπων πολυαλγέα πήματα νούσων,
ἠπιόδωρε, κραταιέ, μόλοις κατάγων ὑγίειαν
καὶ παύων νούσους, χαλεπὰς κῆρας θανάτοιο,
αὐξιθαλής, ἐπίκουρ᾽, ἀπαλεξίκακ᾽, ὀλβιόμοιρε,
Φοίβου Ἀπόλλωνος κρατερὸν θάλος ἀγλαότιμον,
ἐχθρὲ νόσων, Ὑγίειαν ἔχων σύλλεκτρον ἀμεμφῆ,
ἐλθέ, μάκαρ, σωτήρ, βιοτῆς τέλος ἐσθλὸν ὀπάζων.

67. For Asklepios

Incense: manna

Healer of all, Asklepios, Paian
the lord, who touches humans with magic
soothing the agonizing suffering
of disease, strong one, may you come and lead
down Health, ending sickness and the hard fate
of death. You are a helper, promoting
growth, and keeping evil away, sharing
blessings. Strong child of Phoibos Apollon,
your fame shines and you hate disease. You hold
Hygieia as your blameless spouse. Come,
blessed one, savior, send a good end of life.

Note: Health, or Hygeia, is personified and Asklepios is described as leading her or guiding her downward to the earth.

68 Ὑγείας, θυμίαμα μάνναν.

Ἱμερόεσσ', ἐρατή, πολυθάλμιε, παμβασίλεια,
κλῦθι, μάκαιρ' Ὑγίεια, φερόλβιε, μῆτερ ἁπάντων·
ἐκ σέο γὰρ νοῦσοι μὲν ἀποφθινύθουσι βροτοῖσι,
πᾶς δὲ δόμος θάλλει πολυγηθὴς εἵνεκα σεῖο,
καὶ τέχναι βρίθουσι· ποθεῖ δέ σε κόσμος, ἄνασσα,
μοῦνος δὲ στυγέει σ' Ἀίδης ψυχοφθόρος αἰεί,
ἀιθαλής, εὐκταιοτάτη, θνητῶν ἀνάπαυμα·
σοῦ γὰρ ἄτερ πάντ' ἐστὶν ἀνωφελῆ ἀνθρώποισιν·
οὔτε γὰρ ὀλβοδότης πλοῦτος γλυκερὸς θαλίηισιν,
οὔτε γέρων πολύμοχθος ἄτερ σέο γίγνεται ἀνήρ·
πάντων γὰρ κρατέεις μούνη καὶ πᾶσιν ἀνάσσεις.
ἀλλά, θεά, μόλε μυστιπόλοις ἐπιτάρροθος αἰεὶ
ῥυομένη νούσων χαλεπῶν κακόποτμον ἀνίην.

68. For Hygeia

Incense: manna

Charming, lovely, the much-nourishing queen
of all, attend, blessed Hygieia,
bringing happiness, mother of all things;
for by you, the diseases of mortals
perish; and every home blossoms with joy
because of you. The arts ripen, the world
longs for you, lady. And only Hades,
killer of souls, ever hates you, always
blooming, the prayerful respite of mortals.
For without you, everything is harmful
to humans, nor is there sweet wealth, giver
of blessings in abundance, nor do men
achieve much-toiling old age without you.
For you alone rule all things and govern
over everything. But, goddess, arrive
at this mystic rite; ever helpful, draw
off the ill-fated grief of hard disease.

Note: The spelling of the goddess's name in the title is not an error; both spellings are attested, and both appear in this hymn. The Pythagoreans called the pentagram, the five-pointed unicursal star, the Hygieia. The letters of her Greek name—ΥΓΙΕΙΑ—are sometimes arranged around the points of the pentagram, treating the digraph ΕΙ as one letter. Of course, if one uses the spelling in the title, each point can have a single letter.

69 Ἐρινύων, θυμίαμα στύρακα καὶ μάνναν.

Κλῦτε, θεαὶ πάντιμοι, ἐρίβρομοι, εὐάστειραι,
Τισιφόνη τε καὶ Ἀλληκτὼ καὶ δῖα Μέγαιρα·
νυκτέριαι, μυχίοις ὑπὸ κεύθεσιν οἰκί᾽ ἔχουσαι
ἄντρωι ἐν ἠερόεντι παρὰ Στυγὸς ἱερὸν ὕδωρ,
οὐχ ὁσίαις βουλαῖσι βροτῶν κεκοτημέναι αἰεί,
λυσσήρεις, ἀγέρωχοι, ἐπευάζουσαι ἀνάγκαις,
θηρόπεπλοι, τιμωροί, ἐρισθενέες, βαρυαλγεῖς,
Ἀίδεω χθόνιαι, φοβεραὶ κόραι, αἰολόμορφοι,
ἠέριαι, ἀφανεῖς, ὠκυδρόμοι ὥστε νόημα·
οὔτε γὰρ ἡελίου ταχιναὶ φλόγες οὔτε σελήνης
καὶ σοφίης ἀρετῆς τε καὶ ἐργασίμου θρασύτητος
εὔχαρι οὔτε βίου λιπαρᾶς περικαλλέος ἥβης
ὑμῶν χωρὶς ἐγείρει εὐφροσύνας βιότοιο·
ἀλλ᾽ αἰεὶ θνητῶν πάντων ἐπ᾽ ἀπείρονα φῦλα
ὄμμα Δίκης ἐφορᾶτε, δικασπόλοι αἰὲν ἐοῦσαι.
ἀλλά, θεαὶ Μοῖραι, ὀφιοπλόκαμοι, πολύμορφοι,
πραΰνοον μετάθεσθε βίου μαλακόφρονα δόξαν.

69. For the Erinyes

Incense: storax and manna

Hear, all-honored goddesses who loudly
shout: Tisiphone, Alekto, divine
Megaira, nocturnal, who have their homes
in the innermost depths, in murky caves
near the holy water of the river
Styx. You always carry a grudge against
the unholy plans of mortals. You shout,
raving and haughty, over violence;
wrapped in animal skins, very mighty,
avenging and heavily suffering,
beneath the earth of Hades, maidens who
provoke fear, changeable in form, airy
and invisible, you run swift as thought.
Neither the swift flames of the sun or moon,
nor of virtuous wisdom and crafty
audacious charm, nor sleek and beautiful
youth, rouses the mirth of life without you.
But always you, the eye of Dike, watch
over all mortals of boundless nations,
in judgment always. But divine Moirai,
with snaky hair, of many forms, adopt
a gentle and kind opinion of life.

Note: Here the Erinyes are equated to the Fates. See Hymn 59.

70 Εὐμενίδων, θυμίαμα ἀρώματα.

Κλῦτέ μου, Εὐμενίδες μεγαλώνυμοι, εὔφρονι βουλῆι,
ἁγναὶ θυγατέρες μεγάλοιο Διὸς χθονίοιο
Φερσεφόνης τ᾽, ἐρατῆς κούρης καλλιπλοκάμοιο,
αἳ πάντων καθορᾶτε βίον θνητῶν ἀσεβούντων,
τῶν ἀδίκων τιμωροί, ἐφεστηκυῖαι ἀνάγκηι,
κυανόχρωτες ἄνασσαι, ἀπαστράπτουσαι ἀπ᾽ ὄσσων
δεινὴν ἀνταυγῆ φάεος σαρκοφθόρον αἴγλην·
ἀίδιοι, φοβερῶπες, ἀπόστροφοι, αὐτοκράτειραι,
λυσιμελεῖς οἴστρωι, βλοσυραί, νύχιαι, πολύποτμοι,
νυκτέριαι κοῦραι, ὀφιοπλόκαμοι, φοβερῶπες·
ὑμᾶς κικλήσκω γνώμαις ὁσίαισι πελάζειν.

70. For Eumenides

Incense: aromatics

Hear me, Eumenides, greatly famed ones,
with a kind intention, holy daughters
of great chthonic Zeus and Persephone,
lovely maiden with beautiful hair. You
look down upon the lives of all profane
mortals and avenge all injustices.
Set over Necessity, dark-visaged
ladies, your eyes flash forth terrible rays
of shining, flesh-eating light. Eternal,
with dreadful eyes that provoke fear, sovereign,
weakening the arms and legs with madness,
grim, nocturnal, of many fates, maidens
of the night with snaky curls and fearsome
eyes, I call you to approach pious minds.

Note: The Eumenides, lit. "Kindly ones," is a euphemism for the Erinyes
(see hymn 69). It is interesting that this poem makes them the children
of Hades (chthonic Zeus) and Persephone, as they are usually regarded
as the offspring of the blood of Ouranos, but perhaps they are seen as
foster children, because their abode is in Hades.

71 Μηλινόης, θυμίαμα ἀρώματα.

Μηλινόην καλέω, νύμφην χθονίαν, κροκόπεπλον,
ἣν παρὰ Κωκυτοῦ προχοαῖς ἐλοχεύσατο σεμνὴ
Φερσεφόνη λέκτροις ἱεροῖς Ζηνὸς Κρονίοιο,
ἧι ψευσθεὶς Πλούτων' ἐμίγη δολίαις ἀπάταισι,
θυμῶι Φερσεφόνης δὲ δισώματον ἔσπασε χροιήν,
ἣ θνητοὺς μαίνει φαντάσμασιν ἠερίοισιν,
ἀλλοκότοις ἰδέαις μορφῆς τύπον ἐκπροφαίνουσα,
ἄλλοτε μὲν προφανής, ποτὲ δὲ σκοτόεσσα, νυχαυγής,
ἀνταίαις ἐφόδοισι κατὰ ζοφοειδέα νύκτα.
ἀλλά, θεά, λίτομαί σε, καταχθονίων βασίλεια,
ψυχῆς ἐκπέμπειν οἶστρον ἐπὶ τέρματα γαίης,
εὐμενὲς εὐίερον μύσταις φαίνουσα πρόσωπον.

71. For Melinoe

Incense: aromatics
I call Melinoe, the chthonic nymph
in a saffron robe, to whom near the mouth
of the river Kokytos majestic
Persephone gave birth in the sacred
bed of Kronian Zeus. The false Plouton,
with deceitful tricks, snatched in a passion
the two-bodied flesh of Persephone.
She drives mortals mad with airy phantoms,
showing the silhouettes of monstrous shapes
and forms, sometimes bright, sometimes dark, shining
by night, hostile, coming downward from gray
night. But goddess, I pray you, queen below
the earth, to banish the maddening stings
of the soul to the ends of the earth, and show
initiates a kind and holy face.

Note: The meaning of this hymn is uncertain. I have treated Plouton, Πλούτων' (*Ploutōn*), as nominative, and not as accusative or dative with an elided suffix, in the line "The false Plouton/with deceitful tricks." It is unclear what is meant by two-bodied or double-bodied. The lines I have translated as "snatched in a passion" could also mean something like "tore up in a rage," giving a more gruesome take on the myth. It appears to reference a myth, unattested elsewhere, that Zeus disguised himself as Plouton in order to seduce Persephone. The name Melinoe is obscure. W. K. C. Guthrie mentions the name occurring as an epithet of Hekate in some inscriptions,[16] and Anne-France Morand describes a magical tablet containing mention of the name,[17] but otherwise there is no mention of her outside of this hymn. She appears to be a deity of ghosts or of madness.

---

16. William Keith Chambers Guthrie, *Orpheus and Greek Religion* (London: Mehtuen, 1935), 259.
17. Morand, *Études*, 186–188.

72 Τύχης, θυμίαμα λίβανον.

Δεῦρο, Τύχη· καλέω σ', ἀγαθῶν κράντειραν, ἐπευχαῖς,
μειλιχίαν, ἐνοδῖτιν, ἐπ' εὐόλβοις κτεάτεσσιν,
Ἄρτεμιν ἡγεμόνην, μεγαλώνυμον, Εὐβουλῆος
αἵματος ἐκγεγαῶσαν, ἀπρό<σ>μαχον εὖχος ἔχουσαν,
τυμβιδίαν, πολύπλαγκτον, ἀοίδιμον ἀνθρώποισιν.
ἐν σοὶ γὰρ βίοτος θνητῶν παμποίκιλός ἐστιν·
οἷς μὲν γὰρ τεύχεις κτεάνων πλῆθος πολύολβον,
οἷς δὲ κακὴν πενίην θυμῶι χόλον ὁρμαίνουσα.
ἀλλά, θεά, λίτομαί σε μολεῖν βίωι εὐμενέουσαν,
ὄλβοισι πλήθουσαν ἐπ' εὐόλβοις κτεάτεσσιν.

72. For Tyche

Incense: frankincense

I call you here, Tyche, with prayers, who does
good things, gentle one on the road, for rich
wealth, Artemis the guide, much famed, born from
the blood of Eubouleus, having a will
that none can break, funereal, roaming,
and praised in song by humans. Due to you
mortal life is rich with variety;
for to some you give great prosperity,
while to others, vile poverty, with hate
turning over and over in your heart.
But, goddess, I pray you, blissful, to come
gracious to my life with wealthy riches.

Note: The themes of this hymn should seem familiar to those who still
venerate "lady luck." Here she is associated with Artemis, which, considering the role of luck in hunting, makes a certain amount of sense.
She is also described as being "on the road" and "funereal," both themes
of Hekate.

73 Δαίμονος, θυμίαμα λίβανον.

Δαίμονα κικλήσκω μεγάλαν ἡγήτορα φρικτόν,
μειλίχιον Δία, παγγενέτην, βιοδώτορα θνητῶν,
Ζῆνα μέγαν, πολύπλαγκτον, ἀλάστορα, παμβασιλῆα,
πλουτοδότην, ὁπόταν γε βρυάζων οἶκον ἐσέλθηι,
ἔμπαλι δὲ τρύχοντα βίον θνητῶν πολυμόχθων·
ἐν σοὶ γὰρ λύπης τε χαρᾶς κληῖδες ὀχοῦνται.
τοιγάρ τοι, μάκαρ, ἁγνέ, πολύστονα κήδε' ἐλάσσας,
ὅσσα βιοφθορίην πέμπει κατὰ γαῖαν ἅπασαν,
ἔνδοξον βιοτῆς γλυκερὸν τέλος ἐσθλὸν ὀπάζοις.

73. For the Daimon

Incense: frankincense

I invoke the great daimon, the dreadful
but gracious commander Zeus, the father
of all, and giver of life to mortals.
Great Zeus, much-wandering, avenging god
and king of all, you give wealth when you come,
swelling with abundance, into a home;
but then, you give a wasted livelihood
to hard laboring mortals; for the keys
of pain and happiness are held by you.
So, blessed and holy one, drive away
mournful cares that send destruction of life
over the whole earth. And may you provide
a sweet, good, reputable end to life.

Note: The idea of a personal daimon or guardian god is widespread
in Late Antiquity. In Rome, this would be called the genius, while in
Greek religion, the daimon or agathodaimon (lit., good spirit). A word
for "happiness," eudaimonia, simply means having a good daimon.
The mention of Zeus is rather Roman, since a person's daimon could
be called his or her personal Jove, i.e., Jupiter. The dual nature of the
daimon—bringing both good and bad—is reflected in many other
hymns, including the previous one, where the dual nature of the deities
is acknowledged.

74 Λευκοθέας, θυμίαμα ἀρώματα.

Λευκοθέαν καλέω Καδμηίδα, δαίμονα σεμνήν,
εὐδύνατον, θρέπτειραν ἐυστεφάνου Διονύσου.
κλῦθι, θεά, πόντοιο βαθυστέρνου μεδέουσα,
κύμασι τερπομένη, θνητῶν σώτειρα μεγίστη·
ἐν σοὶ γὰρ νηῶν πελαγοδρόμος ἄστατος ὁρμή,
μούνη δὲ θνητῶν οἰκτρὸν μόρον εἰν ἁλὶ λύεις,
οἷς ἂν ἐφορμαίνουσα φίλη σωτήριος ἔλθοις.
ἀλλά, θεὰ δέσποινα, μόλοις ἐπαρωγὸς ἐοῦσα
νηυσὶν ἐπ᾽ εὐσέλμοις σωτήριος εὔφρονι βουλῇι,
μύσταις ἐν πόντωι ναυσίδρομον οὖρον ἄγουσα.

74. For Leukothea

Incense: aromatics
I invoke Leukothea, the daughter
of Kadmos, revered daimon, powerful
nurturer of well-crowned Dionysos.
Hear, goddess, ruler of the wide-breasted
sea, taking joy in waves, mighty savior
of mortals; for the surge of ships, flying
over the sea, unresting, is in you.
For you alone save mortals from a sad
and pitiful doom in the sea, to whom
you come rushing on, a friendly savior.
So, divine mistress, may you come to be
of aid to the ships supplied with many
oars and, kindly savior, bring a fair wind
to speed ships for initiates at sea.

75 Παλαίμονος, θυμίαμα μάνναν.

Σύντροφε βακχεχόροιο Διωνύσου πολυγηθοῦς,
ὃς ναίεις πόντοιο βυθοὺς ἁλικύμονας, ἁγνούς,
κικλήσκω σε, Παλαῖμον, ἐπ' εὐιέροις τελεταῖσιν
ἐλθεῖν εὐμενέοντα, νέωι γήθοντα προσώπωι,
καὶ σώζειν μύστας κατά τε χθόνα καὶ κατὰ πόντον·
ποντοπλάνοις γὰρ ἀεὶ ναυσὶν χειμῶνος ἐναργὴς
φαινομένου σωτὴρ μοῦνος θνητοῖς ἀναφαίνηι,
ῥυόμενος μῆνιν χαλεπὴν κατὰ πόντιον οἶδμα.

75. For Palaimon

Incense: manna

Brought up together with very joyful
Dionysos of the Bacchic dance, you
dwell in the pure depths of the salt-surging
sea. I call you, Palaimon, by these most
holy rites, to come graciously, with joy
upon your youthful face, and to rescue
the initiates, both upon the earth
and upon the sea. For you manifest
as the sole savior to sea-going ships,
appearing to mortals in winter storms.
Shield us from hard rage on the swelling sea.

Note: The name Palaimon means "wrestler," and he was considered a particular patron to those who were shipwrecked.

76 Μουσῶν, θυμίαμα λίβανον.

Μνημοσύνης καὶ Ζηνὸς ἐριγδούποιο θύγατρες,
Μοῦσαι Πιερίδες, μεγαλώνυμοι, ἀγλαόφημοι,
θνητοῖς, οἷς κε παρῆτε, ποθεινόταται, πολύμορφοι,
πάσης παιδείης ἀρετὴν γεννῶσαι ἄμεμπτον,
θρέπτειραι ψυχῆς, διανοίας ὀρθοδότειραι,
καὶ νόου εὐδυνάτοιο καθηγήτειραι ἄνασσαι,
αἳ τελετὰς θνητοῖς ἀνεδείξατε μυστιπ<ο>λεύτους,
Κλειώ τ᾽ Εὐτέρπη τε Θάλειά τε Μαλπομένη τε
Τερψιχόρη τ᾽ Ἐρατώ τε Πολύμνιά τ᾽ Οὐρανίη τε
Καλλιόπηι σὺν μητρὶ καὶ εὐδυνάτηι θεᾶι Ἁγνῆι.
ἀλλὰ μόλοιτε, θεαί, μύσταις πολυποίκιλοι, ἁγναί,
εὔκλειαν ζῆλόν τ᾽ ἐρατὸν πολύυμνον ἄγουσαι.

76. For the Mousai

Incense: frankincense

Daughters of Mnemosyne and thundering
Zeus, Pierian Mousai, great of name
and shining fame: most beloved and with many
forms when you are among mortals. From you
comes the blameless virtue of all learning,
and you feed the soul and set the thoughts straight,
and you guide the great power of the mind.
Ladies, who revealed the mystical rites
to mortals: Clio, Euterpe, Thalia,
Melpomene, Terpsichore, Erato,
Polyhymnia, Ourania, and Kalliope,
with their holy mighty mother goddess.
But come, goddesses, to your worshippers,
various and holy, bringing a zeal
for glory abounding in lovely hymns.

Note: The order of the Mousai listed here is the same as in Hesiod's
Theogony, lines 77–79. The holy mighty mother goddess is, of course,
Mnemosyne (see hymn 77). Some translators have taken Hagne ("holy")
as a proper name; I have translated it as an adjective.

77 Μνημοσύνης, θυμίαμα λίβανον.

Μνημοσύνην καλέω, Ζηνὸς σύλλεκτρον, ἄνασσαν,
ἣ Μούσας τέκνωσ᾽ ἱεράς, ὁσίας, λιγυφώνους,
ἐκτὸς ἐοῦσα κακῆς λήθης βλαψίφρονος αἰεί,
πάντα νόον συνέχουσα βροτῶν ψυχαῖσι σύνοικον,
εὐδύνατον κρατερὸν θνητῶν αὔξουσα λογισμόν,
ἡδυτάτη, φιλάγρυπνος ὑπομνήσκουσά τε πάντα,
ὧν ἂν ἕκαστος ἀεὶ στέρνοις γνώμην κατ<ά>θηται,
οὔτι παρεκβαίνουσ᾽, ἐπεγείρουσα φρένα πᾶσιν.
ἀλλά, μάκαιρα θεά, μύσταις μνήμην ἐπέγειρε
εὐιέρου τελετῆς, λήθην δ᾽ ἀπὸ τῶν<δ᾽> ἀπόπεμπε.

77. For Mnemosyne

Incense: frankincense

I call Mnemosyne, sharing a bed
with Zeus, the lady who bore the holy,
pure, and clear-voiced Mousai, always free from
evil forgetfulness that destroys minds.
Dwelling in the soul, within the whole mind
of mortals, you increase the mighty strength
of human reason. Sweetest and alert
reminder of every thought that each
would always deposit within their breasts,
you do not veer, but you rouse every mind.
So, blessed goddess, wake up memory
for the worshippers of the holy rites
and send away forgetfulness from them.

78 Ἠοῦς, θυμίαμα μάνναν.

Κλῦθι, θεά, θνητοῖς φαεσίμβροτον ἦμαρ ἄγουσα,
Ἠὼς λαμπροφαής, ἐρυθαινομένη κατὰ κόσμον,
ἀγγέλτειρα θεοῦ μεγάλου Τιτᾶνος ἀγαυοῦ,
ἣ νυκτὸς ζοφερήν τε καὶ αἰολόχρωτα πορείην
ἀντολίαις ταῖς σαῖς πέμπεις ὑπὸ νέρτερα γαίης·
ἔργων ἡγήτειρα, βίου πρόπολε θνητοῖσιν·
ἧι χαίρει θνητῶν μερόπων γένος· οὐδέ τίς ἐστιν,
ὃς φεύγει τὴν σὴν ὄψιν καθυπέρτερον οὖσαν,
ἡνίκα τὸν γλυκὺν ὕπνον ἀπὸ βλεφάρων ἀποσείσηις,
πᾶς δὲ βροτὸς γήθει, πᾶν ἑρπετὸν ἄλλα τε φῦλα
τετραπόδων πτηνῶν τε καὶ εἰναλίων πολυεθνῶν·
πάντα γὰρ ἐργάσιμον βίοτον θνητοῖσι πορίζεις.
ἀλλά, μάκαιρ᾽, ἁγνή, μύσταις ἱερὸν φάος αὔξοις.

78. For Eos

Incense: manna
Hear, goddess, who leads the light-bringing day
to mortals, bright-beaming Eos, making
the world red, messenger of the mighty
and noble god Titan. With your risings
you send the dark and swift march of night
down to the underworld. Leader of works,
minister of mortal life, whom the race
of mortal humanity hails. No one
flees your face when it is above, and when
you shake sweet sleep from your eyelids, then each
mortal creature rejoices, all serpents
and each of the species having four legs,
or wings, or dwelling in the teeming sea,
for you provide all working livelihood.
So blessed and holy one, magnify
the sacred light for the initiates.

79 Θέμιδος, θυμίαμα λίβανον.

Οὐρανόπαιδ᾽ ἁγνὴν καλέω Θέμιν εὐπατέρειαν,
Γαίης τὸ βλάστημα, νέην καλυκώπιδα κούρην,
ἢ πρώτη κατέδειξε βροτοῖς μαντήιον ἁγνὸν
Δελφικῶι ἐν κευθμῶνι θεμιστεύουσα θεοῖσ<ι>
Πυθίωι ἐν δαπέδωι, ὅθι Πύθων ἐμβασίλευεν·
ἢ καὶ Φοῖβον ἄνακτα θεμιστοσύνας ἐδίδαξε·
πάντιμ᾽, ἀγλαόμορφε, σεβάσμιε, νυκτιπόλευτε·
πρώτη γὰρ τελετὰς ἁγίας θνητοῖς ἀνέφηνας,
βακχιακὰς ἀνὰ νύκτας ἐπευάζουσα ἄνακτα·
ἐκ σέο γὰρ τιμαὶ μακάρων μυστήριά θ᾽ ἁγνά.
ἀλλά, μάκαιρ᾽, ἔλθοις κεχαρημένη εὔφρονι βουλῆι
εὐιέρους ἐπὶ μυστιπόλου τελετὰς σέο, κούρη.

79. For Themis

Incense: frankincense

I call on Themis, the holy daughter
of her noble father, Ouranos, and
offspring of Gaia, the maiden whose face
is like a budding flower, who first showed
mortals the holy oracle, giving
prophesies to the gods from the abyss
in Delphi on the Pythian plain where
King Python ruled. She taught the lord Phoibos
the oracles. All honored, lovely-shaped,
revered, roaming the night, you brought holy
rites to light for mortals for the first time,
shouting to the lord throughout the Bacchic
nights. For the honors of the blessed ones
and the holy mysteries come from you.
But, blessed maiden, kindly come, welcomed
to holy rites of your solemnity.

Note: It is often thought that Gaia was the first holder of the oracle of
Delphi, but here Themis is given that honor.

80 Βορέου, θυμίαμα λίβανον.

Χειμερίοις αὔραισι δονῶν βαθὺν ἠέρα κόσμου,
κρυμοπαγὴς Βορέα, χιονώδεος ἔλθ' ἀπὸ Θράικης
λῦέ τε παννέφελον στάσιν ἠέρος ὑγροκελεύθου
ῥιπίζων ἱκμάσιν νοτεραῖς ὀμβρηγενὲς ὕδωρ,
αἴθρια πάντα τιθείς, θαλερόμματον αἰθέρα τεύχων
ἀκτίνες ὡς λάμπουσιν ἐπὶ χθονὸς ἠελίοιο.

80. For Boreas

Incense: frankincense

Wintery breezes shaking the deep air
of the world, frost-congealing Boreas,
come from snowy Thrace, break cloudy discord
of water-trailing air. Blow away wet,
moist water born from the rain, and set forth
wholly clear weather, making bright-eyed skies
so that rays of the sun shine on the earth.

Note: Boreas is one of the four winds, governing the north and winter. Hymns to two of the others follow: Zephyros, the western wind and ruler of spring, and Notos the south and summer. The east wind, Euros, is not mentioned in the hymns. Euros is also absent from Hesiod's *Theogony*.

81 Ζεφύρου, θυμίαμα λίβανον.

Αὖραι παντογενεῖς Ζεφυρίτιδες, ἠεροφοῖται,
ἡδύπνοοι, ψιθυραί, θανάτου ἀνάπαυσιν ἔχουσαι,
εἰαριναί, λειμωνιάδες, πεποθημέναι ὅρμοις,
σύρουσαι ναυσὶ τρυφερὸν ὅρμον, ἠέρα κοῦφον·
ἔλθοιτ' εὐμενέουσαι, ἐπιπνείουσαι ἀμεμφεῖς,
ἠέριαι, ἀφανεῖς, κουφόπτεροι, ἀερόμορφοι.

81. For Zephyros

Incense: frankincense

All-begetting western breezes, who roam
the air, fragrant and whispering, you give
a respite from death in spring-time meadows,
and are beloved by harbors, drawing ships
with delicate chains of easy air. Come,
graciously breathe on the blameless at dawn,
airy and invisible with light wings.

Note: There is a pun in the Greek between the word for "harbor" and
the word for "chains." Both are ὅρμος, (*hormos*). See also the note for
Hymn 80.

82 Νότου, θυμίαμα λίβανον.

Λαιψηρὸν πήδημα δι' ἠέρος ὑγροπόρευτον,
ὠκείαις πτερύγεσσι δονούμενον ἔνθα καὶ ἔνθα,
ἔλθοις σὺν νεφέλαις νοτίαις, ὄμβροιο γενάρχα·
τοῦτο γὰρ ἐκ Διός ἐστι σέθεν γέρας ἠερόφοιτον,
ὀμβροτόκους νεφέλας ἐξ ἠέρος εἰς χθόνα πέμπειν.
τοιγάρ τοι λιτόμεσθα, μάκαρ, ἱεροῖσι χαρέντα
πέμπειν καρποτρόφους ὄμβρους ἐπὶ μητέρα γαῖαν.

82. For Notos

Incense: frankincense

In a swift leap through the air, leaving trails
of water, shaken here and there by quick
wings, may you come with moist clouds, ancestors
of rain, for this air-wandering honor
is the gift from Zeus to you, to dispatch
rain-producing clouds from the air to earth.
So we pray to you, to be delighted
with these offerings, blessed one, and send
the rains that nourish fruit on mother earth.

Note: See the note for hymn 80.

83 Ὠκεανοῦ, θυμίαμα ἀρώματα.

Ὠκεανὸν καλέω, πατέρ’ ἄφθιτον, αἰὲν ἐόντα,
ἀθανάτων τε θεῶν γένεσιν θνητῶν τ’ ἀνθρώπων,
ὃς περικυμαίνει γαίης περιτέρμονα κύκλον·
ἐξ οὗπερ πάντες ποταμοὶ καὶ πᾶσα θάλασσα
καὶ χθόνιοι γαίης πηγόρρυτοι ἰκμάδες ἀγναί.
κλῦθι, μάκαρ, πολύολβε, θεῶν ἄγνισμα μέγιστον,
τέρμα φίλον γαίης, ἀργὴ πόλου, ὑγροκέλευθε,
ἔλθοις εὐμενέων μύσταις κεχαρημένος αἰεί.

83. For Okeanos

Incense: aromatics

I call on Okeanos, immortal
and eternal father, parent of both
the deathless gods and mortal humans, who
rises in waves, a border encircling
earth, from whom come rivers and the whole sea
and pure waters flowing from springs below
chthonic earth. Hear, blessed and prosperous
one, the mightiest purification
of the gods, beloved limit of the earth,
ruler of the axis, leaving water
in your path may you come generously
and show kindness to the initiates.

84 Ἑστίας, θυμίαμα ἀρώματα.

Ἑστία εὐδυνάτοιο Κρόνου θύγατερ βασίλεια,
ἣ μέσον οἶκον ἔχεις πυρὸς ἀενάοιο, μεγίστου,
τούσδε σὺ ἐν τελεταῖς ὁσίους μύστας ἀναδείξαις,
θεῖσ' αἰειθαλέας, πολυόλβους, εὔφρονας, ἁγνούς·
οἶκε θεῶν μακάρων, θνητῶν στήριγμα κραταιόν,
ἀιδίη, πολύμορφε, ποθεινοτάτη, χλοόμορφε·
μειδιόωσα, μάκαιρα, τάδ' ἱερὰ δέξο προθύμως,
ὄλβον ἐπιπνείουσα καὶ ἠπιόχειρον ὑγείαν.

84. For Hestia

Incense: aromatics

Hestia, queen and daughter of all-mighty
Kronos, you hold the center of the home,
its eternal and greatest fire. And may
you consecrate these initiates in
the holy rituals, and make them thrive
forever, blessed, cheerful, and holy.
Home of the blessed gods, the strong foundation
of mortals, eternal, many-shaped, loved,
and green as grass. Smiling, blessed one, take
these offerings willingly, and breathe forth
wealthy bliss and Health with her soothing hands.

85 Ὕπνου, θυμίαμα μετὰ μήκωνος.

Ὕπνε, ἄναξ μακάρων πάντων θνητῶν τ᾽ ἀνθρώπων
καὶ πάντων ζώιων, ὁπόσα τρέφει εὐρεῖα χθών·
πάντων γὰρ κρατέεις μοῦνος καὶ πᾶσι προσέρχηι
σώματα δεσμεύων ἐν ἀχαλκεύτοισι πέδηισι,
λυσιμέριμνε, κόπων ἡδεῖαν ἔχων ἀνάπαυσιν
καὶ πάσης λύπης ἱερὸν παραμύθιον ἔρδων·
καὶ θανάτου μελέτην ἐπάγεις ψυχὰς διασώζων·
αὐτοκασίγνητος γὰρ ἔφυς Λήθης Θανάτου τε.
ἀλλά, μάκαρ, λίτομαί σε κεκραμένον ἡδὺν ἱκάνειν
σώζοντ᾽ εὐμενέως μύστας θείοισιν ἐπ᾽ ἔργοις.

85. For Hypnos

Incense: with poppy

Hypnos, the lord of all the blessed ones
and of mortal humans, and all living
things, whatever the wide earth nourishes,
you alone rule over all, and draw near
to all, binding up bodies in shackles
not wrought of metal. Driving care away,
you hold sweet rest from weariness, and you
offer holy abatement for all pain.
And you lead us in a practice for death,
preserving souls, for you are by nature
a brother of Lethe and Thanatos.
But, blessed one, I pray you, sweet tempered,
to come, and with graciousness to preserve
the initiates for the divine works.

Note: Here, sleep is described as a practice for death.

86 Ὀνείρου, θυμίαμα ἀρώματα.

Κικλήσκω σε, μάκαρ, τανυσίπτερε, οὖλε Ὄνειρε,
ἄγγελε μελλόντων, θνητοῖς χρησμῳδὲ μέγιστε·
ἡσυχίαι γὰρ ὕπνου γλυκεροῦ σιγηλὸς ἐπελθών,
προ<σ>φωνῶν ψυχαῖς θνητῶν νόον αὐτὸς ἐγείρεις,
καὶ γνώμας μακάρων αὐτὸς καθ' ὕπνους ὑποπέμπεις,
σιγῶν σιγώσαις ψυχαῖς μέλλοντα προφαίνων,
οἷσιν ἐπ' εὐσεβίῃσι θεῶν νόος ἐσθλὸς ὁδεύει,
ὡς ἂν ἀεὶ τὸ καλὸν μέλλον, γνώμῃσι προληφθέν,
τερπωλαῖς ὑπάγῃ βίον ἀνθρώπων προχαρέντων,
τῶν δὲ κακῶν ἀνάπαυλαν, ὅπως θεὸς αὐτὸς ἐνίσπῃ
εὐχωλαῖς θυσίαις τε χόλον λύσαντες ἀνάκτων.
εὐσεβέσιν γὰρ ἀεὶ τὸ τέλος γλυκερώτερόν ἐστι,
τοῖς δὲ κακοῖς οὐδὲν φαίνει μέλλουσαν ἀνάγκην
ὄψις ὀνειρήεσσα, κακῶν ἐξάγγελος ἔργων,
ὄφρα μὴ εὕρωνται λύσιν ἄλγεος ἐρχομένοιο.
ἀλλά, μάκαρ, λίτομαί σε θεῶν μηνύματα φράζειν,
ὡς ἂν ἀεὶ γνώμαις ὀρθαῖς κατὰ πάντα πελάζῃς
μηδὲν ἐπ' ἀλλοκότοισι κακῶν σημεῖα προφαίνων.

86. For Oneiros

Incense: aromatics

I call you, blessed, long-winged and dreadful
Oneiros, messenger of things to come,
great oracle to mortals. For in sweet
sleep's silence, silently you come. Speaking
to the souls of mortals, you awaken
the mind, and you slip thoughts of the blessed
ones down into sleep. Silently, to hushed
souls, you show forth things to come. By which,
a good mind goes in respect for the gods,
so it always anticipates in thoughts
the future beauty. He leads on the lives
of humans to rejoice in coming joys,
and to rest from evils, as the god bids,
through vows and sacrifices, burning up
the anger of the lords. For to pious
people, the end is always sweeter, but
to the wicked, the face born out of dreams,
the informer of evil works, reveals
no intentions of Necessity, so
that they might find escape from coming pains.
But blessed one, I pray you to reveal
the knowledge of the gods, so that you may
draw near to minds that are ever upright
in all things, and may you never show forth
the omens of evil in obscure forms.

Note: The use of dreams as means of divination is very ancient, often called the first oracle. Here the idea is that Dream will visit those who are righteous to give warning of future events but torment the unrighteous with nightmares. The usual mythological Oneiroi are a class of beings, said by Ovid to rank in the thousands, all sons of Hyp-

nos, whereas here they are collapsed into one. In the *Odyssey*, Penelope explains that there are two kinds of dreams: those that enter the gate of horn, and those that enter the gate of ivory. Those that come in through the gate of horn come true, whereas those that come through the gate of ivory are deceptive. The last line seems to ask Dream to send omens that are recognizable, rather than obscure and difficult to interpret.

87 Θανάτου, θυμίαμα μάνναν.

Κλῦθί μευ, ὃς πάντων θνητῶν οἴηκα κρατύνεις
πᾶσι διδοὺς χρόνον ἁγνόν, ὅσων πόρρωθ' ὑπάρχεις·
σὸς γὰρ ὕπνος ψυχῆν θραύει καὶ σώματος ὁλκόν,
ἡνίκ' ἂν ἐκλύηις φύσεως κεκρατημένα δεσμὰ
τὸν μακρὸν ζώιοισι φέρων αἰώνιον ὕπνον,
κοινὸς μὲν πάντων, ἄδικος δ' ἐνίοισιν ὑπάρχων,
ἐν ταχυτῆτι βίου παύων νεοήλικας ἀκμάς·
ἐν σοὶ γὰρ μούνωι πάντων τὸ κριθὲν τελεοῦται·
οὔτε γὰρ εὐχαῖσιν πείθηι μόνος οὔτε λιταῖσιν.
ἀλλά, μάκαρ, μακροῖσι χρόνοις ζωῆς σε πελάζειν
αἰτοῦμαι, θυσίαισ<ι> καὶ εὐχωλαῖς λιτανεύων,
ὡς ἂν ἔοι γέρας ἐσθλὸν ἐν ἀνθρώποισι τὸ γῆρας.

87. To Thanatos

Incense: manna

Hear me, you who steers the rudder of all
mortals, granting to each a period
of holy time, the amount of which you
set down long ago. For your sleep sunders
the soul and breaks the body's draw. When you
would loosen the strengthened bonds of nature,
you bring to the living a great aeon
of sleep. You are shared by all, but unjust
to some, appointing a quick end to youth
in full bloom, for the decision, alone,
is completed in you. For you alone
are neither persuaded by vows or prayers.
But, blessed one, I beg with sacrifice
and vows, that you close out a long lifespan,
that old age be a noble prize to men.

Note: The first sentence is somewhat obscure in meaning.

The body is described as exerting a force the draws the soul to it,
which Thanatos breaks.

As perhaps grim as the hymn above might be, it does end in a pun,
impossible to preserve in English: The word γέρας (*geras*) means "gift of
honor, privilege, prize." The word γῆρας (*gēras*) means "old age." Immediately after the hymn points out that only Thanatos remains unmoved
by prayer, the author uses the word αἰτοῦμαι (*aitoumai*), "I beg"—the
only occurrence of this word in any of the hymns.

APPENDIX I: CONCORDANCE OF GODS AND PLACES

This concordance of the English translation contains the names of gods and places, as well as a few common nouns used as proper names in context. Numbers in bold indicate reference to the name or word in the title of the hymn. The number zero indicates a reference in the unnumbered initial hymn to Mousaios. See notes for the individual hymns for more mythic context. This concordance is to my English translation, but it may be used with other translations for comparative purposes. The Taylor translation reproduced in appendix II numbers the hymns somewhat differently, including the hymn to Hekate in the introduction to Mousaios. If using the concordance with Taylor's translation, subtract one from the numbers below to find the appropriate hymn.

Pronunciation

Ancient Greek can be pronounced in a number of valid ways. The question of the most authentic pronunciation is confounded by the wide variety of Greek dialects over time. The poems are written in an imitation of the Homeric or Epic dialect, so a reconstructed classical pronunciation might be appropriate in order to maintain the metrical character of the lines. However, they were also written in post-classical antiquity, and so a Koine or Demotic pronunciation might be seen as more appropriate. Many people may also wish to use the Modern Greek pronunciation, to aid in communication with contemporary Greek pagans; this pronunciation is probably fairly close to Koine, the common dialect of late antiquity, from which Demotic—the standard Modern Greek dialect—derives.

The following table will assist you in approximating both pronunciations.

Letter	Reconstructed Classical	Modern
Αα	/a/ (short or long)	/a/
Ββ	/b/	/v/
Γγ	/g/	/ɣ/ before /i/ or /e/, otherwise /g/
Δδ	/d/	/ð/
Εε	/e/	/e/
Ζζ	/z/	/z/
Ηη	/e:/	/i/
Θθ	/θ/	/θ/
Ιι	/i/ (short or long)	/i/
Κκ	/k/	/k/
Λλ	/l/	/l/
Μμ	/m/	/m/
Νν	/n/	/n/
Ξξ	/ks/	/ks/
Οο	/o/	/o/
Ππ	/p/	/p/
Ρρ	/r/	/r/
Σσς	/s/	/s/
Ττ	/t/	/t/
Υυ	/y/ (short or long)	/i/
Φφ	/pʰ/	/f/
Χχ	/kʰ/	/χ/
Ψψ	/ps/	/ps/
Ωω	/o:/	/o/
αυ	/au/	/af/, /av/ (before voiced consonants and vowels)
ου	/u/	/u/

Letter	Reconstructed Classical	Modern
ευ	/eʊ/	/ef/, /ev/ (before voiced consonants and vowels)
οι	/oɪ/	/i/
αι	/aɪ/	/e/
η, ηι	/e:/	/i/
ῳ, ωι	/o:/	/o/
ᾳ, αι (long alpha plus iota)	/a:/	/ɑ/

Classical Greek also uses a number of diacritical marks. Word-initial vowels all hold a breathing mark, which indicates whether or not the vowel is preceded by /h/. The smooth-breathing, ἀ, indicates that there is no /h/ sound, whereas the rough-breathing, ἁ, indicates that the vowel is preceded by /h/. There are also three accent marks, the acute (ά) which indicates a rise in tone, the grave (ὰ) which indicates a fall in tone (or perhaps no tone at all), and a circumflex (ᾶ), only occurring on long vowels, which indicates a rise and a fall of tone.

Modern Greek replaces tone accent with stress accent and does not differentiate between accent marks or include smooth- or soft-breathing marks.

Many people mix and match these pronunciations to some degree. Some also use an artificial pronunciation, Erasmian, which serves the pedagogical function of making every letter maximally distinct. This pronunciation has been used worldwide since the fifteenth century; its motivation is pedagogy, not historical accuracy.

A beginner in Greek can take some comfort in the fact that Greek is a language that has been continuously spoken for thousands of years, through many dialects, across diverse regions. Of course, if you wish to speak in Modern Greek, you should make an effort to learn standard modern Demotic pronunciation, because otherwise you will not be understood. If you wish to speak Ancient Greek, however, you can to some extent choose your pronunciation. Considering that for much of its history it was a second language, I have often said that the most *authentic* way to pronounce Ancient Greek is badly. However, those wishing to read these hymns in Greek should find a pronunciation scheme that appeals to them and learn it carefully.

Most Greek names have an Anglicized version, a specifically English pronunciation that may share no resemblance to the Greek pronunciation. For example, **aigis**, (αἰγίς) would be pronounced in Classical Greek as something like /aigis/ with a raise in tone of voice on the final syllabus. In Modern Greek pronunciation, this word would be pronounced /eɣis/. However, the accepted English spelling and pronunciation is aegis, /ˈidʒɪs/.

Included in the list is the English pronunciation in IPA (the International Phonetic Alphabet). Those unfamiliar with this system of representing speech sounds may learn about it at: https://www.internationalphoneticassociation.org. Note that the English pronunciations listed below are *not* pronunciation guides for the Greek. They are also not the only pronunciations acceptable in English, merely the pronunciations in my dialect of English, North Central American.

The structure of an entry below is as follows:

Headword (Greek spelling) (English spelling, English IPA pronunciation) [poems where word occurs]—definition.

CONCORDANCE
AND GLOSSARY

Acheron (Ἀχέρων) (/'ækəɹɑn/) [18]: According to Virgil, the chief river of Hades from which flow the Styx, the Kokytos, and the Phlegethon. Some sources say that the Kokytos empties into the Acheron. The Acheron is the river of woe.

Adonis (Ἄδωνις) (/ə'dɑnɪs/) [0, 55, 56]: A beautiful youth, beloved by Aphrodite and Persephone. Zeus settled the dispute between the two goddesses by decreeing that Adonis could spend one third of his time with Aphrodite, one third with Persephone, and the last third as he chose. He chose to spend two-thirds of his time with Aphrodite and one-third with Persephone. As a result, he dies and is reborn yearly, leading to a mystery religion that involved mourning for his death and celebrating his return. His origin may be Semitic, since the name is similar to the Phoenician *adon*, meaning "lord." He was associated with the Sumerian deity Tammuz or Damuzid, a consort of Inanna with similar mythology.

Adresteia (Ἀδρήστεια) (Adrasteia, /ɑdɹə'steɪə/) [0]: A nymph of Crete, one of the nurses of Zeus, when Rhea hid him away from his father Kronos.

Aglaia (Ἀγλαΐα) (Aglaea, (/ə'gliə/)) [60]: One of the three Charites, a goddess of beauty. Sometimes a consort of Hephaistos.

Aigis (αἰγίς) (Aegis, /'idʒɪs/) [0, 14]: A shield, borne either by Zeus or Athena, sometimes said to be made from the skin of the Gorgon, a fearsome monster with snakes for hair whose gaze petrified men.

Aion (Αἰών) (Aeon, Eon, /'iɑn/) [0]: The god of time as a whole, the circle of the universe, and the zodiac. He is identified in late antiquity with Dionysos and Phanes, as well as Kronos and Chronus.

Aither (Αἰθήρ) (Aether, /'iθər/) [5, 34]: The upper air.

Alekto (Ἀληκτώ) (Alecto, /ɑ'lɛktou/) [69]: One of the Erinyes or Furies. Along with the other Erinyes, she punishes injustice. Her name means "unceasing," as in "unceasing rage."

Antaia (Ἀνταία) (Antaea, /æn'tiə/) [41]: A name of Demeter.

Antauges (Ἀνταύγης) (/æntɑudʒiz/) [6]: A name of Phanes, meaning "reflection" or "sparkling."

Aphrodite (Ἀφροδίτη) (/ˌæfɪou'dɑɪti/) [0, 46, **55**, 57]: Goddess of love and affection. She was born when Kronos castrated his father Ouranos, throwing his genitals into the sea.

Apollon (Ἀπόλλων) (Apollo, /ə'pɑlou/) [24, **34,** 67]: The god of music, light, poetry, truth, prophesy, healing, and plague. The son of Zeus and brother of Artemis. He is usually depicted as an archer or playing a lyre.

Ares (Ἄρης) (/'ɛɹiz/) [0, 30, 38, 39, **65**]: God of war and bloodshed. In one myth, while Aphrodite was married to Hephaistos, she desired Ares. Hephaistos caught them together and trapped them in an unbreakable net until they confessed their infidelity to all the gods.

Argos (Ἄργος) (Argus, /'ɑɪgəs/) [28]: A monster with a hundred eyes. Hera set Argos as a guard over Io after suspecting Zeus of adultery with her. Hermes killed the monster at Zeus's command.

Artemis (Ἄρτεμις) (/'ɑɹtɪmɪs/) [0, 2, 35, **36**, 72]: Goddess of the hunt and wilderness, twin sister of Apollon and daughter of Leto. In later mythology, conflated with Selene.

Asklepios (Ἀσκληπιός) (Asclepius, /æs'klipiəs/) [0, **67**]: God (or deified Hero) of healing, son of Apollon. Sick people would travel to the temples of Asklepios, make an offering, and then sleep. They would dream of their cure. People would then make a vow or offering, often a small clay model in the shape of the afflicted body part, as thanks to the temple for being healed.

Athena (Ἀθηνᾶ) (/ə'θinə/) [32]: Goddess of wisdom, war, and craft. Patron of Athens. Athena was the daughter of Zeus, who swallowed his consort Metis (Wisdom) when it was prophesied that the child that she bore would overcome him. Nine months later Athena burst from his head. She helped Perseus slay Medusa, one of the Gorgons, and some accounts say that her shield, the Aigis, contains Medusa's head or is made from her skin.

Atlas (Ἄτλας) (/'ætləs/) [0]: A Titan whose role it was to hold up the sky.

Atropos (Ἄτροπος) (/'ætɹəpəs/) [59]: One of the three Moirai. She is the eldest, whose role it is to cut the threads of life.

Attic (Ἀττικός) (/'ætɪk/) [18]: Related to Attica, a region in Greece within which is the city of Athens. Attica gives its name to Attic Greek, a major dialect of ancient Greek.

Attis (Ἄττις) (/'ætɪs/) [0]: The consort of Kybele, a Phrygian deity imported into Greek religion. His priests were reported to castrate themselves. Attis was a vegetative deity, who died and was reborn (c.f. Adonis, Dionysos).

Bacchanal (/'bækənəl/) [0, 30, 47]: A Bakchai, or when used as an adjective, relating to Bakchos.

Bakchai (Βάκχαι) (Bacchae, /'bæki/) [54]: Followers of Bakchos, especially the Mainades.

Bakchos (Βάκχος) (Bacchus, /'bakəs/) [0, 24, 34, 44, 45, 46, 47, 49, 50, 51, 52, 53, 54, 55]: *See* Dionysos.

Bassareus (Βασσαρεύς) (/bæsə'ɹiəs/) [45]: An epithet of Dionysos, meaning "wearing a fox skin." *See also* Bassaros.

Bassaros (Βάσσαρος) [52]: *See* Bassareus.

Boreas (Βορέας) (/'bɔɹiəs/) [80]: The god of the north wind.

Bromios (Βρόμιος) (Bromius, /'bɹɑmiəs/) [40]: An epithet of Dionysos meaning "roaring."

Charites (χάριτες) (/'kærɪtiːz/) [60]: A favorite motif of art, the Charites or Graces are three sisters, daughters of Eunomia, one of the Horai. They are Aglaia, Euphrosyne, and Thalia.

Chronos (Χρόνος) (/ˈkɪoʊnəs/) [0]: Deity of time, often conflated with Kronos.

Chthonian (χθόνιος) (/ˈθoʊniən/) [18]: An epithet of Plouton.

Clouds [21, 22]: Personifications of clouds, νεφέλη or νέφος.

Cyprus (Κύπρος) (/ˈsaɪpɹɪs/) [42, 55, 56]: An island in the Mediterranean, sacred to Aphrodite.

Daimon (δαίμων) (Daemon ,/ˈdimən/, /ˈdaɪmən/) [0, 4, 7, 10, 11, 17, 23, 26, 30, 32, 34, 36, 38, 40, 48, 50, 56, 61, 65, 66, **73**, 74]: A general term for a divine being, often employed as a synonym for "god." But Plato in the Symposium has Diotima draw a distinction between gods and daimons, saying that the latter are intermediary beings between gods and humans. Also a term for the personal genius or private spiritual guardian, or the guardian of a place (such as a home or a plot of land).

Delos (Δῆλος) (/ˈdiloʊs/) [34, 35]: A small barren island in the Cyclades, where Apollon is said to have been born. Delos is only about three square kilometers (a little over a square mile). According to myth, the island itself is a Titan, Leto's sister Asteria, who turned herself into a quail and then into an island to escape the amorous passions of Zeus.. Leto had to take refuge here, because no other place would allow her to give birth to the twins Apollon and Artemis.

Delphi (Δελφοί) (/ˈdɛlfaɪ/) [0, 34]: A city on the slopes of Mt. Parnassus, where Apollon had a famous and influential oracle. According to legend, it was originally guarded by the Python, which Apollon killed. For this reason, the priestesses of the temple are called Pythias.

Demeter (Δημήτηρ) (/dəˈmitəɹ/) [0, 18, **40**]: Goddess of grain. When her daughter Persephone was kidnapped by Hades, her mourning nearly caused all life on earth to die. She established her mystery religion at Eleusis.

Deo (Δηώ) (/ˈdioʊ/) [23, 29, 39, 40, 51, 65]: A name for Demeter

Didymeus (Διδυμεὺς) (/dɪdəˈmeɪəs/) [34]: An epithet of Apollon, for the city Didyma, where he had an oracle and temple.

Dikaiosyne (Δικαιοσύνη) (Dicaeosyne, /disi'ɔsɪni/) [**63**]: Personified justice. C.f. Dike.

Dike (Δίκη) (/'daɪki/) [0, 10, 43, **62**, 69]: Goddess of justice, daughter of Zeus and Themis.

Diktynna (Δίκτυννα) (/dɪktaɪnə/) [36]: Goddess of the Cretan mountain Dikte, the birthplace of Zeus, also known as Britomartis, associated with or identified with Artemis.

Dione (Διώνη) (/daɪ'oʊni/) [0]: A Titan, consort of Zeus, said to be the mother of Aphrodite. Her name is essentially a feminine form of the root of Zeus's name (Dio-).

Dionysos (Διόνυσος) (Dionysus, /ˌdaɪə'naɪsəs/) [0, **30**, 42, 44, **45**, 46, 48, 53, 57, 74, 75]: The central god in Orphic theology and soteriology. According to the Orphic mythologies, Dionysos was born from Persephone and Zeus, then killed by Titans and devoured except for his heart, saved by Athena. Zeus then impregnated Semele by—in some versions of the myth—feeding her the heart. She then was tricked by Hera into begging Zeus to reveal his true form to her. Bound to do what she asked by an unbreakable oath to Styx, Zeus did so, knowing it would destroy her. But the fetus, being divine, survived. Zeus took him from the ashes and sewed him into his thigh, where he grew to term and was born. Thus, Dionysos is born three times. Another reckoning, having him identified with Phanes, would mean that he was born once at the birth of the universe, once from Persephone, and once from Zeus, since the incineration of Semele is not quite a birth. There is no one single unified source for this myth, but it is pieced together from variants.See also Bakchos.

Dioskouroi (Διόσκοροι) (Dioscuri, /diəskjə'ri/) [38]: Twin gods, Kastor and Polydeukes, deified mortals who became the patrons of horsemen and protectors of travelers and guests. Children of Zeus and Leda. The constellation Gemini.

Dysaules (Δυσαύλος) (/daɪ'saʊləs/) [41]: A farmer whom Demeter met on her wanderings in Eleusis. He informed her of the fate of her daughter Persephone.

Earth [21]: Gaia

Echo (Ἠχώ) (/ˈɛkoʊ/) [11]: A nymph, loved by Zeus. Hera cursed her to only be able to repeat the last few words she heard.

Egypt [42, 55]: A country and ancient civilization in the northern part of Africa, at the mouth of the Nile river. Conquered by Alexander the Great, subsequently becoming Hellenistic from 323 BCE to 30 BCE. A source of considerable religious learning and syncretism throughout the Hellenistic and, later, Roman world. The cult of an indigenous goddess, Isis, became particularly popular throughout Rome.

Eileithyia (Εἰλείθυια) (/ɪlɪˈθaɪə/) [0, 2]: Goddess of childbirth.

Eiraphiotes (Εἰραφιώτης) (/ˌaɪɹəfiˈoʊtis/) [48]: An epithet of Dionysos, meaning "sewn inside," a reference to the myth that Zeus sewed Dionysos into his thigh after Semele was destroyed by Zeus's splendor.

Eirene (Εἰρήνη) (/aɪˈɹini/) [43]: Peace. One of the three horai, goddesses of the seasons.

Eleusis (Ἐλευσίς) (/ɪˈlusɪs/) [40, 41, 42]: A town close to Athens, the site of the Eleusian mysteries, which celebrated Demeter and her search for her daughter Persephone.

Eos (Ἠώς) (/ˈiɔs/) [78]: Goddess of the dawn, sister of Helios and Selene.

Epaphios (Ἐπάφιος) [50]: An uncertain epithet of Dionysos, perhaps meaning "one who touches," "one who is possessed," or "son of Epaphos," a reference to the son of Zeus and Io. *See also* Epaphrios.

Epaphrios (Ἐπάφριος) [52]: Probably an alternative spelling of Epaphios.

Erato (Ἐρατώ) (/ˈɛɹətoʊ/) [76]: The muse of lyric poetry.

Erikepaios (Ἡρικεπαῖος) (Ericepaeus, /ɛɹɪsəˈpiəs/) [6, 52]: An epithet of Phanes, of obscure origin and meaning. Perhaps Semitic.

Erinyes (Ἐρινύες) (/ɪˈɹɪniˌiz/) [69]: Daimons who avenge the victims of insolence, inhospitality, and betrayal. The Erinyes or Furies were traditionally the result of Ouranos's blood falling on the earth after his castration. They are particularly concerned with crimes of children against parents, hosts against guests, and other breaches of decorum and order. Also known as Furies and Eumenides.

Eros (Ἔρως) (/ˈiɹoʊs/) [56, **58**]: The god of sexual love. For the Orphics, a primal deity, child of Nyx.

Erotes (Ἔρωτες) (/ɛɹˈoʊtiz/) [55]: Winged daimons of Aphrodite, governing sexual attraction. c.f. Eros.

Eubouleus (Εὐβουλεύς) (Eubulus, /ˈjubələs/) [29, 30, 42, 52, 56, 72]: "Good counsel," an epithet of Dionysos or Zeus, or perhaps a separate god in his own right. Also the name of the son of Dysaules.

Euboulos (Εὔβουλος) [18, 41]: Variant spelling of Eubouleus

Euios (Εὔιος) (Evios, /ˈɛviəs/) [50]: An epithet of Dionysos, in reference to a ritual cry of euoi or euai.

Eumenides (Εὐμενίδες) (juˈmɛnɪdiz) [70]: "Gracious goddesses," an epithet or euphemism for the Erinyes or Furies.

Eunomia (Εὐνομία) (/juˈnɑmiə/) [43, 60]: Goddess of good order and law, one of the three Horai.

Euoi (εὐοῖ) (Evoe, /eɪwoʊeɪ/) [30, 45, 49, 54]: A ritual cry in the worship of Dionysos.

Euphrosyne (Εὐφροσύνη) (/juˈfɹɑzɪni/) [60]: Goddess of joy, one of the Graces or Charites.

Euterpe (Εὐτέρπη) (/juˈtɜɹpi/) [76]: One of the Mousai, who governs music or, according to some sources, lyric poetry.

Evoe [30, 45, 54]: *See* Euoi.

Faith [0]: Pistis (Πίστις), a personification of trust and faith.

Fate, Fates [7, 10, **59**, 70]: The Moirai.

Furies [29]: Erinyes, c.f. Eumenides.

Gaia (Γαῖα) (Gaea, /ˈdʒiə/, /ˈgaɪə/) [0, 13, **26**, 37, 63, 79]: The goddess of the earth. She gave birth to the Titans with her consort Ouranos.

Graces [0, 10, 43, **60**]: The Charites.

Gryneios (Γρύνειος) (/gɹaɪˈneɪəs/) [34]: Epithet of Apollon, for his temple and oracle at Gryneum, a city on the coast of Lydia.

Hades (Ἅδης) (/'heɪdiz/) [3, 18, 29, 41, 68, 69]: The realm of the dead, also the god of that realm, also called Plouton. Not generally regarded as a place of punishment, unlike Tartaros.

Hebe (Ἥβη) (/'hibi/) [0]: Goddess of youth, daughter of Zeus and Hera, wife of Herakles. Cup-bearer of the gods.

Hekate (Ἑκάτη) (Hecate, /'hɛkəti/) [1]: A goddess of doors, crossroads, and—in late antiquity—a cosmic goddess and savior. She is associated at various times with magic, witchcraft, the moon, and the dead.

Helios (Ἥλιος) (/'hiliəs/) [0, 8]: Titan of the sun, brother of Selene and Eos.

Hephaistos (Ἥφαιστος) (Hephaestus, /hɪ'fistəs/) [0, 66]: Craftsman of the gods and god of fire. Often depicted with a limp.

Hera (Ἥρα) (/'hɛɹə/) [0, 16]: Goddess of marriage and women, wife of Zeus and queen of Olympos.

Herakles (Ἡρακλῆς) (Heracles, /'hɛɹəkliz/) [0, 12]: Herakles is a deified hero, son of Zeus and Alkmene. Driven mad, he killed his family and then in grief sought expiation for the sin. The oracle told him to put himself under the service of Eurystheus, who gave him twelve labors to complete. The twelve labors of Herakles were a common motif in art and poetry.

Hermes (Ἑρμῆς) (/'hɛɹmis/) [0, 28, 57]: Son of Zeus and Maia, god of shepherds and herald of the gods. God of commerce, writing, travel, theft, and guide of the souls of the dead. Hermes is god of trickery because shortly after his birth he stole Apollon's cattle, for which Apollon forgave him when he invented Apollon's lyre from a turtle shell and some sinew. Later, he killed the Argos, a many-eyed monster guarding Io, whom Zeus had turned into a heifer to hide her from Hera.

Hestia (Ἑστία) (/'hɛstjə/) [27, 84]: Goddess of the hearth, home, family, and order. Hestia, as goddess of the hearth and domestic fire, is the first god invoked in domestic offerings. She was the first one swallowed by Kronos. One of the virgin goddesses (along with Artemis and Athena), she is the patron of the home.

Hipta (Ἵπτα) (/ˈhɪptə/) [48, 49]: An obscure goddess, nurse of Dionysos who hid him in a winnowing basket on her head.

Horai (Ὧραι) (Horae, /ˈhɔːi/) [43]: Three goddesses governing the seasons: Dike, Eunomia, and Eirene

Hygieia (Ὑγίεια) (/haɪˈdʒiə/) [67, 68]: Goddess of health and hygiene, wife of Asklepios. Also spelled Hygeia. Her name is sometimes associated with the pentagram, around which each of the letters (or digraphs) is sometimes written in Greek.

Hyperion (Ὑπερίων) (/haɪˈpɪiən/) [8]: One of the original twelve Titans, child of Gaia and Ouranos. Father of Helios, Selene, and Eos.

Hypnos (Ὕπνος) (/ˈhɪpnəs/) [85]: God of sleep, son of Nyx, brother of Thanatos. He has many sons called Oneiroi (dreams), among them Phobetor (nightmare), Morpheus (shape), and Phantasos (fantasy).

Iakchos (Ἴακχος) (Iacchus, /ˈjakəs/) [42]: A name of Dionysos or a separate god, perhaps a deification of the ritual cry *ia*.

Ide (Ἴδη) (Ida, /ˈaɪdə/) [49]: A mountain in Phrygia, sacred to Kybele or Rhea.

Idaian Gods (/ɪˈdaɪən/) [0]: The Dactyls, ten beings, born on Mount Ide (Ἴδη) from Rhea. Often associated with the Korybantes

Ie (ἰέ) [34]: A ritual cry.

Ino (Ἰνώ) (/ˈaɪnoʊ/) [0]: Daughter of Kadmos. She fostered Dionysos, for which she was punished by Hera, who drove her husband mad. She fled her mad husband by jumping into the sea with her child in her arms, where she became the goddess Leukothea, and her child became Palaimon.

Isis [42]: Goddess of Egypt, wife and sister of Osiris. Her cult spread throughout the Roman empire in late antiquity, where she was worshipped as a mother goddess.

Justice [63, 64]: *See* Dikaiosyne.

Kabeiroi (Κάβειροι) (Cabeiri, /ˈkabeɪɪaɪ/) [0]: Divine dwarf twins who dance and celebrate in honor of Demeter.

Kadmos (Κάδμος) (Cadmus, /ˈkædməs/) [44, 47, 74]: The founder of the city of Thebes and inventor (according to legend) of the alphabet. Father of Semele.

Kalliope (Καλλιόπη) (Calliope, /kə'lɑɪəpi/) [24, 76]: The muse of epic poetry.

Kleio (κλειώ) (Clio, /'kliou/) [76]: The muse of history.

Klotho (Κλωθώ) (Clotho, /klouθou/) [59]: The youngest of the three Moirai, who spins the threads of life.

Koios (Κοῖος) (Coeus, /siəs/) [35]: A Titan, son of Gaia and Ouranos.

Kokytos (Κωκυτός) (Cocytus, /kou'sɑɪtəs/) [57, 71]: The river of lamentation, one of the rivers of Hades, which flows into (or out of) Acheron.

Korybantes (Κορύβαντες) (Corybants, /kaɹɪ'bɑnts/) [0, 38]: Armed dancers, who dance to honor the mother goddess Kybele. C.f. Kouretes.

Korybas (Κορύβας) (Corybas, /kou'ɹibəs/) [39]: Son of Iasion and Kybele, leader of the Korybantes.

Korykos (Κώρυκος) (Corycus, /'kouɹikəs/) [28]: An ancient city in Anatolia. Sacred to Hermes.

Kosmos (κόσμος) (Cosmos, /'kɑzmous/) [0, 4, 5, 6, 11, 13, 19, 26, 34, 66]: The entire ordered universe.

Kouretes (Κουρῆτες) (Curetes, /kju'ɹitiz/) [0, 31, 38]: Armed dancers, who dance to honor Rhea. According to myth, when Rhea saved Zeus from being swallowed by Kronos, she brought him to a cave where the Kouretes danced to drown out his cries, thus hiding him from Kronos. The Kouretes were identified with the Korybantes, which were worshippers who performed a martial dance in honor of Kybele. C.f. Korybantes.

Kronian (Κρόνιος) (Cronian, /'kɹounian/) [15, 44, 71] An epithet, usually of Zeus, meaning "child of Kronos."

Kronos (Κρόνος) (Cronus, /'kɹounəs/) [0, 4, 13, 14, 27, 84]: A Titan, father of Zeus, son of Ouranos and Gaia. Often conflated with Chronos.

Kydonian (Κυδωνία) (Cydonian, /sɑɪ'dounian/) [36]: An epithet of Artemis, in reference to Cydonia (Κυδωνία), a city-state in Crete.

Kypris (Κύπρις) (Cypris, /'sɑɪpɹis/) [3, 22, 65]: Epithet of Aphrodite, named for the island of Cyprus.

Kythereia (Κυθέρεια) (Cytherea, /sɪθəˈɹiə/) [42]: Epithet of Aphrodite, in reference to the island Cythera, where Aphrodite is said to have washed up when she came out of the foam.

Lachesis (Λάχεσις) (/ˈlækɪsɪs/) [59]: The middle of the Moirai, sisters who weave the thread of life into the tapestry of fate.

Lenaian procession (/lɛˈneɪən/) [54]: A ritual procession in celebration of the Lenaia, a festival held in Athens in honor of Dionysos Lenaios.

Lenaios (ληναῖος) (Lenaeus, /lɛˈneɪəs/) [50]: An epithet of Dionysos, from the word for "wine press."

Lethe (Λήθη) (/ˈliθi/) [85]: The river of oblivion or forgetfulness, one of the rivers of Hades.

Leto (Λητώ) (/ˈlitoʊ/) [0, **35**]: Daughter of the Titans Koios and Phoibe, mother of Apollon and Artemis by Zeus.

Leukothea (Λευκοθέα) (Leucothea, /luˈkaθiə/) [0, **74**]: The White Goddess, a goddess of the sea and protector of mortals. Ino was the daughter of Kadmos, and thus the sister of Semele, mother of Dionysos. When Dionysos was born, his aunt Ino helped care for him. Hera drove Ino insane as punishment (or perhaps drove her husband insane) and she took her youngest son, Melikertes, and leapt into the sea, either out of madness or to escape her husband. The gods transformed her into a sea daimon, as well as her son. Ino became Leukothea, literally, "the white goddess," while he became Palaimon.

Liknites (Λικνίτης) (Licnites, /lɪkˈnaɪtis/) [46]: An epithet of Dionysos, meaning "winnowing fan." Some myths have Dionysos using a winnowing fan as his crib when a child.

Loxias (Λοξίας) (/lɑkˈsiəs/) [34]: An epithet of Apollon, probably from the verb λέγω "to speak," but often popularly thought to be from the adjective λοξός "obscure," due to his oracles.

Lydia (Λυδία) (/ˈlɪdiə/) [49]: An iron-age empire in Anatolia. Later a province of Rome.

Lykoreus (Λυκωρεῦς) (Lycoreus, /laɪˈkɔɹiəs/) [34]: An epithet of Apollon.

Maia (Μαῖα) (/ˈmaɪə/) [28]: A nymph in the Pleiades.

Mainades (μαινάδες) (Maenads, /'miːnædz/) [45]: Followers of Dionysos, women who were said to be driven into a murderous frenzy in his worship. Also Bakchai. Mother of Hermes.

Megaira (Μέγαιρα) (Megaera, /məˈdʒɪəɹə/) [69]: One of the Erinyes, goddess of envy.

Melinoe (Μηλινόη) (/meɪləˈnoʊi/) [71]: An extremely obscure deity, mentioned only in the Orphic hymns, and in some inscriptions as an epithet of Hekate. Appears to be a goddess of ghosts, or perhaps nightmares.

Melpomene (Μελπομένη) (/mɛlˈpɑmɪni/) [76]: The muse of choruses or of tragedy.

Memphis (Μέμφις) (/ˈmɛmfɪs/) [34]: A city in Lower Egypt.

Mēn (Μήν) (/min/) [0]: An Anatolian moon god.

Mene (Μήνη) (/mini/) [0, 9]: A name of Selene.

Mise (Μίση) (/misi/) [42]: An obscure deity, perhaps the feminine version of Iakchos.

Mnemosyne (Μνημοσύνη) (/nɪˈmɑzɪni/) [0, 76, 77]: Titan of memory, mother of the nine Mousai. According to Orphic religion, she has a spring in Hades, near the river Lethe. If one drinks from Lethe after death, he or she will forget his or her life and initiation, but if one drinks from the spring of Mnemosyne, then he or she will remember.

Moirai (Μοῖραι) (Moerae, /ˈmiɹɑɪ/) [69]: The three fates who weave a tapestry of life. Clotho spins the threads. Lachesis measures and weaves them. And Atropos cuts them off. Hence, they represent three phases of life: youth, adulthood, and death. They are said to serve Ananke, or Necessity, an implacable force to whom even Zeus must bow.

Mousai (Μοῦσαι) (Muses, /ˈmjuzɪz/) [0, 34, 76, 77]: Nine deities, daughters of Apollon and Mnemosyne. Clio, Euterpe, Thalia, Melpomene, Terpsichore, Erato, Polyhymnia, Ourania, and Kalliope.

Mousaios (Μουσαῖος) (Musaeus, /mjuˈsaɪəs/) [0]: A legendary Athenian philosopher, mathematician, and musician. Regarded in some legends as the son or student of Orpheus, on others as his father.

Naiades (Ναϊάδες) (Naiads, /ˈneɪædz/) [54]: Water nymphs.

Necessity [57, 59, 70, 86]: A personification of cosmic law, Ἀνάγκη, Ananke in Greek. Even the fates and Zeus are subject to the dictates of Necessity.

Nemesis (Νέμεσις) (/ˈnɛməsɪs/) [61]: The goddess who punishes hubris or wickedness. Hesiod calls her the daughter of Nyx.

Nereus (Νηρεύς) (/ˈnɪəriəs/) [23, 24]: God of the Aegean, son of Pontos, the sea, and Gaia, the earth.

Night [0, 3, 7, 8, 9, 10, 12, 32, 34, 36, 39, 49, 54, 55, 59, 70, 71, 78, 79]: *See* Nyx.

Nike (Νίκη) (/ˈnaɪki/) [0, 32, **33**]: Goddess of victory. Often depicted with wings.

Nomos (Νόμος) (/ˈnoʊməs/) [64]: Personification of the concept of law.

Notos (Νότος) (Notus, /ˈnoʊtəs/) [82]: God of the southern wind.

Nymphs (νύμφη) (/nɪm(p)fs/) [11, 22, 24, 46, **51**, 53, 55]: Nature spirits, often classified according to their domain. Originally, they seem to be connected to certain sacred springs, although there are also nymphs of trees, caves, mountains, and so on.

Nysa (Νῦσα) (/ˈnaɪsə/) [46, 51, 52]: The sacred, mountainous region where Dionysos was raised and from which he gets his name. The actual location of Nysa is unknown; it may have been in Ethiopia or India. Also the name of one of Dionysos's nurses.

Nyx (Νύξ) (/nɪks/) [**3**, 9]: A central goddess in the Orphic cosmology, one of the first gods created, and wife of Phanes.

Okeanos (Ὠκεανός) (Oceanus, /ˌoʊʃiˈænəs/) [0, 11, 17, 18, 22, 38, 51, 55, 58, 64, **83**]: The Titan of the ocean, conceived of as a river that encircles the world.

Olympos (Ὄλυμπος) (Olympus, /əˈlɪmpəs/) [14, 25, 38, 45, 55, 56, 59]: The highest mountain in Greece, regarded as the home of the twelve Olympian gods, ruled by Zeus and Hera.

Oneiros (Ὄνειρος) (Oneirus, /ˈɔneɪəs/) [86]: God of dreams.

Orpheus (Ὀρφεύς) (/ˈɔɪfiəs/) [**0**, 59]: Legendary musician and magician, considered the founder of the Orphic cult. According to myth, descended into the underworld to convince Hades to release Eurydice, his recently killed love.

Orthia (Ὀρθία) (/ɔːθˈiə/) [36]: "Upright." An epithet of Artemis as she was worshipped in Sparta. Spartans boys were flogged at her altar as part of an initiation ritual.

Ortygia (Ὀρτυγία) (/ɔrˈtɪdʒiə/) [35]: A small island, part of the city of Syracuse in Sicily. According to Homer, Leto stopped here to give birth to Artemis, who then helped deliver her brother Apollon on Delos. The island itself, according to legend, is Leto's sister, the Titan Asteria who turned herself into a quail. Other legends suggest that Delos is actually Asteria, not Ortygia.

Paian (Παιάν) (Paean, /ˈpaɪən/) [8, 11, 12, 34, 52, 67]: Physician of the gods, and an epithet of healing gods like Apollon and Asklepios.

Palaimon (Παλαίμων) (Palaemon, /pæˈleɪmən/) [0, **75**]: Deified son of Leukothea.

Pallas (Παλλάς) (/ˈpæləs/) [0, 32]: An epithet of Athena, of obscure origin. A number of myths exist in which she has a companion named Pallas, whom she kills. There is also a story of her killing and flaying a giant of this name.

Pan (Πάν) (/pæn/) [0, **11**, 34, 51]: A pastoral god with feet and horns of a goat, often depicted playing on pipes.

Paphos (Πάφος) (/ˈpæfəs/) [57]: A city of Cyprus, cult center of Aphrodite, where she was said to have washed up after birth.

Peitho (Πειθώ) (/peɪθoʊ/) [10]: "Persuasion," either an epithet of or a separate attendant to Aphrodite.

Perikionios (Περικιόνιος) (/pɛɹikiˈoʊniəs/) [47]: "Wrapped around the pillar," an epithet of Dionysos.

Persephone (Περσεφόνη, Φερσεφόνη) (/pəɹˈsɛfəni/) [0, 24, 29, 30, 41, 43, 44, 46, 53, 56, 57, 70, 71]: Daughter of Demeter, consort of Hades, who kidnapped her from a meadow. The myth of Persephone's abduction by Hades is central to the mysteries of Eleusis. One day as a young girl, picking flowers in a meadow, she was startled by the sudden appearance of Hades, who captured her and took her to the underworld to be his wife. Demeter went in search of her daughter, mourning for her and thereby nearly destroying the earth. When she arrived at Eleusis, she discovered what had happened and appealed to Zeus. Eventually, a deal was brokered where Persephone would have to return to Demeter. But while in Hades, Persephone had eaten some seeds of the pomegranate, and since she had eaten in that realm she was, according to guest laws, part of it. So she must spend part of each year in Hades, and part on earth with her mother. The Orphic mythology also has her as the first mother of Dionysos.

Perses (Πέρσης) (/ˈpɛɹsiz/) [1]: Titan, whose name means "Destroyer." Father of Hekate.

Phanes (Φάνης) (/ˈfeɪnis/) [6]: In Orphic cosmology, the first god. Associated with Dionysos and Eros.

Phlegraian giants (Φλεγραῖα) (/flɛˈɡɹaɪən ˈdʒaɪənts/) [32]: Giants dwelling in a volcanic region in Macedonia, said to be the site of a battle in the Gigantomachy, or battle between the gods and giants.

Phoibos (Φοῖβος) (Phoebus, /ˈfibəs/) [0, 34, 35, 67, 79]: "Bright." An epithet of Apollon.

Phrygia (Φρύγια) (/ˈfɹɪdʒiə/) [27, 48, 49]: An ancient kingdom in western Anatolia.

Physis (Φύσις) (/ˈfaɪsɪs/) [10]: Self-created goddess of nature.

Pierian (Πιερία) (/paɪˈɹiən/) [76]: Of or from Pieria, in reference to the Pierian spring, sacred to the Mousai. According to Ovid, the spring was formed when the winged horse Pegasus struck the ground with his hoof.

Plouton (Πλούτων) (Pluto, /ˈplutoʊ/) [18, 29, 71]: An epithet and euphemism for Hades, meaning "wealthy."

Polyhymnia (Πολυύμνια) (/pɑliˈhɪmniə/) [76]: The muse of sacred poetry.

Poseidon (Ποσειδῶν) (/poʊˈsaɪdən/) [0, 17]: Poseidon is god of the seas, and also of horses and earthquakes. When he came forth with his brothers and sisters from Kronos, he and the other gods discussed how to divide up the world. It was decided that Hades would get the lower realms of the earth, Zeus would get the upper realms of the air, and Poseidon would get the oceans.

Praxidike (Πραξιδίκη) (/ˌpɹæksə'dikeɪ/) [29]: Goddess of judicial punishment. Also an epithet or aspect of Persephone.

Priapos (Πρίαπος) (Priapus, /pɹaɪ'eɪpəs/) [6]: God of gardens and fertility, often depicted with an erection.

Prometheus (Προμηθεύς) (/pɹou'miθiəs/) [13]: A titan, "Forethought," who stole fire from the gods and gave it to mankind, for which crime Zeus punished him.

Pronoia (Πρόνοια) (/pɹou'nɔɪə/) [0]: Personification of care.

Proteus (Πρωτεύς) (/'pɹoutiəs/) [25]: A sea god, capable of transforming into multiple forms. Said to be all-knowing. In the *Odyssey*, Menelaus is told that Proteus can reveal which god he has offended if only Menelaus can wrestle him into submission. Proteus constantly transforms his shape in an attempt to escape, but Menelaus succeeds in capturing him.

Prothyraia (Προθυραία) (/pɹouθə'ɹaɪə/) [2]: "Near the door," an epithet of several goddesses of childbirth, as well as of Hekate.

Protogonos (Πρωτόγονος) (/ˌpɹoutə'gounəs/) [6, 14]: Firstborn, epithet of Phanes.

Pythios (Πύθιος) (Pythius, /'paɪθiəs/) [34]: An epithet of Apollon, a reference to the Pythia priestess of Delphi.

Python (Πύθων) (/'paɪθan/) [34, 79]: A serpent who dwelt at Delphi, slain by Apollon.

Rhea (Ῥέα) (/'ɹiə/) [0, 13, 14]: A mother deity, often associated with Kybele. When Zeus and the other gods were born, Kronos swallowed them out of fear that they would displace him as he had done to Ouranos. Rhea tricked him by giving him a stone to swallow instead of Zeus, whom she hid away. When Zeus came of age, he overthrew Kronos and released the other gods from within him.

Sabazios (Σαβάζιος) (/sə'baziəs/) [48]: A Phrygian god identified with both Zeus and Dionysos.

Sabos (Σάβος) [49]: Another name for Sabazios.

Samothrace (Σαμοθράκη) (/'sæməθɹaɪs/) [38]: An island in the Northern Aegean, site of a large temple complex and home to a mystery religion.

Satyros (Σάτυρος) (Satyr, /'seɪtəɹ/) [54]: One of several male nature spirits, consorts of nymphs.

Seasons [0, 8, 10, 11, 26, 29, 32, 38, 51, 54, 56]: The Horai.

Seilenos (Σειληνός) (Silenus, /saɪ'linəs/) [54]: One of the Satyrs, teacher of the young Dionysos.

Selene (Σελήνη) (/sɪ'lini/) [9]: Titan of the moon, sister of Helios and Eos.

Semele (Σεμέλη) (/'sɛməli/) [0, 44]: Mother of Dionysos, destroyed by Zeus when he revealed his full splendor to her, at her request. Some myths recount Dionysos descending into Hades to bring her back after her death to dwell with him on Olympos, a myth strikingly similar to the Orpheus myth.

Smintheus (Σμινθεύς) (/'smɪnθiəs/) [34]: An epithet for Apollon, derived from the town of Sminthe, where he had a famous temple. Sometimes thought to be derived from the word for "mouse."

Stars [7, 9, 11, 26, 64, 66]: The seven planets or wandering stars were considered to be signs of fate.

Styx (Στύξ) (/stɪks/) [0, 69]: A river of Hades. An oath sworn by its waters by a god is said to be unbreakable. The waters of Styx could make a mortal invulnerable. Achilles, the hero of the *Iliad*, was bathed in the Styx as a child, all but his heel, which became his only vulnerable point.

Syria (Συρία) (/'sɪɹiə/) [55]: A western Asian nation.

Tartaros (Τάρταρος) (/'taɹtəɹəs/) [18, 37, 56, 57, 58]: An abyss within the realm of Hades, regarded as a place of judgment and punishment for wickedness and the prison of the Titans.

Terpsichore (Τερψιχόρη) (/təɹp'sɪkəɹi/) [76]: The muse of chorus and dance.

Tethys (Τηθύς) (/'tɛθəs/) [0, 22]: A Titan, wife of Okeanos. Tethys, according to the *Theogony*, was the daughter and consort of Okeanos, and the mother of rivers.

Thalia (Θαλία) (/'θæliə/) [60, 76]: "Abundance," one of the Charites. Also the name of the muse of comedy.

Thanatos (Θάνατος) (/'θænətoʊs/) [85, 87]: Death, son of Nyx, brother of Oneiros. Thanatos is the personification of death. While he cannot be moved by prayers or vows, he has been tricked before: Sisyphus once bound him up until Ares freed him. For punishment, Sisyphus must roll a rock up a mountain in Tartaros. Every time he gets to the top, it rolls back down and he must start over.

Themis (Θέμις) (/'θiməs/) [0, 43, 79]: Titan of divine law. C.f. Nomos.

Thesmodoteira (Θεσμοδότειρα) (/ˌθɛzmədoʊ'teɪɹə/) [0]: "Giver of law."

Thrace (Θράκη) (/θɹeɪs/) [80]: A region of Europe comprising parts of contemporary Bulgaria, European Turkey, and Greece. Considered sacred to Ares.

Tisiphone (Τισιφόνη) (/tɪ'sɪfəni/) [69]: One of the Erinyes, who avenges murder.

Titan (Τιτάν) (/'taɪtən/) [8, 12, 13, 34, 37, 78]: Primal divine beings, children of Gaia and Ouranos. Hesiod recounts a battle between Titans and gods, which established Zeus and the Olympians as ruling deities. In the Orphic mythology, Titans killed and partially devoured Dionysos. Destroyed by Zeus, their ashes formed humanity. Also an epithet of Apollon and Helios.

Titanis (Τιτανίς) (/taɪ'teɪnəs/) [36]: An epithet of Artemis.

Tityos (Τιτυός) (Tityus, /'tɪtjəs/) [34]: A giant who attempted to rape Leto. Killed by Artemis and Apollon.

Tmolos (Τμῶλος) (/'moʊləs/) [48, 49]: Mountain in Lydia.

Tritogeneia (Τριτογένεια) (/ˌtɹaɪtədʒə'neɪə/) [32]: An epithet of Athena, of obscure origin. It may indicate "born from Triton" or "thrice-born."

Tritones (Τρίτονες) (Tritons, /'tɹaɪtənz/) [24]: Daimons of the sea, messengers of Poseidon.

Tyche (Τύχη) (/'taɪki/) [72]: Goddess of good fortune.

Ourania (Οὐρανία) (Urania, /jʊ'ɹeɪniə/ [0, 76]: The muse of astronomy and astrology.

Ouranos (Οὐρανός) (Uranus, /jʊ'ɹeɪnəs/) [4, 13, 37, 79]: Titan of the sky. He created the other Titans with his wife, Gaia, the Earth. But he locked the more unruly of the Titans inside of Gaia's body. She convinced her son Kronos to rebel, and gave him a sickle with which he castrated his father. This made Kronos king of the universe, but of course his own children, the gods, would do a very similar thing to him later.

Zephyros (Ζέφυρος) (/ˈzɛfərəs/) [81]: The god of the western wind.

Zeus (Ζεύς) (/zus/) [0, 5, 8, 11, 14, **15**, 16, 18, **19**, **20**, 28, 29, 30, 32, 35, 36, 41, 43, 44, 46, 50, 52, 59, 60, 62, 63, 70, 71, 73, 76, 77, 82]: King of the gods, son of Rhea and Kronos. Father of Dionysos. In myth, Zeus is often depicted as a philanderer, but in religious practice he was regarded with respect as the ruler of the gods. According to one legend, Zeus impregnated and then swallowed the goddess Metis because of a prophesy that her son would overthrow him. In swallowing Metis, who represented cosmic wisdom, he gained all the wisdom of Phanes, hence he contains all things. Nine months after swallowing Metis, Zeus suffered a great headache which eventually split his skull, releasing the full-grown goddess Athena.

APPENDIX II:
THOMAS TAYLOR'S TRANSLATION
OF THE ORPHIC HYMNS

Preface

Note: I have worked from a photographic facsimile of the 1792 edition of Taylor's translation, correcting a text scan of that document. I did not modernize spelling or punctuation, other than replacing his long ſ with the more contemporary short s. Taylor's original translation contains a very long introduction (over one hundred pages) that he calls the "dissertation." For those interested in his Neoplatonic interpretation of the hymns, it is worth reading not only for its insight into Taylor's early Neopaganism, but also as a work of scholarship itself. However, including it here as well as the extensive footnotes to the hymns would render this book unwieldy and would require extensive editing in order to make the Greek legible to modern audiences, as he uses many abbreviations and ligatures no longer in common use. A full scan of the introduction is available at the internet Sacred Texts archive. www.sacred-texts.com/cla/hoo/index.htm

I am indebted to them for making their scan of Taylor's text available. It saved me countless hours of work.

THE INITIATIONS OF ORPHEUS

TO MUSÆUS.

ATTEND Musæus to my sacred song,
And learn what rites to sacrifice belong.
Jove I invoke, the earth, and solar light,
The moon's pure splendor, and the stars of night;
Thee Neptune, ruler of the sea profound,
Dark-hair'd, whose waves begirt the solid ground;
Ceres abundant, and of lovely mien,
And Proserpine infernal Pluto's queen;
The huntress Dian, and bright Phœbus rays,
Far-darting God, the theme of Delphic praise;
And Bacchus, honour'd by the heav'nly choir,
And raging Mars, and Vulcan god of fire;
The mighty pow'r who rose from foam to light,
And Pluto potent in the realms of night;
With Hebe young, and Hercules the strong,
And you to whom the cares of births belong:
Justice and Piety august I call,
And much-fam'd nymphs, and Pan the god of all.
To Juno sacred, and to Mem'ry fair,
And the chaste Muses I address my pray'r;
The various year, the Graces, and the Hours,
Fair-hair'd Latona, and Dione's pow'rs;
Armed Curetes, household Gods I call,
With those who spring from Jove the king of all:
Th' Idæan Gods, the angel of the skies,
And righteous Themis, with sagacious eyes;
With ancient night, and day-light I implore,
And Faith, and Justice dealing right adore;
Saturn and Rhea, and great Thetis too,
Hid in a veil of bright celestial blue:
I call great Ocean, and the beauteous train

Of nymphs, who dwell in chambers of the main;
Atlas the strong, and ever in its prime,
Vig'rous Eternity, and endless Time;
The Stygian pool, and placid Gods beside,
And various Genii, that o'er men preside;
Illustrious Providence, the noble train
Of dæmon forms, who fill th' ætherial plain;
Or live in air, in water, earth, or fire,
Or deep beneath the solid ground retire.
Bacchus and Semele the friends of all,
And white Leucothea of the sea I call;
Palæmon bounteous, and Adrastria great,
And sweet-tongu'd Victory, with success elate;
Great Esculapius, skill'd to cure disease,
And dread Minerva, whom fierce battles please;
Thunders and winds in mighty columns pent,
With dreadful roaring struggling hard for vent;
Attis, the mother of the pow'rs on high,
And fair Adonis, never doom'd to die,
End and beginning he is all to all,
These with propitious aid I gently call;
And to my holy sacrifice invite,
The pow'r who reigns in deepest hell and night;
I call Einodian Hecate, lovely dame,
Of earthly, wat'ry, and celestial frame,
Sepulchral, in a saffron veil array'd,
Pleas'd with dark ghosts that wander thro' the shade;
Persian, unconquerable huntress hail!
The world's key-bearer never doom'd to fail;
On the rough rock to wander thee delights,
Leader and nurse be present to our rites;
Propitious grant our just desires success,
Accept our homage, and the incense bless.

I. TO THE GODDESS PROTHYRÆA.
The FUMIGATION from STORAX.

O Venerable goddess, hear my pray'r,
For labour pains are thy peculiar care;
in thee, when stretch'd upon the bed of grief,
The sex as in a mirror view relief.
Guard of the race, endued with gentle mind,
To helpless youth, benevolent and kind;
Benignant nourisher; great Nature's key
Belongs to no divinity but thee.
Thou dwell'st with all immanifest to sight,
And solemn festivals are thy delight.
Thine is the talk to loose the virgin's zone,
And thou in ev'ry work art seen and known.
With births you sympathize, tho' pleas'd to see
The numerous offspring of fertility;
When rack'd with nature's pangs and sore distress'd,
The sex invoke thee, as the soul's sure rest;
For thou alone can'st give relief to pain,
Which art attempts to ease, but tries in vain;
Assisting goddess, venerable pow'r,
Who bring'st relief in labour's dreadful hour;
Hear, blessed Dian, and accept my pray'r,
And make the infant race thy constant care.

II. TO NIGHT.
The FUMIGATION with TORCHES.

NIGHT, parent goddess, source of sweet repose,
From whom at first both Gods and men arose,
Hear, blessed Venus, deck'd with starry light,
In sleep's deep silence dwelling Ebon night!
Dreams and soft case attend thy dusky train,
Pleas'd with the length'ned gloom and feastful strain.
Dissolving anxious care, the friend of Mirth,
With darkling coursers riding round the earth.
Goddess of phantoms and of shadowy play,

Whose drowsy pow'r divides the nat'ral day:
By Fate's decree you constant send the light
To deepest hell, remote from mortal sight;
For dire Necessity which nought withstands,
Invests the world with adamantine bands.
Be present, Goddess, to thy suppliant's pray'r,
Desir'd by all, whom all alike revere,
Blessed, benevolent, with friendly aid
Dispell the fears of Twilight's dreadful shade.

III. TO HEAVEN.

The FUMIGATION from FRANKINCENSE.

GREAT Heav'n, whose mighty frame no respite knows,
Father of all, from whom the world arose:
Hear, bounteous parent, source and end of all,
Forever whirling round this earthly ball;
Abode of Gods, whose guardian pow'r surrounds
Th' eternal World with ever during bounds;
Whose ample bosom and encircling folds
The dire necessity of nature holds.
Ætherial, earthly, whose all-various frame
Azure and full of forms, no power can tame.
All-seeing Heav'n, progenitor of Time,
Forever blessed, deity sublime,
Propitious on a novel mystic shine,
And crown his wishes with a life divine.

IV. TO FIRE.

The FUMIGATION from SAFFRON.

O Ever untam'd Fire, who reign'st on high
In Jove's dominions ruler of the sky;
The glorious sun with dazzling lustre bright,
And moon and stars from thee derive their light;
All taming pow'r, ætherial shining fire,
Whose vivid blasts the heat of life inspire:
The world's best element, light-bearing pow'r,

With starry radiance shining, splendid flow'r,
O hear my suppliant pray'r, and may thy frame
Be ever innocent, serene, and tame.

V. TO PROTOGONUS, Or the FIRST-BORN.
The FUMIGATION from MYRRH.

O Mighty first-begotten, hear my pray'r,
Two-fold, egg-born, and wand'ring thro' the air,
Bull-roarer, glorying in thy golden wings,
From whom the race of Gods and mortals springs.
Ericapæus, celebrated pow'r,
Ineffable, occult, all shining flow'r.
From eyes obscure thou wip'st the gloom of night,
All-spreading splendour, pure and holy light;
Hence Phanes call'd, the glory of the sky,
On waving pinions thro' the world you fly.
Priapus, dark-ey'd splendour, thee I sing,
Genial, all-prudent, ever-blessed king,
With joyful aspect on our rights divine
And holy sacrifice propitious shine.

VI. TO THE STARS.
The FUMIGATION from AROMATICS.

WITH holy voice I call the stars on high,
Pure sacred lights and genii of the sky.
Celestial stars, the progeny of Night,
In whirling circles beaming far your light,
Refulgent rays around the heav'ns ye throw,
Eternal fires, the source of all below.
With flames significant of Fate ye shine,
And aptly rule for men a path divine.
In seven bright zones ye run with wand'ring flames,
And heaven and earth compose your lucid frames:
With course unwearied, pure and fiery bright
Forever shining thro' the veil of Night.
Hail twinkling, joyful, ever wakeful fires!

Propitious shine on all my just desires;
These sacred rites regard with conscious rays,
And end our works devoted to your praise.

VII. TO THE SUN.

The FUMIGATION from FRANKINCENSE and MANNA.

HEAR golden Titan, whose eternal eye
With broad survey, illumines all the sky.
Self-born, unwearied in diffusing light,
And to all eyes the mirrour of delight:
Lord of the seasons, with thy fiery car
And leaping coursers, beaming light from far:
With thy right hand the source of morning light,
And with thy left the father of the night.
Agile and vig'rous, venerable Sun,
Fiery and bright around the heav'ns you run.
Foe to the wicked, but the good man's guide,
O'er all his steps propitious you preside:
With various sounding, golden lyre, 'tis thine
To fill the world with harmony divine.
Father of ages, guide of prosp'rous deeds,
The world's commander, borne by lucid steeds,
Immortal Jove, all-searching, bearing light,
Source of existence, pure and fiery bright:
Bearer of fruit, almighty lord of years,
Agil and warm, whom ev'ry pow'r reveres.
Great eye of Nature and the starry skies,
Doom'd with immortal flames to set and rise:
Dispensing justice, lover of the stream,
The world's great despot, and o'er all supreme.
Faithful defender, and the eye of right,
Of steeds the ruler, and of life the light:
With sounding whip four fiery steeds you guide,
When in the car of day you glorious ride.
Propitious on these mystic labours shine,
And bless thy suppliants with a life divine.

VIII. TO THE MOON.

The FUMIGATION from AROMATICS.

HEAR, Goddess queen, diffusing silver light,
Bull-horn'd and wand'ring thro' the gloom of Night.
With stars surrounded, and with circuit wide
Night's torch extending, thro' the heav'ns you ride:
Female and Male with borrow'd rays you shine,
And now full-orb'd, now tending to decline.
Mother of ages, fruit-producing Moon,
Whose amber orb makes Night's reflected noon:
Lover of horses, splendid, queen of Night,
All-seeing pow'r bedeck'd with starry light.
Lover of vigilance, the foe of strife,
In peace rejoicing, and a prudent life:
Fair lamp of Night, its ornament and friend,
Who giv'st to Nature's works their destin'd end.
Queen of the stars, all-wife Diana hail!
Deck'd with a graceful robe and shining veil;
Come, blessed Goddess, prudent, starry, bright,
Come moony-lamp with chaste and splendid light,
Shine on these sacred rites with prosp'rous rays,
And pleas'd accept thy suppliant's mystic praise.

IX. TO NATURE.

The FUMIGATION from AROMATICS.

NATURE, all parent, ancient, and divine,
O much-mechanic mother, art is thine;
Heav'nly, abundant, venerable queen,
In ev'ry part of thy dominions seen.
Untam'd, all-taming, ever splendid light,
All ruling, honor'd, and supremly bright.
Immortal, first-born, ever still the same,
Nocturnal, starry, shining, glorious dame.
Thy feet's still traces in a circling course,
By thee are turn'd, with unremitting force.

Pure ornament of all the pow'rs divine,
Finite and infinite alike you shine;
To all things common and in all things known,
Yet incommunicable and alone.
Without a father of thy wond'rous frame,
Thyself the father whence thy essence came.
All-flourishing, connecting, mingling soul,
Leader and ruler of this mighty whole.
Life-bearer, all-sustaining, various nam'd,
And for commanding grace and beauty fam'd.
Justice, supreme in might, whose general sway
The waters of the restless deep obey.
Ætherial, earthly, for the pious glad,
Sweet to the good, but bitter to the bad.
All-wife, all bounteous, provident, divine,
A rich increase of nutriment is thine;
Father of all, great nurse, and mother kind,
Abundant, blessed, all-spermatic mind:
Mature, impetuous, from whose fertile seeds
And plastic hand, this changing scene proceeds.
All-parent pow'r, to mortal eyes unseen,
Eternal, moving, all-sagacious queen.
By thee the world, whose parts in rapid flow,
Like swift descending streams, no respite know,
On an eternal hinge, with steady course
Is whirl'd, with matchless, unremitting force.
Thron'd on a circling car, thy mighty hand
Holds and directs, the reins of wide command.
Various thy essence, honor'd, and the best,
Of judgement too, the general end and test.
Intrepid, fatal, all-subduing dame,
Life-everlasting, Parca, breathing flame.
Immortal, Providence, the world is thine,
And thou art all things, architect divine.
O blessed Goddess, hear thy suppliant's pray'r,

And make my future life, thy constant care;
Give plenteous seasons, and sufficient wealth,
And crown my days with lasting peace and health.

X. TO PAN.
The FUMIGATION from VARIOUS ODORS.

I Call strong Pan, the substance of the whole,
Etherial, marine, earthly, general soul,
Immortal fire; for all the world is thine,
And all are parts of thee, O pow'r divine.
Come, blessed Pan, whom rural haunts delight,
Come, leaping, agile, wand'ring, starry light;
The Hours and Seasons, wait thy high command,
And round thy throne in graceful order stand.
Goat-footed, horned, Bacchanalian Pan,
Fanatic pow'r, from whom the world began,
Whose various parts by thee inspir'd, combine
In endless dance and melody divine.
In thee a refuge from our fears we find,
Those fears peculiar to the human kind.
Thee shepherds, streams of water, goats rejoice,
Thou lov'st the chace, and Echo's secret voice:
The sportive nymphs, thy ev'ry step attend,
And all thy works fulfill their destin'd end.
O all-producing pow'r, much-fam'd, divine,
The world's great ruler, rich increase is thine.
All-fertile Pæan, heav'nly splendor pure,
In fruits rejoicing, and in caves obscure.
True serpent-horned Jove, whose dreadful rage
When rous'd, 'tis hard for mortals to asswage.
By thee the earth wide-bosom'd deep and long,
Stands on a basis permanent and strong.
Th' unwearied waters of the rolling sea,
Profoundly spreading, yield to thy decree.
Old Ocean too reveres thy high command,
Whose liquid arms begirt the solid land.

The spacious air, whose nutrimental fire,
And vivid blasts, the heat of life inspire
The lighter frame of fire, whose sparkling eye
Shines on the summit of the azure sky,
Submit alike to thee, whole general sway
All parts of matter, various form'd obey.
All nature's change thro' thy protecting care,
And all mankind thy lib'ral bounties share:
For these where'er dispers'd thro' boundless space,
Still find thy providence support their race.
Come, Bacchanalian, blessed power draw near,
Fanatic Pan, thy humble suppliant hear,
Propitious to these holy rites attend,
And grant my life may meet a prosp'rous end;
Drive panic Fury too, wherever found,
From human kind, to earth's remotest bound.

XI. TO HERCULES.

The FUMIGATION from FRANKINCENSE.

HEAR, pow'rful, Hercules untam'd and strong,
To whom vast hands, and mighty works belong,
Almighty Titan, prudent and benign,
Of various forms, eternal and divine,
Father of Time, the theme of gen'ral praise,
Ineffable, ador'd in various ways.
Magnanimous, in divination skill'd
And in the athletic labours of the field.
'Tis thine strong archer, all things to devour,
Supreme, all-helping, all-producing pow'r;
To thee mankind as their deliv'rer pray,
Whose arm can chase the savage tribes away:
Uweary'd, earth's best blossom, offspring fair,
To whom calm peace, and peaceful works are dear.
Self-born, with primogenial fires you shine,
And various names and strength of heart are thine.
Thy mighty head supports the morning light,

And bears untam'd, the silent gloomy night;
From east to west endu'd with strength divine,
Twelve glorious labours to absolve is thine;
Supremely skill'd, thou reign'st in heav'n's abodes,
Thyself a God amid'st th' immortal Gods.
With arms unshaken, infinite, divine,
Come, blessed pow'r, and to our rites incline;
The mitigations of disease convey,
And drive disasterous maladies away.
Come, shake the branch with thy almighty arm,
Dismiss thy darts and noxious fate disarm.

XII. TO SATURN.

The FUMIGATION from STORAX.

ETHERIAL father, mighty Titan, hear,
Great fire of Gods and men, whom all revere:
Endu'd with various council, pure and strong,
To whom perfection and decrease belong.
Consum'd by thee all forms that hourly die,
By thee restor'd, their former place supply;
The world immense in everlasting chains,
Strong and ineffable thy pow'r contains;
Father of vast eternity, divine,
O mighty Saturn, various speech is thine:
Blossom of earth and of the starry skies,
Husband of Rhea, and Prometheus wife.
Obstetric Nature, venerable root,
From which the various forms of being shoot;
No parts peculiar can thy pow'r enclose,
Diffus'd thro' all, from which the world arose,
O, best of beings, of a subtle mind,
Propitious hear to holy pray'rs inclin'd;
The sacred rites benevolent attend,
And grant a blameless life, a blessed end.

XIII. TO RHEA.
The FUMIGATION from AROMATICS.

DAUGHTER of great Protogonus, divine,
Illustrious Rhea, to my pray'r incline,
Who driv'st thy holy car with speed along,
Drawn by fierce lions, terrible and strong.
Mother of Jove, whose mighty arm can wield
Th' avenging bolt, and shake the dreadful shield.
Drum-beating, frantic, of a splendid mien,
Brass-sounding, honor'd, Saturn's blessed queen.
Thou joy'st in mountains and tumultuous fight,
And mankind's horrid howlings, thee delight.
War's parent, mighty, of majestic frame,
Deceitful saviour, liberating dame.
Mother of Gods and men, from whom the earth
And lofty heav'ns derive their glorious birth;
Th' ætherial gales, the deeply spreading sea
Goddess ærial form'd, proceed from thee.
Come, pleas'd with wand'rings, blessed and divine,
With peace attended on our labours shine;
Bring rich abundance, and wherever found
Drive dire disease, to earth's remotest bound.

XIV. TO JUPITER.
The FUMIGATION from STORAX.

O Jove much-honor'd, Jove supremely great,
To thee our holy rites we consecrate,
Our pray'rs and expiations, king divine,
For all things round thy head exalted shine.
The earth is thine, and mountains swelling high,
The sea profound, and all within the sky.
Saturnian king, descending from above,
Magnanimous, commanding, sceptred Jove;
All-parent, principle and end of all,
Whose pow'r almighty, shakes this earthly ball;

Ev'n Nature trembles at thy mighty nod,
Loud-sounding, arm'd with light'ning, thund'ring God.
Source of abundance, purifying king,
O various-form'd from whom all natures spring;
Propitious hear my pray'r, give blameless health,
With peace divine, and necessary wealth.

XV. TO JUNO.

The FUMIGATION from AROMATICS.

O Royal Juno of majestic mien,
Aerial-form'd, divine, Jove's blessed queen,
Thron'd in the bosom of cærulean air,
The race of mortals is thy constant care.
The cooling gales thy pow'r alone inspires,
Which nourish life, which ev'ry life desires.
Mother of clouds and winds, from thee alone
Producing all things, mortal life is known:
All natures share thy temp'rament divine,
And universal sway alone is thine.
With sounding blasts of wind, the swelling sea
And rolling rivers roar, when shook by thee.
Come, blessed Goddess, fam'd almighty queen,
With aspect kind, rejoicing and serene.

XVI. TO NEPTUNE.

The FUMIGATION from MYRRH.

HEAR, Neptune, ruler of the sea profound,
Whose liquid grasp begirts the solid ground;
Who, at the bottom of the stormy main,
Dark and deep-bosom'd, hold'st thy wat'ry reign;
Thy awful hand the brazen trident bears,
And ocean's utmost bound, thy will reveres:
Thee I invoke, whose steeds the foam divide,
From whose dark locks the briny waters glide;
Whose voice loud sounding thro' the roaring deep,
Drives all its billows, in a raging heap;

When fiercely riding thro' the boiling sea,
Thy hoarse command the trembling waves obey.
Earth shaking, dark-hair'd God, the liquid plains
(The third division) Fate to thee ordains,
'Tis thine, cærulian dæmon, to survey
Well pleas'd the monsters of the ocean play,
Confirm earth's basis, and with prosp'rous gales
Waft ships along, and swell the spacious sails;
Add gentle Peace, and fair-hair'd Health beside,
And pour abundance in a blameless tide.

XVII. TO PLUTO.

PLUTO, magnanimous, whose realms profound
Are fix'd beneath the firm and solid ground,
In the Tartarian plains remote from fight,
And wrapt forever in the depths of night;
Terrestrial Jove, thy sacred ear incline,
And, pleas'd, accept thy mystic's hymn divine.
Earth's keys to thee, illustrious king belong,
Its secret gates unlocking, deep and strong.
'Tis thine, abundant annual fruits to bear,
For needy mortals are thy constant care.
To thee, great king, Avernus is assign'd,
The seat of Gods, and basis of mankind.
Thy throne is fix'd in Hade's dismal plains,
Distant, unknown to rest, where darkness reigns;
Where, destitute of breath, pale spectres dwell,
In endless, dire, inexorable hell;
And in dread Acheron, whose depths obscure,
Earth's stable roots eternally secure.
O mighty dæmon, whose decision dread,
The future fate determines of the dead,
With captive Proserpine, thro' grassy plains,
Drawn in a four-yok'd car with loosen'd reins,
Rapt o'er the deep, impell'd by love, you flew
'Till Eleusina's city rose to view;

There, in a wond'rous cave obscure and deep,
The sacred maid secure from search you keep,
The cave of Atthis, whose wide gates display
An entrance to the kingdoms void of day.
Of unapparent works, thou art alone
The dispensator, visible and known.
O pow'r all-ruling, holy, honor'd light,
Thee sacred poets and their hymns delight:
Propitious to thy mystic's works incline,
Rejoicing come, for holy rites are thine.

XVIII. TO THUNDRING JOVE.

The FUMIGATION from STORAX.

O Father Jove, who shak'st with fiery light
The world deep-sounding from thy lofty height:
From thee, proceeds th' ætherial lightning's blaze,
Flashing around intolerable rays.
Thy sacred thunders shake the blest abodes,
The shining regions of th' immortal Gods:
Thy pow'r divine, the flaming lightning shrouds,
With dark investiture, in fluid clouds.
'Tis thine to brandish thunders strong and dire,
To scatter storms, and dreadful darts of fire;
With roaring flames involving all around,
And bolts of thunder of tremendous sound.
Thy rapid dart can raise the hair upright,
And shake the heart of man with wild afright.
Sudden, unconquer'd, holy, thund'ring God,
'With noise unbounded, flying all abroad;
With all-devouring force, entire and strong,
Horrid, untam'd, thou roll'st the flames along.
Rapid, ætherial bolt, descending fire,
The earth all-parent, trembles at thy ire;
The sea all-shining; and each beast that hears
The sound terrific, with dread horror fears:
When Nature's face is bright with flashing fire,

And in the heavens resound thy thunders dire.
Thy thunders white, the azure garments tear,
And burst the veil of all surrounding air.
O Jove, all-blessed, may thy wrath severe,
Hurl'd in the bosom of the deep appear,
And on the tops of mountains be reveal'd,
For thy strong arm is not from us conceal'd.
Propitious to these sacred rites incline,
And crown my wishes with a life divine:
Add royal health, and gentle peace beside,
With equal reason, for my constant guide.

XIX. TO JOVE, as the AUTHOR of LIGHTNING.
The FUMIGATION from FRANKINCENSE and MANNA.
I Call the mighty, holy, splendid light,
Aerial, dreadful-sounding, fiery-bright;
Flaming, aerial-light, with angry voice,
Lightning thro' lucid clouds with horrid noise.
Untam'd, to whom resentments dire belong,
Pure, holy pow'r, all-parent, great and strong:
Come, and benevolent these rites attend,
And grant my days a peaceful, blessed end.

XX. TO THE CLOUDS.
The FUMIGATION from MYRRH.
Ærial clouds, thro' heav'n's resplendent plains
Who wander, parents of prolific rains;
Who nourish fruits, whose water'y frames are hurl'd,
By winds impetuous, round the mighty world;
All-thund'ring, lion-roaring, flashing fire,
In Air's wide bosom, bearing thunders dire;
Impell'd by ev'ry stormy, sounding gale,
With rapid course, along the skies ye sail.
With blowing winds your wat'ry frames I call,
On mother Earth with fruitful show'rs to fall.

XXI. TO THE SEA, OR TETHYS.

The FUMIGATION from FRANKINCENSE and MANNA.

TETHYS I call, with eyes cærulean bright,
Hid in a veil obscure from human sight;
Great Ocean's empress, wand'ring thro' the deep,
And pleas'd with gentle gales, the earth to sweep;
Whose blessed waves in swift succession go,
And lash the rocky shore with endless flow:
Delighting in the Sea serene to play,
In ships exulting and the wat'ry way.
Mother of Venus, and of clouds obscure,
Great nurse of beasts, and source of fountains pure.
O venerable Goddess, hear my pray'r,
And make benevolent my life thy care;
Send, blessed queen, to ships a prosp'rous breeze,
And waft them safely o'er the stormy seas.

XXII. TO NEREUS.

The FUMIGATION from MYRRH.

O Thou, who dost the roots of Ocean keep
In seats cærulean, dæmon of the deep,
With fifty nymphs (attending in thy train,
Fair virgin artists) glorying thro' the main:
The dark foundation of the rolling sea
And Earth's wide bounds, belong much-fam'd to thee;
Great dæmon, source of all, whose pow'r can make
The Earth's unmeasur'd, holy basis shake,
When blust'ring winds in secret caverns pent,
By thee excited, struggle hard for vent:
Come, blessed Nereus, listen to my pray'r,
And cease to shake the earth with wrath severe;
Send on our sacred rites abundant health,
With peace divine and necessary wealth.

XXIII. TO THE NEREIDS.
The FUMIGATION from AROMATICS.

DAUGHTERS of Nereus, resident in caves
Merg'd deep in Ocean, sporting thro' the waves;
Fanatic fifty nymphs, who thro' the main
Delight to follow in the Triton's train,
Rejoicing close behind their cars to keep;
Whose forms half wild, are nourish'd by the deep,
With other nymphs of different degree
Leaping and wand'ring thro' the liquid sea:
Bright, wat'ry dolphins, sonorous and gay,
Well pleas'd to sport with bachanalian play;
Nymphs beauteous-ey'd, whom sacrifice delights,
Send rich abundance on our mystic rites;
For you at first disclos'd the rites divine,
Of holy Bacchus and of Proserpine,
Of fair Calliope from whom I spring,
And of Apollo bright, the Muse's king.

XXIV. TO PROTEUS.
The FUMIGATION from STORAX.

PROTEUS I call, whom Fate decrees, to keep
The keys which lock the chambers of the deep;
First-born, by whose illustrious pow'r alone
All Nature's principles are clearly shewn:
Matter to change with various forms is thine,
Matter unform'd, capacious, and divine.
All-honor'd, prudent, whose sagacious mind
Knows all that was, and is, of ev'ry kind,
With all that shall be in succeeding time;
So vast thy wisdom, wond'rous, and sublime:
For all things Nature first to thee consign'd,
And in thy essence omniform confin'd.
Come, blessed father, to our rites attend,
And grant our happy lives a prosp'rous end.

XXV. TO THE EARTH.

The FUMIGATION from every kind of SEED, except BEANS and AROMATICS.

O Goddess, Earth, of Gods and men the source,
Endu'd with fertile, all destroying force;
All-parent, bounding, whose prolific pow'rs,
Produce a store of beauteous fruits and flow'rs,
All-various maid, th' eternal world's strong base
Immortal, blessed, crown'd with ev'ry grace;
From whose wide womb, as from an endless root,
Fruits, many-form'd, mature and grateful shoot.
Deep bosom'd, blessed, pleas'd with grassy plains,
Sweet to the smell, and with prolific rains.
All flow'ry dæmon, centre of the world,
Around thy orb, the beauteous stars are hurl'd
With rapid whirl, eternal and divine,
Whose frames with matchless skill and wisdom shine.
Come, blessed Goddess, listen to my pray'r,
And make increase of fruits thy constant care;
With fertile Seasons in thy train, draw near,
And with propitious mind thy suppliant hear.

XXVI. TO THE MOTHER OF THE GODS.

The FUMIGATION from a Variety of ODORIFEROUS SUBSTANCES.

Mother of Gods, great nurse of all, draw near,
Divinely honor'd, and regard my pray'r:
Thron'd on a car, by lions drawn along,
By bull-destroying lions, swift and strong,
Thou sway'st the sceptre of the pole divine,
And the world's middle seat, much-fam'd, is thine.
Hence earth is thine, and needy mortals share
Their constant food, from thy protecting care:
From thee at first both Gods and men arose;

From thee, the sea and ev'ry river flows.
Vesta, and source of good, thy name we find
To mortal men rejoicing to be kind;
For ev'ry good to give, thy soul delights;
Come, mighty pow'r, propitious to our rites,
All-taming, blessed, Phrygian saviour, come,
Saturn's great queen, rejoicing in the drum.
Celestial, ancient, life-supporting maid,
Fanatic Goddess, give thy suppliant aid;
With joyful aspect on our incense shine,
And, pleas'd, accept the sacrifice divine.

XXVII. TO MERCURY.
The FUMIGATION from FRANKINCENSE.
HERMES, draw near, and to my pray'r incline,
Angel of Jove, and Maia's son divine;
Studious of contests, ruler of mankind,
With heart almighty, and a prudent mind.
Celestial messenger, of various skill,
Whose pow'rful arts could watchful Argus kill:
With winged feet, 'tis thine thro' air to course,
O friend of man, and prophet of discourse:
Great life-supporter, to rejoice is thine,
In arts gymnastic, and in fraud divine:
With pow'r endu'd all language to explain,
Of care the loos'ner, and the source of gain.
Whose hand contains of blameless peace the rod,
Corucian, blessed, profitable God;
Of various speech, whose aid in works we find,
And in necessities to mortals kind:
Dire weapon of the tongue, which men revere,
Be present, Hermes, and thy suppliant hear;
Assist my works, conclude my life with peace,
Give graceful speech, and memory's increase.

XXVIII. TO PROSERPINE.

A HYMN

DAUGHTER of Jove, almighty and divine,
Come, blessed queen, and to these rites incline:
Only-begotten, Pluto's honor'd wife,
O venerable Goddess, source of life:
'Tis thine in earth's profundities to dwell,
Fast by the wide and dismal gates of hell:
Jove's holy offspring, of a beauteous mien,
Fatal, with lovely locks, infernal queen:
Source of the furies, whose blest frame proceeds
From Jove's ineffable and secret seeds:
Mother of Bacchus, sonorous, divine,
And many-form'd, the parent of the vine:
The dancing Hours attend thee, essence bright,
All-ruling virgin, bearing heav'nly light:
Illustrious, horned, of a bounteous mind,
Alone desir'd by those of mortal kind.
O, vernal queen, whom grassy plains delight,
Sweet to the smell, and pleasing to the sight:
Whose holy form in budding fruits we view,
Earth's vig'rous offspring of a various hue:
Espous'd in Autumn: life and death alone
To wretched mortals from thy power is known:
For thine the task according to thy will,
Life to produce, and all that lives to kill.
Hear, blessed Goddess, send a rich increase
Of various fruits from earth, with lovely Peace;
Send Health with gentle hand, and crown my life
With blest abundance, free from noisy strife;
Last in extreme old age the prey of Death,
Dismiss we willing to the realms beneath,
To thy fair palace, and the blissful plains
Where happy spirits dwell, and Pluto reigns.

XXIX. TO BACCHUS.

The FUMIGATION from STORAX.

BACCHUS I call, loud-sounding and divine,
Fanatic God, a two-fold shape is thine:
Thy various names and attributes I sing,
O, first-born, thrice begotten, Bacchic king:
Rural, ineffable, two-form'd, obscure,
Two-horn'd, with ivy crown'd, euion, pure.
Bull-fac'd, and martial, bearer of the vine,
Endu'd with counsel prudent and divine:
Triennial, whom the leaves of vines adorn,
Of Jove and Proserpine, occultly born.
Immortal dæmon, hear my suppliant voice,
Give me in blameless plenty to rejoice;
And listen gracious to my mystic pray'r,
Surrounded with thy choir of nurses fair.

XXX. TO THE CURETES.

A HYMN.

LEAPING Curetes, who with dancing feet
And circling measures, armed footsteps beat:
Whose bosom's mad, fanatic transports fire,
Who move in rythm to the sounding lyre:
Who traces deaf when lightly leaping tread,
Arm bearers, strong defenders, rulers dread:
Propitious omens, guards of Proserpine,
Preserving rites, mysterious and divine:
Come, and benevolent my words attend,
(In herds rejoicing), and my life defend.

XXXI. TO PALLAS.

A HYMN.

ONLY-Begotten, noble race of Jove,
Blessed and fierce, who joy'st in caves to rove:
O, warlike Pallas, whose illustrious kind,

Ineffable and effable we find:
Magnanimous and fam'd, the rocky height,
And groves, and shady mountains thee delight:
In arms rejoicing, who with Furies dire
And wild, the souls of mortals dost inspire.
Gymnastic virgin of terrific mind,
Dire Gorgons bane, unmarried, blessed, kind:
Mother of arts, imperious; understood,
Rage to the wicked, wisdom to the good:
Female and male, the arts of war are thine,
Fanatic, much-form'd dragoness, divine:
O'er the Phlegrean giants rous'd to ire,
Thy coursers driving, with destruction dire.
Sprung from the head of Jove, of splendid mien,
Purger of evils, all-victorious queen.
Hear me, O Goddess, when to thee I pray,
With supplicating voice both night and day,
And in my latest hour, peace and health,
Propitious times, and necessary wealth,
And, ever present, be thy vot'ries aid,
O, much implor'd, art's parent, blue eyed maid.

XXXII. TO VICTORY.

The FUMIGATION from MANNA.

O Powerful Victory, by men desir'd,
With adverse breasts to dreadful fury fir'd,
Thee I invoke, whose might alone can quell
Contending rage, and molestation fell:
'Tis thine in battle to confer the crown,
The victor's prize, the mark of sweet renown;
For thou rul'st all things, Victory divine!
And glorious strife, and joyful shouts are thine.
Come, mighty Goddess, and thy suppliant bless,
With sparkling eye, elated with success;
May deeds illustrious thy protection claim,
And find, led on by thee immortal Fame.

XXXIII. TO APOLLO.

The FUMIGATION from MANNA.

Blest Pæan, come, propitious to my pray'r,
Illustrious pow'r, whom Memphian tribes revere,
Slayer of Tityus, and the God of health,
Lycorian Phœbus, fruitful source of wealth.
Spermatic, golden-lyr'd, the field from thee
Receives it's constant, rich fertility.
Titanic, Grunian, Smynthian, thee I sing,
Python-destroying, hallow'd, Delphian king:
Rural, light-bearer, and the Muse's head,
Noble and lovely, arm'd with arrows dread:
Far-darting, Bacchian, two-fold, and divine,
Pow'r far diffused, and course oblique is thine.
O, Delian king, whose light-producing eye
Views all within, and all beneath the sky:
Whose locks are gold, whose oracles are sure,
Who, omens good reveal'st, and precepts pure:
Hear me entreating for the human kind,
Hear, and be present with benignant mind;
For thou survey'st this boundless æther all,
And ev'ry part of this terrestrial ball
Abundant, blessed; and thy piercing sight,
Extends beneath the gloomy, silent night;
Beyond the darkness, starry-ey'd, profound,
The stable roots, deep fix'd by thee are found.
The world's wide bounds, all-flourishing are thine,
Thyself all the source and end divine:
'Tis thine all Nature's music to inspire,
With various-sounding, harmonising lyre;
Now the last string thou tun'st to sweet accord,
Divinely warbling now the highest chord;
Th' immortal golden lyre, now touch'd by thee,
Responsive yields a Dorian melody.
All Nature's tribes to thee their diff'rence owe,
And changing seasons from thy music flow:

Hence, mix'd by thee in equal parts, advance
Summer and Winter in alternate dance;
This claims the highest, that the lowest string,
The Dorian measure tunes the lovely spring .
Hence by mankind, Pan-royal, two-horn'd nam'd,
Emitting whistling winds thro' Syrinx fam'd;
Since to thy care, the figur'd seal's consign'd,
Which stamps the world with forms of ev'ry kind.
Hear me, blest pow'r, and in these rites rejoice,
And save thy mystics with a suppliant voice.

XXXIV. TO LATONA.

The FUMIGATION from MYRRH.

DARK veil'd Latona, much invoked queen,
Twin-bearing Goddess, of a noble mien;
Cæantis great, a mighty mind is thine,
Offspring prolific, blest of Jove divine:
Phœbus proceeds from thee, the God of light,
And Dian fair, whom winged darts delight;
She in Ortygia's honor'd regions born,
In Delos he, which mountains high adorn.
Hear me, O Goddess, with propitious mind,
And end these holy rites, with aspect kind.

XXXV. TO DIANA.

The FUMIGATION from MANNA.

HEAR me, Jove's daughter, celebrated queen,
Bacchian and Titan, of a noble mien:
In darts rejoicing and on all to shine,
Torch-bearing Goddess, Dictynna divine;
O'er births presiding, and thyself a maid,
To labour-pangs imparting ready aid:
Dissolver of the zone and wrinkl'd care,
Fierce huntress, glorying in the Sylvan war:
Swift in the course, in dreadful arrows skill'd,
Wandering by night, rejoicing in the field:

Of manly form, erect, of bounteous mind,
Illustrious dæmon, nurse of human kind:
Immortal, earthly, bane of monsters fell,
'Tis thine; blest maid, on woody hills to dwell:
Foe of the stag, whom woods and dogs delight,
In endless youth who flourish fair and bright.
O, universal queen, august, divine,
A various form, Cydonian pow'r, is thine:
Dread guardian Goddess, with benignant mind
Auspicious, come to mystic rites inclin'd;
Give earth a store of beauteous fruits to bear,
Send gentle Peace, and Health with lovely hair,
And to the mountains drive Disease and Care.

XXXVI. TO THE TITANS.
The FUMIGATION from FRANKINCENSE.

O Mighty Titans, who from heav'n and earth
Derive your noble and illustrious birth,
Our fathers fires, in Tartarus profound
Who dwell, deep merg'd beneath the solid ground:
Fountains and principles, from whom began
Th' afflicted, miserable, race of man:
Who not alone in earth's retreats abide,
But in the ocean and the air reside;
Since ev'ry species from your nature flows,
Which all prolific, nothing barren knows:
Avert your rage, if from th' infernal seats
One of your tribe should visit our retreats.

XXXVII. TO THE CURETES.
The FUMIGATION from FRANKINCENSE.

BRASS-beating Salians, ministers of Mars,
Who guard his arms the instruments of wars;
Whose blessed frames, heav'n, earth, and sea compose,
And from whose breath all animals arose:
Who dwell in Samothracia's sacred ground,

Defending mortals thro' the sea profound.
Deathless Curetes, by your pow'r alone,
Initial rites to men at first were shewn:
Who shake old Ocean thund'ring to the sky,
And stubborn oaks with branches waving high.
'Tis your's in glittering arms the earth to beat,
With lightly-leaping, rapid, sounding feet;
Then every beast the noise terrific flies,
And the loud tumult wanders thro' the skies:
The dust your feet excites with matchless force,
Flies to the clouds amidst their whirling course;
And ev'ry flower of variegated hue,
Grows in the dancing motion form'd by you.
Immortal dæmons, to your pow'rs consign'd
The task to nourish, and destroy mankind.
When rushing furious with loud tumult dire,
O'erwhelm'd, they perish in your dreadful ire;
And live replenish'd with the balmy air,
The food of life, committed to your care.
When shook by you, the seas, with wild uproar,
Wide-spreading, and profoundly whirling, roar:
The concave heav'ns, with Echo's voice resound,
When leaves with ruffling noise bestrew the ground.
Curetes, Corybantes, ruling kings,
Whose praise the land of Samothracia sings:
From Jove descended; whose immortal breath
Sustains the soul, and wafts her back from death;
Aerial-form'd, much-fam'd, in heav'n ye shine
Two-fold, in heav'n all-lucid and divine:
Blowing, serene, from whom abundance springs,
Nurses of seasons, fruit-producing kings.

XXXVIII. TO CORYBAS.

The FUMIGATION from FRANKINCENSE.

THE mighty ruler of this earthly ball,
For ever flowing, to these rites I call;

Martial and blest, unseen by mortal sight,
Preventing fears, and pleas'd with gloomy night:
Hence, fancy's terrors are by thee allay'd,
All-various king, who lov'st the desart shade:
Each of thy brothers killing, blood is thine,
Two-fold Curete, many-form'd, divine.
By thee transmuted Ceres' body pure,
Became a dragon's savage and obscure:
Avert thy anger, hear me when I pray,
And by fix'd fate, drive fancy's fears away.

XXXIX. TO CERES.
The FUMIGATION from STORAX.

O Universal mother, Ceres fam'd
August, the source of wealth, and various nam'd:
Great nurse, all-bounteous, blessed and divine,
Who joy'st in peace, to nourish corn is thine:
Goddess of seed, of fruits abundant, fair,
Harvest and threshing, are thy constant care;
Who dwell'st in Eleusina's seats retir'd,
Lovely, delightful queen, by all desir'd.
Nurse of all mortals, whose benignant mind,
First ploughing oxen to the yoke confin'd;
And gave to men, what nature's wants require,
With plenteous means of bliss which all desire.
In verdure flourishing, in honor bright,
Assessor of great Bacchus, bearing light:
Rejoicing in the reapers sickles, kind,
Whose nature lucid, earthly, pure, we find.
Prolific, venerable, Nurse divine,
Thy daughter loving, holy Proserpine:
A car with dragons yok'd, 'tis thine to guide,
And orgies singing round thy throne to ride:
Only-begotten, much-producing queen,
All flowers are thine and fruits of lovely green.
Bright Goddess, come, with Summer's rich increase

Swelling and pregnant, leading smiling Peace;
Come, with fair Concord and imperial Health,
And join with these a needful store of wealth.

XL. TO THE CERALIAN MOTHER.
The FUMIGATION from AROMATICS.

CERALIAN queen, of celebrated name,
From whom both men, and Gods immortal came;
Who widely wand'ring once, oppress'd with grief,
In Eleusina's valley found'st relief,
Discovering Proserpine thy daughter pure
In dread Avernus, dismal and obscure;
A sacred youth while thro' the world you stray
Bacchus, attending leader of the way;
The holy marriage of terrestrial Jove
Relating, while oppress'd with grief you rove;
Come, much invok'd, and to these rites inclin'd,
Thy mystic suppliant bless, with fav'ring mind.

XLI. TO MISES.
The FUMIGATION from STORAX.

I Call Thesmophorus, spermatic God,
Of various names, who bears the leafy rod:
Mises, ineffable, pure, sacred queen,
Two-fold Iacchus, male and female seen:
Illustr'ous, whether to rejoice is thine
In incense offer'd, in the fane divine;
Or if in Phrygia most thy soul delights,
Performing with thy mother sacred rites;
Or if the land of Cyprus is thy care,
Well pleas'd to dwell with Cytherea fair;
Or if exulting in the fertile plains
With thy dark mother Isis, where she reigns,
With nurses pure attended, near the flood

Of sacred Egypt, thy divine abode:
Wherever resident, blest pow'r attend,
And with benignant mind these labours end.

XLII. TO THE SEASONS.
The FUMIGATION from AROMATICS.

DAUGHTERS of Jove and Themis, seasons bright,
Justice, and blessed peace, and lawful right,
Vernal and grassy, vivid, holy pow'rs,
Whose balmy breath exhales in lovely flow'rs
All-colour'd seasons, rich increase your care,
Circling, for ever flourishing and fair:
Invested with a veil of shining dew,
A flow'ry veil delightful to the view:
Attending Proserpine, when back from night,
The Fates and Graces lead her up to light;
When in a band-harmonious they advance,
And joyful round her, form the solemn dance:
With Ceres triumphing, and Jove divine;
Propitious come, and on our incense shine;
Give earth a blameless store of fruits to bear,
And make a novel mystic's life your care.

XLIII. TO SEMELE.
The FUMIGATION from STORAX.

CADMEAN Goddess, universal queen,
Thee, Semele I call, of beauteous mien;
Deep-bosom'd, lovely flowing locks are thine,
Mother of Bacchus, joyful and divine,
The mighty offspring, whom Jove's thunder bright,
Forc'd immature, and fright'ned into light:
Born from the deathless counsels, secret, high,
Of Jove Saturnian, regent of the sky;
Whom Proserpine permits to view the light,

And visit mortals from the realms of night:
Constant attending on the sacred rites,
And feast triennial, which thy soul delights;
When thy son's wond'rous birth mankind relate,
And secrets deep, and holy celebrate.
Now I invoke thee, great Cadmean queen,
To bless these rites with countenance serene.

XLIV. TO DIONYSIUS BASSAREUS TRIENNALIS.
A HYMN.

COME, blessed Dionysius, various nam'd,
Bull-fac'd, begot from Thunder, Bacchus fam'd.
Bassarian God, of universal might,
Whom swords, and blood, and sacred rage delight:
In heav'n rejoicing, mad, loud-sounding God,
Furious inspirer, bearer of the rod:
By Gods rever'd, who dwell'st with human kind,
Propitious come, with much-rejoicing mind.

XLV. TO LIKNITUS BACCHUS.
The FUMIGATION from MANNA.

LIKNITAN Bacchus, bearer of the vine,
Thee I invoke to bless these rites divine:
Florid and gay, of nymphs the blossom bright,
And of fair Venus, Goddess of delight,
'Tis thine mad footsteps with mad nymphs to beat,
Dancing thro' groves with lightly leaping feet:
From Jove's high counsels nurst by Proserpine,
And born the dread of all the pow'rs divine:
Come, blessed pow'r, regard thy suppliant's voice,
Propitious come, and in these rites rejoice.

XLVI. TO BACCHUS PERICIONIUS.
The FUMIGATION from AROMATICS.

BACCHUS Pericionius, hear my pray'r,
Who mad'st the house of Cadmus once thy care,

With matchless force, his pillars twining round,
(When burning thunders shook the solid ground,
In flaming, sounding torrents borne along),
Propt by thy grasp indissolubly strong.
Come mighty Bacchus to these rites inclin'd,
And bless thy suppliants with rejoicing mind.

XLVII. TO SABASIUS.
The FUMIGATION from AROMATICS.

HEAR me, illustrious father, dæmon fam'd.
Great Saturn's offspring, and Sabasius nam'd;
Inserting Bacchus, bearer of the vine,
And sounding God, within thy thigh divine,
That when mature, the Dionysian God
Might burst the bands of his conceal'd abode,
And come to sacred Tmolus, his delight,
Where Ippa dwells, all beautiful and bright.
Come blessed Phrygian God, the king of all,
And aid thy mystics, when on thee they call.

XLVIII. TO IPPA.
The FUMIGATION from STORAX.

GREAT nurse of Bacchus, to my pray'r incline,
For holy Sabus' secret rites are thine,
The mystic rites of Bacchus' nightly choirs,
Compos'd of sacred, loud-resounding fires:
Hear me, terrestrial mother, mighty queen,
Whether on Phyrgia's holy mountain seen,
Or if to dwell in Tmolus thee delights,
With holy aspect come, and bless these rites.

XLIX. TO LYSIUS LENÆUS.
A HYMN.

HEAR me, Jove's son, blest Bacchus, God of wine,
Born of two mothers, honor'd and divine;
Lysian, Euion Bacchus, various-nam'd,

Of Gods the offspring secret, holy, fam'd:
Fertile and nourishing whose liberal care
Earth's fruits increases, flourishing and fair;
Sounding, magnanimous, Lenæan pow'r
O various form'd, medic'nal, holy flow'r:
Mortals in thee, repose from labour find,
Delightful charm, desir'd by all mankind:
Fair-hair'd Euion, Bromian, joyful God,
Lysian, invested with the leafy rod.
To these our rites, benignant pow'r incline,
When fav'ring men, or when on Gods you shine;
Be present to thy mystic's suppliant pray'r,
Rejoicing come, and fruits abundant bear.

L. TO THE NYMPHS.
The FUMIGATION from AROMATICS.

NYMPHS, who from Ocean's stream derive your birth,
Who dwell in liquid caverns of the earth;
Nurses of Bacchus secret-coursing pow'r,
Who fruits sustain, and nourish ev'ry flow'r:
Earthly, rejoicing, who in meadows dwell,
And caves and dens, whose depths extend to hell:
Holy, oblique, who swiftly soar thro' air,
Fountains and dews, and mazy streams your care:
Seen and unseen, who joy with wand'rings wide
And gentle course, thro' flow'ry vales to glide;
With Pan exulting on the mountains height,
Loud-sounding, mad, whom rocks and woods delight:
Nymphs od'rous, rob'd in white, whose streams exhale
The breeze refreshing, and the balmy gale;
With goats and pastures pleas'd, and beasts of prey,
Nurses of fruits, unconscious of decay:
In cold rejoicing, and to cattle kind,
Sportive thro' ocean wand'ring unconfin'd:
Nysian, fanatic Nymphs, whom oaks delight,
Lovers of Spring, Pæonian virgins bright.

With Bacchus, and with Ceres, hear my pray'r.
And to mankind abundant favour bear;
Propitious listen to your suppliants voice,
Come, and benignant in these rites rejoice;
Give plenteous Seasons, and sufficient wealth,
And pour, in lasting streams, continued Health.

LI. TO TRIETERICUS.

The FUMIGATION from AROMATICS.

BACCHUS fanatic, much-nam'd, blest, divine,
Bull-fac'd Lenæan, bearer of the vine;
From fire descended, raging, Nysian king,
From whom initial ceremonies spring:
Liknitan Bacchus, pure and fiery bright,
Prudent, crown-bearer, wandering in the night;
Pupil of Proserpine, mysterious pow'r,
Triple, ineffable, Jove's secret flow'r:
Ericapæus, first-begotten nam'd,
Of Gods the father, and the offspring fam'd:
Bearing a sceptre, leader of the choir,
Whose dancing feet, fanatic Furies fire,
When the triennial band thou dost inspire.
Loud-sounding, Tages, of a fiery light,
Born of two mothers, Amphietus bright:
Wand'ring on mountains, cloth'd with skins of deer,
Apollo, golden-ray'd, whom all revere.
God of the grape with leaves of ivy crown'd,
Bassarian, lovely, virgin-like, renown'd
Come blessed pow'r, regard thy mystics voice,
Propitious come, and in these rites rejoice.

LII. To AMPHIETUS BACCHUS.

The FUMIGATION from every AROMATIC except FRANKINCENSE.

TERRESTRIAL Dionysius, hear my pray'r,
Awak'ned rise with nymphs of lovely hair:

Great Amphietus Bacchus, annual God,
Who laid asleep in Proserpine's abode,
Did'st lull to drowsy and oblivious rest,
The rites triennial, and the sacred feast;
Which rous'd again by thee, in graceful ring,
Thy nurses round thee mystic anthems sing;
When briskly dancing with rejoicing pow'rs,
Thou mov'st in concert with the circling hours.
Come, blessed, fruitful, horned, and divine,
And on these rites with joyful aspect shine;
Accept the general incense and the pray'r,
And make prolific holy fruits thy care.

LIII. To SILENUS, SATYRUS, and the PRIESTESSES of BACCHUS.

The FUMIGATION from MANNA.

GREAT nurse of Bacchus, to my pray'r incline,
Silenus, honor'd by the pow'rs divine;
And by mankind at the triennial feast
Illustrious dæmon, reverenc'd as the best:
Holy, august, the source of lawful rites,
Rejoicing pow'r, whom vigilance delights;
With Sylvans dancing ever young and fair,
Head of the Bacchic Nymphs, who ivy bear.
With all thy Satyrs on our incense shine,
Dæmons wild form'd, and bless the rites divine;
Come, rouse to sacred Joy thy pupil kin,
And Brumal Nymphs with rites Lenæan bring;
Our orgies shining thro' the night inspire,
And bless triumphant pow'r the sacred choir.

LIV. TO VENUS.

A HYMN.

HEAV'NLY, illustrious, laughter-loving queen,
Sea-born, night-loving, of an awful mien;

Crafty, from whom necessity first came,
Producing, nightly, all-connecting dame:
'Tis thine the world with harmony to join,
For all things spring from thee, O pow'r divine.
The triple Fates are rul'd by thy decree,
And all productions yield alike to thee:
Whate'er the heav'ns, encircling all contain,
Earth fruit-producing, and the stormy main,
Thy sway confesses, and obeys thy nod,
Awful attendant of the brumal God:
Goddess of marriage, charming to the sight,
Mother of Loves, whom banquetings delight;
Source of persuasion, secret, fav'ring queen,
Illustrious born, apparent and unseen:
Spousal, lupercal, and to men inclin'd,
Prolific, most-desir'd, life-giving., kind:
Great sceptre-bearer of the Gods, 'tis thine,
Mortals in necessary bands to join;
And ev'ry tribe of savage monsters dire
In magic chains to bind, thro' mad desire.
Come, Cyprus-born, and to my pray'r incline,
Whether exalted in the heav'ns you shine,
Or pleas'd in Syria's temple to preside,
Or o'er th' Egyptian plains thy car to guide,
Fashion'd of gold; and near its sacred flood,
Fertile and fam'd to fix thy blest abode;
Or if rejoicing in the azure shores,
Near where the sea with foaming billows roars,
The circling choirs of mortals, thy delight,
Or beauteous nymphs, with eyes cerulean bright,
Pleas'd by the dusty banks renown'd of old,
To drive thy rapid, two-yok'd car of gold;
Or if in Cyprus with thy mother fair,
Where married females praise thee ev'ry year,
And beauteous virgins in the chorus join,

Adonis pure to sing and thee divine;
Come, all-attractive to my pray'r inclin'd,
For thee, I call, with holy, reverent mind.

LV. TO ADONIS.
The FUMIGATION from AROMATICS.

MUCH-nam'd, and best of dæmons, hear my pray'r,
The desart-loving, deck'd with tender hair;
Joy to diffuse, by all desir'd is thine,
Much form'd, Eubulus; aliment divine:
Female and Male, all charming to the sight,
Adonis ever flourishing and bright;
At stated periods doom'd to set and rise,
With splendid lamp, the glory of the skies.
Two-horn'd and lovely, reverenc'd with tears,
Of beauteous form, adorn'd with copious hairs.
Rejoicing in the chace, all-graceful pow'r,
Sweet plant of Venus, Love's delightful flow'r:
Descended from the secret bed divine,
Of lovely-hair'd, infernal Proserpine.
'Tis thine to sink in Tartarus profound,
And shine again thro' heav'ns illustrious round,
With beauteous temp'ral orb restor'd to sight;
Come, with earth's fruits, and in these flames delight.

LVI. TO THE TERRESTRIAL HERMES.
The FUMIGATION from STORAX.

HERMES I call, whom Fate decrees to dwell
In the dire path which leads to deepest hell:
O Bacchic Hermes, progeny divine
Of Dionysius, parent of the vine,
And of celestial Venus Paphian queen,
Dark eye-lash'd Goddess of a lovely mien:
Who constant wand'rest thro' the sacred seats
Where hell's dread empress, Proserpine, retreats;
To wretched souls the leader of the way

When Fate decrees, to regions void of day:
Thine is the wand which causes sleep to fly,
Or lulls to slumb'rous rest the weary eye;
For Proserpine thro' Tart'rus dark and wide
Gave thee forever flowing souls to guide.
Come, blessed pow'r the sacrifice attend,
And grant our mystic works a happy end.

LVII. TO CUPID, OR LOVE.
The FUMIGATION from AROMATICS.

I Call great Cupid, source of sweet delight,
Holy and pure, and lovely to the sight;
Darting, and wing'd, impetuous fierce desire,
With Gods and mortals playing, wand'ring fire:
Cautious, and two-fold, keeper of the keys
Of heav'n and earth, the air, and spreading seas;
Of all that Ceres' fertile realms contains,
By which th' all-parent Goddess life sustains,
Or dismal Tartarus is doom'd to keep,
Widely extended, or the sounding, deep;
For thee, all Nature's various realms obey,
Who rul'st alone, with universal sway.
Come, blessed pow'r, regard these mystic fires,
And far avert, unlawful mad desires.

LVIII. TO THE FATES.
The FUMIGATION from AROMATICS.

DAUGHTERS of darkling night, much-nam'd, draw near
Infinite Fates, and listen to my pray'r;
Who in the heav'nly lake (where waters white
Burst from a fountain hid in depths of night,
And thro' a dark and stony cavern glide,
A cave profound, invisible) abide;
From whence, wide coursing round the boundless earth,
Your pow'r extends to those of mortal birth;
To men with hope elated, trifling, gay,

A race presumptuous, born but to decay;
Whose life 'tis your's in darkness to conceal
To sense impervious, in a purple veil,
When thro' the fatal plain they joyful ride
In one great car, Opinion for their guide;
'Till each completes his heav'n-appointed round
At Justice, Hope, and Care's concluding bound,
The terms absolv'd, prescrib'd by ancient law
Of pow'r immense, and just without a flaw;
For Fate alone with vision unconfin'd,
Surveys the conduct of the mortal kind.
Fate is Jove's perfect and eternal eye,
For Jove and Fate our ev'ry deed descry.
Come, gentle pow'rs, well born, benignant, fam'd,
Atropos, Lachesis, and Clotho nam'd:
Unchang'd, aerial, wand'ring in the night,
Restless, invisible to mortal sight;
Fates all-producing, all-destroying hear,
Regard the incense and the holy pray'r;
Propitious listen to these rites inclin'd,
And far avert distress with placid mind.

LIX. TO THE GRACES.

The FUMIGATION from STORAX.

HEAR me, illustrious Graces, mighty nam'd,
From Jove descended and Eunomia fam'd;
Thalia, and Aglaia fair and bright,
And blest Euphrosyne whom joys delight:
Mothers of mirth, all lovely to the view,
Pleasure abundant pure belongs to you:
Various, forever flourishing and fair,
Desir'd by mortals, much invok'd in pray'r:
Circling, dark-ey'd, delightful to mankind,
Come, and your mystics bless with bounteous mind.

LX. TO NEMESIS.

A HYMN.

THEE, Nemesis I call, almighty queen,
By whom the deeds of mortal life are seen:
Eternal, much rever'd, of boundless sight,
Alone rejoicing in the just and right:
Changing the counsels of the human breast
For ever various, rolling without rest.
To every mortal is thy influence known,
And men beneath thy righteous bondage groan;
For ev'ry thought within the mind conceal'd
Is to thy sight perspicuously reveal'd.
The soul unwilling reason to obey
By lawless passion rul'd, thy eyes survey.
All to see, hear, and rule, O pow'r divine
Whose nature Equity contains, is thine.
Come, blessed, holy Goddess, hear my pray'r,
And make thy mystic's life, thy constant care:
Give aid benignant in the needful hour,
And strength abundant to the reas'ning pow'r;
And far avert the dire, unfriendly race
Of counsels impious, arrogant, and base.

LXI. TO JUSTICE.

The FUMIGATION from FRANKINCENSE.

THE piercing eye of Justice bright, I sing,
Plac'd by the throne of heav'n's almighty king,
Perceiving thence, with vision unconfin'd,
The life and conduct of the human kind:
To thee, revenge and punishment belong,
Chastising ev'ry deed, unjust and wrong;
Whose pow'r alone, dissimilars can join,
And from th' equality of truth combine:
For all the ill, persuasion can inspire,
When urging bad designs, with counsel dire,

'Tis thine alone to punish; with the race
Of lawless passions, and incentives base;
For thou art ever to the good inclin'd,
And hostile to the men of evil mind.
Come, all-propitious, and thy suppliant hear,
When Fate's predestin'd, final hour draws near.

LXII. TO EQUITY.

The FUMIGATION from FRANKINCENSE.

O Blessed Equity, mankind's delight,
Th' eternal friend of conduct just and right:
Abundant, venerable, honor'd maid,
To judgments pure, dispensing constant aid,
A stable conscience, and an upright mind;
For men unjust, by thee are undermin'd,
Whose souls perverse thy bondage ne'er desire,
But more untam'd decline thy scourges dire:
Harmonious, friendly power, averse to strife,
In peace rejoicing, and a stable life;
Lovely, loquacious, of a gentle mind,
Hating excess, to equal deeds inclin'd:
Wisdom, and virtue of whate'er degree,
Receive their proper bound alone in thee.
Hear, Goddess Equity, the deeds destroy
Of evil men, which human life annoy;
That all may yield to thee of mortal birth,
Whether supported by the fruits of earth,
Or in her kindly fertile bosom found,
or in the depths of Marine Jove profound.

LXIII. TO LAW.

A HYMN.

THE holy king of Gods and men I call,
Celestial Law, the righteous seal of all;
The seal which stamps whate'er the earth contains,
Nature's firm basis, and the liquid plains:

Stable, and starry, of harmonious frame,
Preserving laws eternally the same:
Thy all-composing pow'r in heaven appears,
Connects its frame, and props the starry spheres;
And shakes weak Envy with tremendous sound,
Toss'd by thy arm in giddy whirls around.
'Tis thine, the life of mortals to defend,
And crown existence with a blessed end;
For thy command alone, of all that lives
Order and rule to ev'ry dwelling gives:
Ever observant of the upright mind,
And of just actions the companion kind;
Foe to the lawless, with avenging ire,
Their steps involving in destruction dire.
Come, blest, abundant pow'r, whom all revere,
By all desir'd, with favr'ing mind draw near;
Give me thro' life, on thee to fix my sight,
And ne'er forsake the equal paths of right.

LXIV. TO MARS.
The FUMIGATION from FRANKINCENSE.

Magnanimous, unconquer'd, boistrous Mars,
In darts rejoicing, and in bloody wars:
Fierce and untam'd, whose mighty pow'r can make
The strongest walls from their foundations shake:
Mortal destroying king, defil'd with gore,
Pleas'd with war's dreadful and tumultuous roar:
Thee, human blood, and swords, and spears delight,
And the dire ruin of mad savage fight.
Stay, furious contests, and avenging strife,
Whose works with woe, embitter human life;
To lovely Venus, and to Bacchus yield,
To Ceres give the weapons of the field;
Encourage peace, to gentle works inclin'd,
And give abundance, with benignant mind.

LXV. TO VULCAN.

The FUMIGATION from FRANKINCENSE and MANNA.

STRONG, mighty Vulcan, bearing splendid light,
Unweary'd fire, with flaming torrents bright:
Strong-handed, deathless, and of art divine,
Pure element, a portion of the world is thine:
All-taming artist, all-diffusive pow'r,
'Tis thine supreme, all substance to devour:
Æther, Sun, Moon, and Stars, light pure and clear,
For these thy lucid parts to men appear.
To thee, all dwellings, cities, tribes belong,
Diffus'd thro' mortal bodies bright and strong.
Hear, blessed power, to holy rites incline,
And all propitious on the incense shine:
Suppress the rage of fires unweary'd frame,
And still preserve our nature's vital flame.

LXVI. TO ESCULAPIUS.

The FUMIGATION from MANNA.

GREAT Esculapius, skill'd to heal mankind,
All-ruling Pæan, and physician kind;
Whose arts medic'nal, can alone assuage
Diseases dire, and stop their dreadful rage:
Strong lenient God, regard my suppliant pray'r,
Bring gentle Health, adorn'd with lovely hair;
Convey the means of mitigating pain,
And raging, deadly pestilence restrain.
O pow'r all-flourishing, abundant, bright,
Apollo's honor'd offspring, God of light;
Husband of blameless Health, the constant foe
Of dread Disease the minister of woe:
Come, blessed saviour, and my health defend,
And to my life afford a prosp'rous end.

LXVII. TO HEALTH.

The FUMIGATION from MANNA.

O Much-desir'd, prolific, gen'ral queen,
Hear me, life-bearing Health, of beauteous mien,
Mother of all; by thee diseases dire,
Of bliss destructive, from our life retire;
And ev'ry house is flourishing and fair,
If with rejoicing aspect thou art there:
Each dædal art, thy vig'rous force inspires,
And all the world thy helping hand desires;
Pluto life's bane alone resists thy will,
And ever hates thy all-preserving skill.
O fertile queen, from thee forever flows
To mortal life from agony repose;
And men without thy all-sustaining ease,
Find nothing useful, nothing form'd to please;
Without thy aid, not Plutus' self can thrive,
Nor man to much afflicted age arrive;
For thou alone of countenance serene,
Dost govern all things, universal queen.
Assist thy mystics with propitious mind,
And far avert disease of ev'ry kind.

LXVIII. TO THE FURIES.

The FUMIGATION from AROMATICS.

VOCIFEROUS Bacchanalian Furies, hear!
Ye, I invoke, dread pow'rs, whom all revere;
Nightly, profound, in secret who retire,
Tisiphone, Alecto, and Megara dire:
Deep in a cavern merg'd, involv'd in night,
Near where Styx flows impervious to the sight;
Ever attendant on mysterious rites,
Furious and fierce, whom Fate's dread law delights;
Revenge and sorrows dire to you belong,
Hid in a savage veil, severe and strong,

Terrific virgins, who forever dwell
Endu'd with various forms, in deepest hell;
Aerial, and unseen by human kind,
And swiftly coursing, rapid as the mind.
In vain the Sun with wing'd refulgence bright,
In vain the Moon, far darting milder light,
Wisdom and Virtue may attempt in vain;
And pleasing, Art, our transport to obtain;
Unless with these you readily conspire,
And far avert your all-destructive ire.
The boundless tribes of mortals you descry,
And justly rule with Right's impartial eye.
Come, snaky-hair'd, Fates many-form'd, divine,
Suppress your rage, and to our rites incline.

LXIX. TO THE FURIES.

The FUMIGATION from AROMATICS.

HEAR me, illustrious Furies, mighty nam'd,
Terrific pow'rs, for prudent counsel fam'd;
Holy and pure, from Jove terrestrial born
And Proserpine, whom lovely locks adorn:
Whose piercing sight, with vision unconfin'd,
Surveys the deeds of all the impious kind:
On Fate attendant, punishing the race
(With wrath severe) of deeds unjust and base.
Dark-colour'd queens, whose glittering eyes, are bright
With dreadful, radiant, life-destroying, light:
Eternal rulers, terrible and strong,
To whom revenge, and tortures dire belong;
Fatal and horrid to the human sight,
With snaky tresses wand'ring in the night;
Hither approach, and in these rites rejoice,
For ye, I call, with holy, suppliant voice.

LXX. TO MELINOE.

The FUMIGATION from AROMATICS.

I Call Melinoe, saffron-veil'd, terrene,
Who from infernal Pluto's sacred queen,
Mixt with Saturnian Jupiter, arose,
Near where Cocytus' mournful river flows;
When under Pluto's semblance, Jove divine
Deceiv'd with guileful arts dark Proserpine.
Hence, partly black thy limbs and partly white,
From Pluto dark, from Jove etherial, bright
Thy colour'd members, men by night inspire
When seen in specter'd forms with terrors dire;
Now darkly visible, involv'd in night,
Perspicuous now they meet the fearful fight.
Terrestrial queen expel wherever found
The soul's mad fears to earth's remotest bound;
With holy aspect on our incense shine,
And bless thy mystics, and the rites divine.

LXXI. TO FORTUNE.

The FUMIGATION from FRANKINCENSE.

Approach strong Fortune, with propitious mind
And rich abundance, to my pray'r inclin'd
Placid, and gentle Trivia, mighty nam'd,
Imperial Dian, born of Pluto fam'd;
Mankind's unconquer'd, endless praise is thine,
Sepulch'ral, widely-wand'ring pow'r divine!
In thee, our various mortal life is found,
And some from thee in copious wealth abound;
While others mourn thy hand averse to bless,
In all the bitterness of deep distress.
Bc present, Goddess, to thy vot'ry kind,
And give abundance with benignant mind.

LXXII. TO THE DÆMON, OR GENIUS.
The FUMIGATION from FRANKINCENSE.

THEE, mighty-ruling, Dæmon dread, I call,
Mild Jove, life-giving, and the source of all:
Great Jove, much-wand'ring, terrible and strong,
To whom revenge and tortures dire belong.
Mankind from thee, in plenteous wealth abound,
When in their dwellings joyful thou art found;
Or pass thro' life afflicted and distress'd,
The needful means of bliss by thee supprest.
'Tis thine alone endu'd with boundless might,
To keep the keys of sorrow and delight.
O holy, blessed father, hear my pray'r,
Disperse the seeds of life-consuming care;
With fav'ring mind the sacred rites attend,
And grant my days a glorious, blessed end.

LXXIII. TO LEUCOTHEA.
The FUMIGATION from AROMATICS.

I Call Leucothea, of great Cadmus born,
And Bacchus' nurse, whom ivy leaves adorn.
Hear, pow'rful Goddess, in the mighty deep
Wide and profound, thy station doom'd to keep:
In waves rejoicing, guardian of mankind;
For ships from thee alone deliv'rance find
Amidst the fury of th' unstable main,
When art no more avail, and strength is vain;
When rushing billows with tempestuous ire
O'erwhelm the mariner in ruin dire,
Thou hear'st, with pity touch'd, his suppliant pray'r,
Resolv'd his life to succour and to spare.
Be ever present, Goddess! in distress,
Waft ships along with prosperous success:
Thy mystics thro' the stormy sea defend,
And safe conduct them to their destin'd end.

LXXIV. TO PALÆMON.

The FUMIGATION from MANNA.

O Nurs'd with Dionysius, doom'd to keep
Thy dwelling in the widely-spreading deep:
With joyful aspect to my pray'r incline,
Propitious come, and bless the rites divine:
Thro' earth and sea thy ministers attend,
And from old Ocean's stormy waves defend:
For ships their safety ever owe to thee,
Who wand'rest with them thro' the raging sea.
Come, guardian pow'r, whom mortal tribes desire,
And far avert the deep's destructive ire.

LXXV. TO THE MUSES.

The FUMIGATION from FRANKINCENSE.

Daughters of Jove, dire-sounding and divine,
Renown'd Pierian, sweetly speaking Nine;
To those whose breasts your sacred furies fire
Much-form'd, the objects of supreme desire:
Sources of blameless virtue to mankind,
Who form to excellence the youthful mind;
Who nurse the soul, and give her to descry
The paths of right with Reason's steady eye.
Commanding queens who lead to sacred light
The intellect refin'd from Error's night;
And to mankind each holy rite disclose,
For mystic knowledge from your nature stows.
Clio, and Erato, who charms the sight,
With thee Euterpe minist'ring delight:
Thalia flourishing, Polymina fam'd,
Melpomene from skill in music nam'd:
Terpischore, Urania heav'nly bright,
With thee who gav'st me to behold the light.
Come, venerable, various, pow'rs divine,
With fav'ring aspect on your mystics shine;

Bring glorious, ardent, lovely, fam'd desire,
And warm my bosom with your sacred fire.

LXXVI. To MNEMOSYNE,
or the GODDESS of MEMORY.
The FUMIGATION from FRANKINCENSE.

THE consort I invoke of Jove divine,
Source of the holy, sweetly-speaking Nine;
Free from th' oblivion of the fallen mind,
By whom the soul with intellect is join'd:
Reason's increase, and thought to thee belong,
All-powerful, pleasant, vigilant, and strong:
'Tis thine, to waken from lethargic rest
All thoughts deposited within the breast;
And nought neglecting, vigorous to excite
The mental eye from dark oblivion's night.
Come, blessed power, thy mystic's mem'ry wake
To holy rites, and Lethe's fetters break.

LXXVII. TO AURORA.
The FUMIGATION from MANNA.

HEAR me, O Goddess! whose emerging ray
Leads on the broad refulgence of the day;
Blushing Aurora, whose celestial light
Beams on the world with red'ning splendours bright:
Angel of Titan, whom with constant round,
Thy orient beams recall from night profound:
Labour of ev'ry kind to lead is thine,
Of mortal life the minister divine.
Mankind in thee eternally delight,
And none presumes to shun thy beauteous sight.
Soon as thy splendours break the bands of rest,
And eyes unclose with pleasing sleep oppress'd;
Men, reptiles, birds, and beasts, with gen'ral voice,
And all the nations of the deep, rejoice;
For all the culture of our life is thine.

Come, blessed pow'r! and to these rites incline:
Thy holy light increase, and unconfin'd
Diffuse its radiance on thy mystic's mind.

LXXVIII. TO THEMIS.
The FUMIGATION from FRANKINCENSE.

ILLUSTRIOUS Themis, of celestial birth,
Thee I invoke, young blossom of the earth;
Beauteous-eyed virgin; first from thee alone,
Prophetic oracles to men were known,
Giv'n from the deep recesses of the fane
In sacred Pytho, where renown'd you reign;
From thee, Apollo's oracles arose,
And from thy pow'r his inspiration flows.
Honour'd by all, of form divinely bright,
Majestic virgin, wand'ring in the night:
Mankind from thee first learnt initial rites,
And Bacchus' nightly choirs thy soul delights;
For holy honours to disclose is thine,
With all the culture of the pow'rs divine.
Be present, Goddess, to my pray'r inclin'd,
And bless the mystic rites with fav'ring mind.

LXXIX. TO THE NORTH WIND.
The FUMIGATION from FRANKINCENSE.

BOREAS, whose wint'ry blasts, terrific, tear
The bosom of the deep surrounding air;
Cold icy pow'r, approach, and fav'ring blow,
And Thrace a while desert expos'd to snow:
The misty station of the air dissolve,
With pregnant clouds, whose frames in show'rs resolve:
Serenely temper all within the sky,
And wipe from moisture, Æther's beauteous eye.

LXXX. TO THE WEST WIND.
The FUMIGATION from FRANKINCENSE.

SEA-born, aerial, blowing from the west,
Sweet gales, who give to weary'd labour rest:
Vernal and grassy, and of gentle sound,
To ships delightful, thro' the sea profound;
For these, impell'd by you with gentle force,
Pursue with prosp'rous Fate their destin'd course.
With blameless gales regard my suppliant pray'r,
Zephyrs unseen, light-wing'd, and form'd from air.

LXXXI. TO THE SOUTH WIND.
The FUMIGATION from FRANKINCENSE.

WIDE coursing gales, whose lightly leaping feet
With rapid wings the air's wet bosom beat,
Approach benevolent, swift-whirling pow'rs,
With humid clouds the principles of show'rs:
For show'ry clouds are portion'd to your care,
To send on earth from all surrounding air.
Hear, blessed pow'rs, these holy rites attend,
And fruitful rains on earth all-parent send.

LXXXII. TO OCEAN.
The FUMIGATION from AROMATICS.

OCEAN I call, whose nature ever flows,
From whom at first both Gods and men arose;
Sire incorruptible, whose waves surround,
And earth's concluding mighty circle bound:
Hence every river, hence the spreading sea,
And earth's pure bubbling fountains spring from thee:
Hear, mighty sire, for boundless bliss is thine,
Whose waters purify the pow'rs divine:
Earth's friendly limit, fountain of the pole,
Whose waves wide spreading and circumfluent roll.
Approach benevolent, with placid mind,
And be for ever to thy mystics kind.

LXXXIII. TO VESTA.

The FUMIGATION from AROMATICS.

Daughter of Saturn, venerable dame,
The seat containing of unweary'd flame;
In sacred rites these ministers are thine,
Mystics much-blessed, holy and divine.
In thee, the Gods have fix'd place,
Strong, stable, basis of the mortal race:
Eternal, much-form'd ever-florid queen,
Laughing and blessed, and of lovely mien;
Accept these rites, accord each just desire,
And gentle health, and needful good inspire.

LXXXIV. TO SLEEP.

The FUMIGATION from a Poppy.

SLEEP, king of Gods, and men of mortal birth,
Sov'reign of all sustain'd by mother Earth;
For thy dominion is supreme alone,
O'er all extended, and by all things known.
'Tis thine all bodies with benignant mind
In other bands than those of brass to bind:
Tamer of cares, to weary toil repose,
From whom sweet solace in affliction flows.
Thy pleasing, gentle chains preserve the soul,
And e'en the dreadful cares of death controul;
For death and Lethe with oblivious stream,
Mankind thy genuine brothers justly deem.
With fav'ring aspect to my pray'r incline,
And save thy mystics in their works divine.

LXXXV. TO THE DIVINITY OF DREAMS.

The FUMIGATION from AROMATICS.

THEE I invoke, blest pow'r of dreams divine,
Angel of future fates, swift wings are thine:
Great source of oracles to human kind,

When stealing soft, and whisp'ring to the mind,
Thro' sleep's sweet silence and the gloom of night,
Thy pow'r awakes th' intellectual sight;
To silent souls the will of heav'n relates,
And silently reveals their future fates.
For ever friendly to the upright mind
Sacred and pure, to holy rites inclin'd;
For these with pleasing hope thy dreams inspire,
Bliss to anticipate, which all desire.
Thy visions manifest of fate disclose,
What methods best may mitigate our woes;
Reveal what rites the Gods immortal please,
And what the means their anger to appease:
For ever tranquil is the good man's end,
Whose life, thy dreams admonish and defend.
But from the wicked turn'd averse to bless,
Thy form unseen, the angel of distress;
No means to cheek approaching ill they find,
Pensive with fears, and to the future blind.
Come, blessed pow'r, the signatures reveal
Which heav'n's decrees mysteriously conceal,
Signs only present to the worthy mind,
Nor omens ill disclose of monst'rous kind.

LXXXVI. TO DEATH.

The FUMIGATION from MANNA.

HEAR me, O Death, whose empire unconfin'd,
Extends to mortal tribes of ev'ry kind.
On thee, the portion of our time depends,
Whose absence lengthens life, whose presence ends.
Thy sleep perpetual bursts the vivid folds,
By which the soul, attracting body holds:
Common to all of ev'ry sex and age,
For nought escapes thy all-destructive rage;
Not youth itself thy clemency can gain,
Vig'rous and strong, by thee untimely slain.

In thee, the end of nature's works is known,
In thee, all judgment is absolv'd alone:
No suppliant arts thy dreadful rage controul,
No vows revoke the purpose of thy soul;
O blessed pow'r regard my ardent pray'r,
And human life to age abundant spare.

APPENDIX III:
INDEX OF PURPOSES
OF THE HYMNS

This list organizes ways that the hymns might be used for particular religio-magical goals, whether mentioned in the hymn itself or related to the god to whom the hymn is dedicated. The numbers refer to the number of the hymn. If using Thomas Taylor's translation, subtract one from the number listed here to find the corresponding hymn, since he includes Hekate in the introductory hymn.

BIBLIOGRAPHY

Athanassakis, Apostolos N., and Benjamin M. Wolkow. *The Orphic Hymns.* Baltimore: Johns Hopkins UP, 2013.

Dunn, Patrick. *The Practical Art of Divine Magic: Contemporary & Ancient Techniques of Theurgy.* Woodbury, MN: Llewellyn Worldwide, 2015.

Graf, Fritz. "Serious Singing: The Orphic Hymns as Ritual Text." *Kernos* 22 (2009): 169–182.

Graf, Fritz, and Sarah Iles Johnston. *Ritual Texts for the Afterlife: Orpheus and the Bacchic Gold Tablets.* London: Routledge, 2013.

Guthrie, William Keith Chambers. *Orpheus and Greek Religion.* London: Mehtuen, 1935.

Hesiod. "Theogony." *Internet Sacred Texts Archive.* 29 June 2017. http://www.sacred-texts.com/cla/hesiod/theogony.htm.

Lord, Albert B. *The Singer of Tales.* New York: Atheneum, 1973.

Morand, Anne-France. *Études sur les Hymnes Orphiques.* Leiden: Brill, 2001.

Taylor, Thomas. "The Hymns of Orpheus." *Internet Sacred Texts Archive.* 29 June 2017. http://www.sacred-texts.com/cla/hoo/index.htm.

yronwode, catherine. "Mikhail Strabo: A Pseudonym of Sydney J. Rosenfeld Steiner." Lucky Mojo Curio Company. 30 June 2017. http://www.luckymojo.com/strabo.html.